iPhoto

THE MISSING MANUAL

*The book that
should have been
in the box*

iPhoto

THE MISSING MANUAL

David Pogue, Joseph Schorr, and Derrick Story

POGUE PRESS™

O'REILLY®

Beijing • Cambridge • Farnham • Köln • Paris • Sebastopol • Taipei • Tokyo

iPhoto: The Missing Manual

by David Pogue, Joseph Schorr, and Derrick Story

Copyright © 2002 Pogue Press, LLC. All rights reserved.
Printed in the United States of America.

Published by Pogue Press/O'Reilly & Associates, Inc.,
1005 Gravenstein Highway North, Sebastopol, CA 95472.

July 2002:   First Edition.
August 2002:   Second Printing.
October 2002:   Third Printing.

ISBN: 0-596-00365-x

Table of Contents

Part Two: iPhoto Basics

Part Three: Meet Your Public

The Missing Credits

About the Authors

 David Pogue is the weekly computer columnist for the *New York Times* and the creator of the Missing Manual series. He's the author or co-author of 20 books, including five in this series and six in the "For Dummies" line (including *The Flat-Screen iMac, Magic, Opera,* and *Classical Music*). In his other life, David is a former Broadway show conductor, a magician, and an incorrigible pianist (photos await at *www.davidpogue.com*).

He welcomes feedback about Missing Manual title by email: *david@pogueman.com*. (If you're seeking technical help, however, please refer to the help sources listed in Appendix C.)

 Joseph Schorr is a frequent contributor to *Macworld* and the senior product manager for digital asset management software at Extensis, Inc. in Portland, Oregon. A former *Macworld* contributing editor, he wrote the magazine's "Secrets" column for several years and co-authored six editions of *Macworld Mac Secrets.* He began collaborating with David Pogue in 1982—on musical comedies at Yale.

Joseph made his first foray into the world of photography long before the digital era—at age eight, when he built his own pinhole camera for a school science project using a cardboard box and set up a darkroom in the family laundry room. He'd be pleased to receive your feedback and suggestions about this book by email at *schorr@earthlink.net.*

 Derrick Story is the managing editor of O'Reilly Network (*www.oreillynet.com*). His interests include Mac OS X, digital photography, multimedia, Web development, wireless connectivity, and mobile computing. Derrick created the Mac DevCenter (*www.macdevcenter.com*) for O'Reilly & Associates and oversees its daily operations. After graduating with a BA in English, Derrick's professional experience includes more than 15 years as a photojournalist, former managing editor of Web Review, and a conference speaker for CMP, IDG, and O'Reilly. He also manages his commercial photo business, Story Photography (*www.storyphoto.com*). His photographs are featured in Chapters 1, 2, and 3 and elsewhere in this book.

About the Creative Team

Nan Barber (copy editor) co-authored *Office X for the Macintosh: The Missing Manual* and *Office 2001 for Macintosh: The Missing Manual.* She's the principal copy editor for the Missing Manual series, having edited the Missing Manual titles on Mac OS 9, AppleWorks 6, iMovie, Dreamweaver 4, and Windows XP. She's also managing editor for *Salamander (www.salamandermag.org)* and contributing copy editor for *www.thespook.com.* Email: *nanbarber@mac.com.*

John Cacciatore (copy editor) works out of his home office in Woburn, Mass., where he is ardently engaged in the English major's freelance trinity: writing, editing, and proofing. A collaborator on the past several Missing Manual volumes, John now understands the inner workings of Mac and Windows PCs more intimately than he ever dreamed possible. Email: *j_cacciatore@yahoo.com.*

Rose Cassano (cover illustration) has worked as an independent designer and illustrator for 20 years. Assignments have spanned everything from the nonprofit sector to corporate clientele. She lives in beautiful Southern Oregon, grateful for the miracles of modern technology that make living and working there a reality. Email: *cassano@cdsnet.net.* Web: *www.rosecassano.com.*

Dennis Cohen (technical reviewer), a veteran of the Jet Propulsion Laboratory, Claris, Ashton-Tate, and Aladdin, has served as the technical reviewer for many bestselling Mac books, including several editions of *Macworld Mac Secrets* and most Missing Manual titles. He's the co-author of *AppleWorks 6 for Dummies, Macworld Apple-Works 6 Bible, Macworld Microsoft Office 2001 Bible,* and *Macworld Mac OS X Bible.* Email: *drcohen@mac.com.*

Phil Simpson (book design and layout) has been involved with computer graphics since 1977, when he worked with one of the first graphics-generating computers, which were an offspring of flight-simulation technology. He now works out of his office in Stamford, Connecticut, where he has had his graphic design business since 1982. He is experienced in many facets of graphic design, including corporate identity, publication design, and corporate and medical communications. Email: *pmsimpson@earthlink.net.*

Acknowledgements

Special thanks to Ancil Nance, the amazing Portland photographer whose work added a measurable touch of class to my photo libraries (and whose gorgeous photos you can spot in many of the iPhoto screen illustrations in the latter chapters of this book). I'm also grateful to the engineering and marketing teams at Extensis who helped answer my technical questions and test some of the hardware and software mentioned in the book. Finally, my deepest thanks to my three favorite photographic subjects—Allison, Alexandria, and Zachary—who bring all the best things in life into my world every day.

—*Joseph Schorr*

Every photograph I publish reflects the help and generosity of these people: The late Don Swanson, who gave me my first camera (Argus C3) and inspired my vision; Al McCombs, who published my first photo in the *Chino Champion* when I was eleven years old; Jerry Saba, who showed me the magic of a print coming to life in a tray of developer; Dennis Tannen, who freely shared everything he learned at Brooks Institute of Photography and never asked for anything in return; and Jan Blanchard, who took my PR photo and has helped me through countless wedding assignments.

—*Derrick Story*

The Missing Manual series is a joint venture between Pogue Press (the dream team introduced on these pages) and O'Reilly & Associates (a dream publishing partner). I'm indebted, as always, to Tim O'Reilly, Mark Brokering, Cathy Record, and the rest of the gang.

I'm also grateful to proofreaders Chuck Brandstater, Stephanie English, and Danny Marcus; to beta reader Elizabeth Tonis; to Glenn Reid, the genius; to the wonderful Astrid Vanatalu; and to David Rogelberg for believing in the idea. Above all, thanks to Jennifer, Kelly, and Tia, who make these books—and everything else—possible.

—*David Pogue*

The Missing Manual Series

Missing Manuals are witty, superbly written guides to computer products that don't come with printed manuals (which is just about all of them). Each book features a handcrafted index; cross-references to specific page numbers (not just "see Chapter 14"); and an ironclad promise never to use an apostrophe in the possessive word *its*.

Recent and upcoming titles include:

- *DreamWeaver MX: The Missing Manual* by David Sawyer McFarland
- *Mac OS X: The Missing Manual* (2nd Edition) by David Pogue
- *Mac OS 9: The Missing Manual* by David Pogue
- *Office X for Macintosh: The Missing Manual* by Nan Barber, Tonya Engst, and David Reynolds
- *Office 2001 for Macintosh: The Missing Manual* by Nan Barber and David Reynolds
- *AppleWorks 6: The Missing Manual* by Jim Elferdink and David Reynolds
- *iMovie 2: The Missing Manual* by David Pogue
- *Windows 2000 Pro: The Missing Manual* by Sharon Crawford
- *Windows XP Home Edition: The Missing Manual* by David Pogue
- *Windows XP Pro: The Missing Manual* by David Pogue, Craig Zacker, and Linda Zacker

Introduction

In case you haven't heard, the digital camera market is exploding. One-third of all the cameras sold last year—close to *seven million*—were digital. What's more, industry experts are in universal agreement that within the next three or four years, companies like Nikon, Kodak, and Olympus will be selling far more digital cameras than the traditional film-based models.

It's taken a few decades—the underlying technology used in most digital cameras was invented in 1969. But film is finally on the decline.

And why not? The appeal of digital photography is huge. When you shoot digitally, you never have to pay a cent for film or photo processing. You get instant results, viewing your photos just moments after shooting them, making even Polaroids seem painfully slow by comparison. As a digital photographer, you can even be your own darkroom technician—without the darkroom. You can retouch and enhance photos, make enlargements, and print out greeting cards using your home computer. Sharing your pictures with others is far easier, too, since you can burn them to CD, email them to friends, or post them on the Web. As one fan puts it: "There are no 'negatives' in digital photography."

But there is one problem: When most people try to make all this cool stuff actually happen, they find themselves drowning in a sea of technical details—JPEG compression, EXIF tags, file format compatibility, image resolutions, FTP clients, and so on. It isn't pretty.

The cold reality is that while digital photography is full of promise, it's also been full of headaches. During the early years of digital cameras, just making the camera-to-computer connection was a nightmare. You had to mess with serial or USB cables, install device drivers, and use proprietary software to transfer, open, and convert camera images into a standard file format. If you handled all these tasks perfectly— and sacrificed a young male goat during the spring equinox—you ended up with good digital pictures.

iPhoto Arrives

Apple recognized this mess and finally decided to do something about it. When Steve Jobs gave his keynote address at Macworld Expo in January 2002, he referred to the "chain of pain" ordinary people experienced when attempting to download, store, edit, and share their digital photos.

He also focused on another growing problem among digital camera users: once you start shooting free, filmless photos, they pile up quickly. Before you know it, you have 6,000 pictures of your kid playing soccer. Just organizing and keeping track of all these photos is enough to drive you insane.

Apple's answer to all these problems is iPhoto, a simple and uncluttered program designed to organize, edit, and distribute digital photos without the nightmarish hassles. Like Apple's other iProducts (iMovie, iTunes, and iDVD), iPhoto isn't the most powerful image-management software in the world. Its design subscribes to its own little 80/20 rule: 80 percent of us really don't need more than about 20 percent of the features you'd find in a full-blown, $650 digital-asset management program. And iPhoto is free.

Two months after releasing iPhoto, Apple reported over one million downloads. Evidently, there were a lot of digital camera users out there feeling the pain and hoping that iPhoto would provide some much-needed relief.

About This Book

Don't let the rumors fool you. iPhoto may be simple, but it isn't simplistic. It offers a wide range of tools, shortcuts, and database-like features; a complete arsenal of photo-presentation features; and sophisticated multimedia and Internet hooks. Unfortunately, many of the best techniques aren't covered in the only "manual" you get with iMovie, its sparse electronic help screens.

This book was born to address two needs. First, it's designed to serve as the iPhoto manual—as the book that should have been in the box. It explores each iPhoto feature in depth, offers shortcuts and workarounds, and unearths features that the online help doesn't even mention.

Second, this book is designed to give you a grounding in professional photography. Together, the digital camera and iPhoto can produce presentations of stunning visual quality; they give you the *technical* tools to produce amazing photos. But most people don't have much experience with the *artistic* side of shooting—like lighting, manual shutter control, and composition—or even how to use the dozens of features packed into the modern digital camera. This book will tell you all you need to know.

About the Outline

This book is divided into four parts, each containing several chapters:

- Part 1, **Digital Cameras: The Missing Manual,** is a special treat. It's the course in photography and digital cameras promised above. These three chapters cover buying, using, and exploiting your digital camera, choosing the proper image resolution settings, and getting the most out of batteries and memory cards. This section of the book creates a bridge between everyday snapshots and the kinds of emotionally powerful shots you see in magazines and newspapers.

- Part 2, **iPhoto Basics,** covers the fundamentals of getting your photos into iPhoto, organizing and filing them, searching and finding them, and editing them to compensate for weak lighting (or weak photography).

- Part 3, **Meet Your Public,** is all about the payoff, the moment you've presumably been waiting for ever since you snapped the shots—showing them off. It covers the many ways iPhoto can show those photos to other people: as a slide show, as prints you order from the Internet or make yourself, as a handsome hardbound gift book, as a Web page, by email, or as a QuickTime-movie slide show that you post on the Web or distribute on CD or even DVD.

- Part 4, **iPhoto Stunts,** takes you way beyond the basics. It covers a miscellaneous potpourri of additional iPhoto features, including turning photos into screen savers or desktop pictures on your own Mac, exporting the photos in various formats, using iPhoto plug-ins and accessory programs, and managing (or even switching) iPhoto libraries.

At the end of the book, Appendix A offers troubleshooting guidance, Appendix B goes through iPhoto's menus one by one to make sure that every last feature has been covered, and Appendix C lists some Web sites that will help to fuel your growing addiction to digital photography.

The Very Basics

You'll find very little jargon or nerd terminology in this book. You will, however, encounter a few terms and concepts that you'll see frequently in your Macintosh life. They include:

- **Clicking.** This book offers three kinds of instructions that require you to use the mouse or trackpad attached to your Mac. To *click* means to point the arrow cursor at something onscreen and then—without moving the cursor at all—press and release the clicker button on the mouse (or laptop trackpad). To *double-click,* of course, means to click twice in rapid succession, again without moving the cursor at all. And to *drag* means to move the cursor while keeping the button continuously pressed.

  When you're told to ⌘-*click* something, you click while pressing the ⌘ key (next to the Space bar). Such related procedures as *Shift-clicking, Option-clicking,* and

Control-clicking work the same way—just click while pressing the corresponding key on the bottom row of your keyboard.

- **Menus.** The *menus* are the words in the lightly striped bar at the top of your screen. You can either click one of these words to open a pull-down menu of commands (and then click again on a command), or click and *hold* the button as you drag down the menu to the desired command (and release the button to activate the command). Either method works fine.

- **Keyboard shortcuts.** Every time you take your hand off the keyboard to move the mouse, you lose time and potentially disrupt your creative flow. That's why many experienced Mac fans use keystroke combinations instead of menu commands wherever possible. ⌘-P opens the Print dialog box, ⌘-S saves whatever document you're currently working in, and ⌘-M minimizes the current window to the Dock.

When you see a shortcut like ⌘-W (which closes the current window), it's telling you to hold down the ⌘ key, and, while it's down, type the letter W, and then release both keys.

About→These→Arrows

Throughout this book, and throughout the Missing Manual series, you'll find sentences like this one: "Open the System folder→Libraries→Fonts folder." That's shorthand for a much longer instruction that directs you to open three nested folders in sequence. That instruction might read: "On your hard drive, you'll find a folder called System. Open that. Inside the System folder window is a folder called Libraries. Open that. Inside *that* folder is yet another one called Fonts. Double-click to open it, too."

Similarly, this kind of arrow shorthand helps to simplify the business of choosing commands in menus, as shown in Figure I-1.

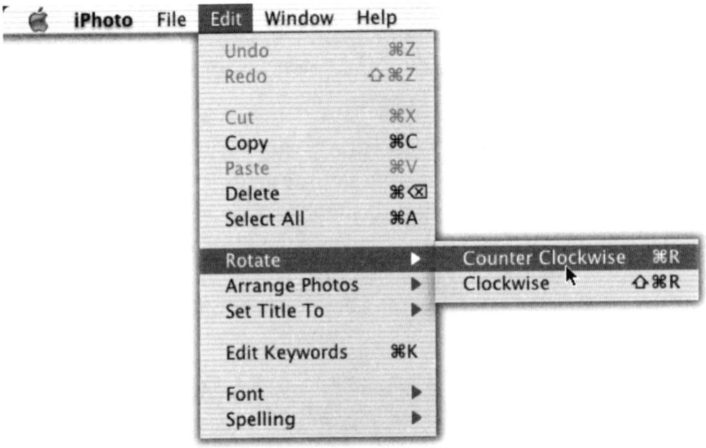

Figure I-1:
When you read "Choose Edit→Rotate→Counter Clockwise" in a Missing Manual, that means: "Click the Edit menu to open it; click Rotate in that menu; choose Counter Clockwise in the resulting submenu."

About MissingManuals.com

At the *missingmanuals.com* Web site, you'll find news, articles, and updates to the books in this series.

But if you click the name of this book and then the Errata link, you'll find a unique resource: a list of corrections and updates that have been made in successive printings of this book. You can mark important corrections right into your own copy of the book, if you like.

In fact, the same Errata page offers an invitation for you to submit such corrections and updates yourself. In an effort to keep the book as up-to-date and accurate as possible, each time we print more copies of this book, we'll make any confirmed corrections you've suggested. Thanks in advance for reporting any glitches you find!

In the meantime, we'd love to hear your own suggestions for new books in the Missing Manual line. There's a place for that on the Web site, too, as well as a place to sign up for free email notification of new titles in the series.

Part One:
Digital Cameras:
The Missing Manual

1

Welcome to Digital Photography

pple's marketing team came up with a cute slogan for iPhoto: "Shoot like Ansel; organize like Martha." The truth is, of course, that iPhoto doesn't help you shoot like Ansel Adams at all. In fact, it does absolutely nothing for your photography skills.

But this book will. The first three chapters cover both the basics and the secrets that the pros use to take consistently good photographs. After all, if you're going to the trouble of mastering a new program, then you should be rewarded with stunning results. Or, put another way: Beautiful pictures in, beautiful pictures out.

Meet Digital Photography

When you use a film camera, your pictures are "memorized" by billions of silver halide crystals suspended on celluloid. Most digital cameras, on the other hand, store your pictures on a memory card.

It's a special kind of memory: *flash* memory. Unlike the RAM in your Macintosh, the contents of flash memory survive even when the machine is turned off, just as in a Palm organizer. You can erase and reuse a digital camera's memory card over and over again—a key to the great economy of digital photography.

At this millisecond of technology time, digital cameras are slightly slower than film cameras in almost every regard. They're slower to turn on, slower to autofocus, and slower to recover from one shot before it's ready to take another.

Once you've captured a picture, however, digital cameras provide almost nothing but advantages over film.

Instant Feedback

You can view a miniature version of the photo on the camera's built-in screen. If there's something about the picture that bothers you—like the telephone pole growing out of your best friend's head—you can simply erase it and try again. Once the shooting session is over, you leave knowing that nothing but good photos are on your camera. By contrast, with traditional film photography you have no real idea how your pictures turned out until you open that sealed drugstore envelope and flip through the prints. More often than not, there are one or two pictures that you really like, and the rest are wasted money.

Instant feedback becomes a real benefit when you're under pressure to deliver excellent photographs. Imagine the hapless photographer who, having offered to shoot candid photos during a friend's wedding reception, later opens the envelope of prints and discovers that the flash had malfunctioned all evening, resulting in three rolls of shadowy figures in a darkened hotel ballroom. A digital camera would have alerted the photographer to the problem immediately.

In short, digital photographers sleep much better at night. They never worry about how the day's pictures will turn out—they already know!

Cheap Pix

Digital cameras also save you a great deal of money. Needless to say, you don't spend anything on developing. Printing out pictures on a photo printer at home costs money, but few people print every single shot they take. And where are most of your prints now? In a shoebox somewhere?

Printing out 4 x 6 prints at home, using an inkjet photo printer, costs about the same amount as you'd pay at the drugstore. But when you want enlargements, printing your own is vastly less expensive. Even on the glossy $1-per-sheet inkjet photo paper, an 8 x 10 costs about $1.50 or so (ink cartridges are expensive), compared with $8 from the drugstore. A poster-sized print from a wide-format photo printer (13 x 10) will cost you about $3.50 at home, compared with $20 from a photo lab.

Take More Risks

Because you have nothing to lose by taking a shot—and everything to gain—digital photography allows your creative juices to flow. If you don't like that shot of randomly piled shoes on the front porch, then, what the heck, erase it.

With the expense of developing taken out of the equation, you're free to shoot everything that catches your eye and decide later whether to keep it or not. This is how a digital camera can make you a better photographer—by freeing up your creativity. Your risk-taking will lead to more exciting images than you ever dreamed you'd take.

More Fun

Add it all up, and digital photography is more fun than traditional shooting. No more disappointing prints and wasted money. Instead, you enjoy the advantages of instant feedback, flexibility, and creativity.

But that's just the beginning, since now there's iPhoto. Suddenly photography isn't just about producing a stack of 4 x 6 pieces of paper. Thanks to iPhoto, now your photos are infinitely more flexible. At the end of the day, you get to sit down with your Mac and create instant slide shows, screen savers, desktop pictures, professional Web pages, and email attachments. Shoot the most adorable shot ever taken of your daughter, and minutes later it's on its way to Grandma.

Photography doesn't get any better than this.

Buying a Digital Camera

Citizens of the world bought nearly 18 million digital cameras in 2001, and we're just getting started. By 2005, in fact, analysts expect digital cameras to outsell film cameras.

The major players in this market are Sony, Olympus, Nikon, HP, Kodak, and Canon. They're not alone, however. Every company ever associated with electronics or cameras—Panasonic, Casio, Leica, Kyocera, Minolta, Konica, and so on—also has a finger in the pie. Each company offers a variety of models and a wide range of prices, which compete fiercely for your dollars. Some of these companies release new models *every six months*. And, exactly as in other high-tech industries, each generation offers better features, improved resolution, and lower prices.

If you're in the market for a new digital camera, the rest of this chapter is for you. It's dedicated to helping you find that diamond in the rough: the camera with the features you *really* need at a price you can afford.

Don't worry about the different marketing categories for cameras—entry level, consumer, prosumer, pro, whatever. Just read about the features available in the following pages—presented here roughly in order of importance—and consider how much they're worth to you.

Image Resolution

The first number you probably see in the description of a digital camera is the number of *megapixels* it offers.

A pixel (short for *picture element*) is one tiny colored dot, one of the thousands or millions that compose a single digital photograph. You can't escape learning this term, since pixels are everything in computer graphics.

You need one million pixels—that is, one megapixel—for something as simple as a 4 x 6 inch print. Thus the shorthand: Instead of saying that your camera has 3,300,000 pixels, you'd say that it's a 3.3-megapixel camera.

What you're describing is its *resolution*. For instance, a 5-megapixel camera has better resolution than a 3-megapixel camera. (It also costs a lot more.)

So how many pixels you need?

Pictures on the screen

Many digital photos are destined to be shown solely on a computer screen. That includes pictures that you:

- Send by email.
- Post on a Web page.
- Paste into a FileMaker database.
- Turn into a screen saver that parades full-screen pictures across your monitor when you're not using it.
- Choose as a desktop background.

If this is what you have in mind when you think about digital photography, congratulations. You're about to save a lot of money on a camera, because you can get by with one that has very few megapixels.

For example, a 1.3-megapixel camera typically produces graphics files that measure 1280 x 960 pixels. Remember that the screen of an iBook laptop has a resolution of 1024 x 768 pixels, which is even smaller. So even a very inexpensive 1.3-megapixel camera ($200 or less) takes pictures that are actually too big to display on the iBook screen. If you want to see the whole picture, you'll have to zoom out (or trim off some of the margins).

Printing out pictures

If you intend to print out your photos, however, it's a very different story.

The typical computer screen displays 72 pixels per square inch. But to look smooth like a real photograph, a printer has to pack the color dots much closer together on the paper—150 pixels per square inch or more.

Remember the 1.3-megapixel photo that would fill the iBook screen? It has barely adequate resolution for a 4 x 6 print (see Figure 1-1). If you try to print that photo as an 8 x 10, you'll see jagged dots. The resulting speckled effect makes it look as though everybody in your circle of friends has some kind of skin disorder.

If you intend to make prints of your photos—and you'll be in very good company—shop for your camera with this table in mind:

Camera Resolution to Print Size

Megapixels	Max Print Size
0.3 megapixels (640 x 480)	3 x 4 inches
1.3 megapixels	5 x 7 inches
2 megapixels	8 x 10 inches
3.3 megapixels	11 x 14 inches
4 megapixels	12 x 16 inches

These are extremely crude guidelines, by the way. Many factors contribute to the quality of an 8 x 10 print—lens quality, file compression, exposure, camera shake, paper quality, the number of different color cartridges your printer has, and so on. But these figures do provide a rough guide regarding the number of megapixels you need in a camera for various uses.

Figure 1-1:
What went wrong? The top image, shot with a 1.3-megapixel camera, is what you saw on your computer screen. But when you made an 8 x 10 print, the results looked like the bottom: filled with "jaggies." The answer is that printers need more megapixels than computer screens. So if you want photo-quality 8 x 10 prints, get a camera with at least 2 megapixels (3 is better) so you can avoid the jaggies.

Memory Capacity

Memory cards are like suitcases: They're never big enough. But unlike suitcases, you can't sit on a memory card to squeeze more inside.

One thing, however, is for sure: The memory card that came with your camera is a joke. It probably holds only about six or eight best-quality pictures. It's nothing more than a cost-saving placeholder, foisted on you by a camera company that knew full well that you'd have to go buy a bigger one.

When you're shopping for a camera, then, it's imperative that you also factor in the cost of a bigger card.

It's impossible to overstate how glorious it is to have a huge memory card in your camera (or several smaller ones in your camera bag). You quit worrying that you're about to run out of storage, and so you shoot more freely, increasing the odds that you'll get truly phenomenal pictures. You can go on longer trips without dragging a laptop along, too, because you won't feel the urge to run back to your hotel room every three hours to offload your latest pictures.

You'll be worrying plenty about your camera's limited *battery* life. The last thing you need is another chronic headache in the form of your memory card. Bite the bullet and buy a bigger one.

Here's a table that helps you calculate how much storage you'll need to record images at the high-quality setting. Find the column that represents the resolution of your camera, in megapixels, and then read down to see how many best-quality photos each size card will hold.

Camera Resolution	640 x 480 (.3 MP)	1280 x 960 (.3 MP)	1600 x 1200 (.3 MP)	2048 x 1536 (.3 MP)	2272 x 1704 (4.1 MP)
Card Capacity	How many pictures	How many pictures	How many pictures	How many pictures	How many pictures
8 MB	29	10	7	3	2
16 MB	58	24	14	8	7
32 MB	120	49	30	17	14
64 MB	241	88	61	35	30
128 MB	483	177	123	71	61

Memory Cards

The *kind* of memory card your camera uses isn't nearly as important as the factors listed earlier in this discussion. But once you've narrowed down your potential purchase to a short list of candidates, it's worth weighing the pros and cons of the cards they use.

- **Compact Flash**—Compact Flash cards are popular and relatively inexpensive; you can buy them in capacities all the way up to 1 GB . That's a *lot* of pictures—hundreds and hundreds. *Pros:* Readily available; affordable; wide selection to meet just about every need. *Con:* They're the largest of any memory-card format, which dictates a bigger camera. Current prices for a 128 MB Compact Flash card range from $50 to $80 depending on the *write speed* of the card (how fast it stores the picture). However, tests haven't proven conclusively that they're actually any faster in the real world.

Tip: Some Compact Flash cameras can also accommodate the IBM Microdrive, which is literally a miniature hard drive in the form of a Compact Flash card. These cards (hard drives) have enormous capacity: 340 MB or 1 GB.

- **SmartMedia**—These cards are wafer-thin and reasonably priced. Unfortunately, storage capacity is limited—at this writing, SmartMedia cards top out at 128 MB. *Pros:* Perfect for small cameras; readily available; affordable. *Con:* Storage capacity limited to 128 MB. Current prices for a 128 MB SmartMedia card range from $50 to $85.

- **Memory Stick**—Sony created the Memory Stick as an interchangeable memory card for its cameras, camcorders, and laptops. Memory Sticks are great if you're already knee-deep in Sony equipment, but few other companies use them. *Pro:* Works with most Sony digital devices. *Cons:* Works primarily with Sony gear;

limited in capacity to 128 MB. Current price range for a 128 MB Memory Stick is $62 to $150, depending on the brand (Sony's own are the most expensive).

- **MultiMedia/Secure Digital (SD)**—These extremely tiny cards are no bigger than postage stamps, which is why you also find them in Palm organizers and MP3 players. *Pro:* Very compact size, perfect for subcompact cameras. *Cons:* Somewhat limited availability; maximum size of about 128 MB; expensive. Current prices for a 128 MB Multimedia card range from $80 to $95.

If you already have an existing supply of memory cards from a previous camera, you have a good incentive to buy a new camera that uses the same format. Otherwise, compare price per megabyte, availability, and what works with your other digital gear.

If all other factors are equal, however, choose a camera that takes Compact Flash cards. They're plentiful, inexpensive, and have huge capacity.

Tip: When buying memory cards, ignore the brand: there's no quality difference between big name brands and lesser-known companies. Furthermore, premium cards labeled "high performance" aren't significantly faster than standard cards. In truth, the speed of a camera depends on its electronics much more than the type of memory card.

Battery Life

In many ways, digital cameras have arrived. They're not like cellphones, which drop calls on a daily basis, or wireless palmtops, which are excruciatingly slow connecting to the Internet. Digital cameras are reliable, high quality, and generally extremely rewarding.

Except for battery life.

Thanks to that LCD screen on the back, digital cameras go through batteries like Kleenex. The battery, as it turns out, will probably be the one limiting factor to your photo shoots. When the juice is gone, your session is over.

Battery type could be a deal-breaker for a certain model that you'd had your eye on. Here's what you'll find as you shop for various cameras:

- **Proprietary, built-in rechargeable**—Many smaller cameras come with a "brick" battery—a dark gray, lithium-ion rechargeable battery. (These subcompact cameras are simply too small to accommodate four AA-style batteries, as described next.)

  The problem with proprietary batteries is that you can't replace them when you're on the road. If you're only three hours into your day at Disney World when the battery dies, that's just tough—your shooting session is over. You can't exactly duck into a drugstore to buy a new one.

  Some cameras come with a separate, external charger for this battery. The advantage here is that you can buy a second battery (usually for $60 or so). You can keep one battery in the charger at all times. That way, when the main battery gives up the ghost, you can swap it with the one in the charger, and your day goes on. (Or, in Disney World situations, you can take both batteries with you for the day.)

All of this is something of a pain, and not nearly as handy as the rechargeable AAs described next.

But it sure beats the system used by Sony and other companies, in which the camera *is* the battery charger. When the battery dies, so does your creative muse. You have no choice but to return home and plug in the camera itself, taking it out of commission for several hours as it recharges the battery.

• **Two or four AA-size batteries**—Most other cameras accept AA batteries, and may even come with a set of alkalines to get you started.

If you learn nothing else from this chapter, however, learn this: *Don't use standard alkaline AAs.* You'll get a better return on your investment by tossing $5 bills out your car window on the highway.

Alkalines may be fine for flashlights and radios, but they're no match for the massive power drain of the modern digital camera (not even "premium" alkalines). A set of four AAs might last 20 minutes in the digital camera, if you're lucky.

So what are you supposed to put in there? Something you may have never even heard of: *rechargeable nickel-metal-hydride (NiMH)* AAs. They last *much* longer than alkalines, and because you can use them over and over again, they're far less expensive.

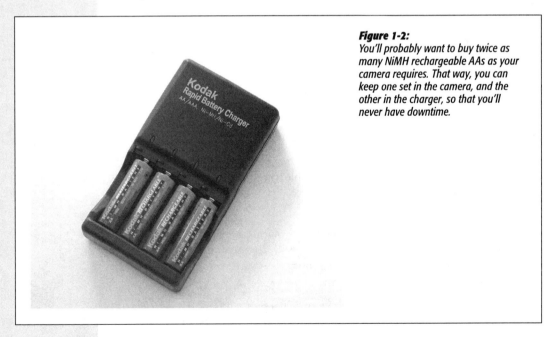

Figure 1-2:
You'll probably want to buy twice as many NiMH rechargeable AAs as your camera requires. That way, you can keep one set in the camera, and the other in the charger, so that you'll never have downtime.

You generally won't find NiMHs in department stores, but they're easy to find online (for example, *www.shopper.com*). A charger and a set of four NiMH AAs cost about $30 (see Figure 1-2).

The beauty of digital cameras that accept AAs is that they accommodate so many different kinds of batteries. In addition to rechargeable NiMH batteries, most cameras can also accept something called AA *photo lithium* batteries. They're a lot like alkalines, in that they're disposable and can't be recharged. However, because they last many times longer than regular AAs, they're much more expensive. They're also ideal to carry in the camera case for emergency backup.

The final advantage of this kind of camera is that, in a pinch—yes, in the middle of your Disney World day—you can even hit up a drugstore for a set of standard alkaline AAs. Sure enough, you'll be tossing them in the trash after only about 20 minutes of use in the camera—but in an emergency, 20 minutes is a lot better than nothing.

Tip: Some cameras offer the best of all worlds. The Nikon CoolPix 5000 camera, for example, comes with a proprietary lithium-ion "brick" and a matching charger. In addition, the camera also accepts all kinds of AAs, including alkalines, rechargeables, and the Duracell CRV3 battery (a disposable lithium battery that looks like two AAs fused together at the seam). You should always be able to get juice on the road with *this* baby.

Size and Shape

You could have the best 4-megapixel camera on the planet, but if it's bulkier than a Volvo, you're probably going to leave it at home and miss lots of good shots.

The trick is to balance the features you need with the package you want; unfortunately, the smaller the camera, the fewer the features you usually get. For example, you'll rarely see a connector for an external flash (a *hotshoe*) or a rotating flip screen on a camera that fits in your shirt pocket.

Once you've balanced features against size, do whatever you can to get your hands on your leading candidate. Is it too small to hold comfortably? Does your index finger naturally align with the shutter release? Are you constantly smudging the lens with your other fingers?

Your camera should become a natural extension of your vision. If you're not bonding with it, your pictures will reflect that—or, rather, your *lack* of pictures.

Lens Quality

In the early days of digital photography, cameras had interesting electronics, but only so-so lenses. And if you've ever tried reading fine print through a cheesy magnifying glass, then you have some idea of how the world looks though bad optics…in a word, lousy.

Fortunately, the scene is much sharper now. Sony, Olympus, Canon, Leica, and Nikon all take pride in the lenses for their digital cameras, and they have solid reputations for great glass, as a result. (Interestingly, the camera makers not listed here generally buy their lenses *from* Olympus, Canon, and Nikon.)

This particular criterion, important though it may be, isn't something you'll have much control over. There's no measurement for the quality of a lens, and no way for you to tell how good it is simply by looking. The closest you can come is to read the reviews in photo magazines or the Web sites listed in Appendix C.

Zoom

When you read the specs for a camera—or read the logos painted on its body—you frequently encounter numbers like this: "3X/10X ZOOM!" The number before the slash tells you how many times the camera can magnify a distant image, much like a telescope. That number measures the *optical* zoom, which is the actual amount that the lenses themselves can zoom in. Such zooming, of course, is useful when you want to shoot something that's far away.

Note: If you're used to traditional photography, here's what you can expect: A typical 3X digital camera zoom ranges from 6.5mm (wide angle) to 19.5mm (telephoto). That would be about the same as a 38mm to 105mm zoom lens in film-camera talk (35mm).

Then there's *digital* zoom, the number after the slash. Much as computer owners mistakenly jockey for superiority by comparing the megahertz rating of their computers—little suspecting that higher megahertz ratings don't necessarily make faster computers—camera makers seem to think that what consumers want most in a digital camera is a powerful digital zoom. "7X!" your camera may say on the box. "10X! 20X!"

When a camera uses its *digital* zoom, it simply reinterprets the individual pixels, in effect enlarging them. The image gets bigger, but it doesn't get any *sharper;* in fact, image quality actually degrades. Digital zooms are handy in a pinch, but they're not something worth paying extra for.

Base your camera-buying decision on the *optical* zoom range—that's the zoom that counts.

Flip Screen

Every digital camera has a little LCD screen, but on some specially endowed models, you can flip and swivel the screen around to allow multiple viewing angles (Figure 1-3). These cameras let you hold it any way you want—at your waist, above your head, even at your ankles—and still frame the shot without contorting yourself into a pretzel.

If you're stuck in the middle of a crowd, but want a shot of the parade, then tilt the screen, raise the camera over your head, frame the shot, and shoot. Want to create that low-angle Orson Welles shot for added drama, or snap a terrific baby's-eye-view photo without having to crawl around in the dirt? It's easy with a flip screen.

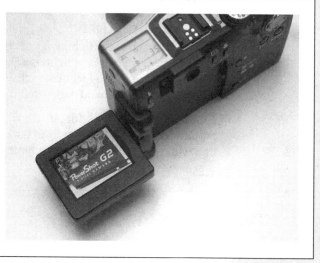

Figure 1-3:
Flip screens first appeared on camcorders and were soon adapted to digital cameras. The best ones flip all the way out from the camera, providing multiple viewing angles. Others just allow slight tilting upward and downward and remain attached to the camera back.

Manual Controls

Entry-level digital cameras are often called *point-and-shoot* models with good reason: You point, you shoot. The camera is stuck in perennial *program mode,* which means it does all the thinking.

More expensive cameras, on the other hand, provide a selection of manual settings that let you take your camera off autopilot.

Don't assume that all you'll ever need is a point-and-shoot. Read Chapter 3 first. There you'll learn all the amazing, special-situation photos—sports photos, night-time shots, fireworks, indoor portraits, and so on—you can take *only* if your camera offers manual controls. (And if all of that sounds too esoteric, *then* buy a point-and-shoot.)

If you opt for a camera with manual controls, shop for these features:

- *Aperture priority mode* lets you specify how wide the camera's shutter opens when you take the shot. It's probably the most popular manual control mode, because it's easy to use but offers lots of control. In Chapter 3, you'll learn how to use aperture priority to create soft background portraits and other great effects.

- *Shutter priority mode* is particularly handy for freezing—or blurring—shots. It lets you tell the camera how *fast* the shutter should open and close: fast to freeze sports shots; slow for nighttime shots, or to turn a babbling brook into an abstract, fuzzy blur.

• *Manual mode* allows you to set the aperture and the shutter speed independently. When you hit the right combination, the camera lets you know that you've set the right exposure and can take the picture.

If you're looking for a camera that you can grow with as your photo skills increase, then manual controls are features worth paying for.

Autofocus Assist Light

Even though autofocus technology has been around for years, it's still not a perfect science. There are plenty of lighting conditions, such as dark interiors, where your camera will struggle to focus correctly. Autofocus works by looking for patches of *contrast* between light and dark—and if there's no light, there's no focusing.

An autofocus assist light (or *AF assist*) is a clever invention that neatly solves the problem (Figure 1-4). In dim light, the camera briefly beams stripes of white light, or a subtle red pattern, onto the subject so the camera has enough visual information on which to focus.

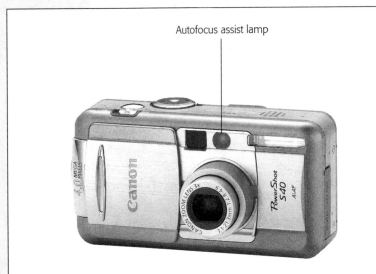

Autofocus assist lamp

Figure 1-4:
An AF assist light, like the one on this Canon PowerShot S40, will greatly improve your percentage of properly focused shots. You might want to put this item near the top of your desirable-features list. (Ditto for the sliding, built-in lens cover, which makes the camera self-contained and handy.)

Variable "Film" Speeds

Back in the old days, when photographers had to walk through ten-foot snow drifts just to get to school (uphill both ways), they also had to carry around different film types for different lighting situations. They would use *400-speed* film in dim lighting, *100-speed* film in bright outdoor light, and so on. You might have heard these film speeds referred to as the *ISO settings*.

Even though digital cameras don't need different kinds of film, most still let you "bump up" the speed by pushing a button (Figure 1-5).

You'll find out more about speeds in Chapters 2 and 3. For now, it's enough to note that a choice of film speeds gives you greater flexibility when shooting indoors or outside at night.

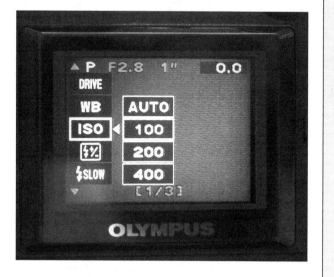

Figure 1-5:
Some cameras provide a menu of film speed options, often under the label "ISO," which is a measurement of light sensitivity familiar to film photographers.

Built-In Sliding Lens Cover

Let's call a spade a spade: Detachable lens covers are a pain. If you tie it to the camera with that little loop of black thread, it bangs against your hand, or the lens, when it's windy. If it's loose, it's destined to fall behind the couch cushions, pop off in your camera bag, or get mixed in with the change in your pocket. They seem to end up everywhere but protecting the lens of your camera.

Some cameras, especially compact models, eliminate this madness. They have sliding lens covers that protect the optics (and your sanity), as shown in Figure 1-4. Just sliding the cover open both turns the camera on and makes its zoom lens extend, ready for action. When you're done shooting, the lens retracts and the cover slides back in place.

The drawback to built-in lens protectors is that they generally prevent you from adding filters, telephoto lenses, and other attachments. If you're looking for a portable travel mate to take on vacation, the sliding lens cover should be high on your list. On the other hand, if a serious picture-making tool is your focus, then make sure it accepts attachments.

Attachments

Digital camera owners never even consider attaching filters, telephoto lenses, and external flashes. But if you're coming from a traditional film-camera background, and you're a fairly serious photographer, this may be one of the first features you think about.

In general, most of the big, heavy, traditional-design digital cameras can accept such attachments. Most tiny, capsule-shaped, subcompact pocket cameras can't.

The trick to a happy accessory life is calculating how hard they are to attach. The process often entails fitting the camera with tubular lens adapters (attachable via tiny threads). Nothing is more frustrating than stripping the threads on your camera body because you couldn't get the adapter ring to screw in properly (Figure 1-6).

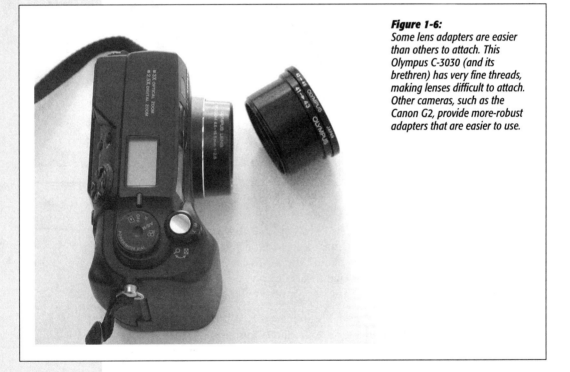

Figure 1-6:
Some lens adapters are easier than others to attach. This Olympus C-3030 (and its brethren) has very fine threads, making lenses difficult to attach. Other cameras, such as the Canon G2, provide more-robust adapters that are easier to use.

So after you find a camera that accepts the attachments you want, then pay attention to *how* they attach. Usually the smaller the adapter and the finer the threads, the more patience you'll need. Your sanity may be at stake here.

iPhoto Compatibility

As Chapter 4 makes clear, transferring your digital pictures into iPhoto is a piece of cake. You simply plug the camera into your Mac, turn it on, and let iPhoto slurp up the pictures over the USB cable.

Unfortunately, as hundreds of crestfallen Mac fans have discovered, iPhoto doesn't recognize every digital camera ever built. If you are indeed shopping for a camera right now, you're almost certainly covered, since most cameras released *since* iPhoto's debut work with it. But older cameras may not.

A list of officially approved cameras awaits at *www.apple.com/iphoto/compatibility*. This is not a comprehensive list, however. It represents only a few models that Apple has actually tested. Dozens of other models work just fine but haven't yet been tested and listed on the Web site.

If it turns out that your camera can't talk to iPhoto, all is not lost; Chapter 4 explains several workarounds for iPhoto-incompatible cameras.

Shutter Lag

You won't see *shutter lag* times included on most camera spec sheets, but it represents one of the biggest frustrations with digital cameras.

Shutter lag is the time it takes for the camera to calculate the correct focus and exposure before it actually captures the scene. In most camera models under $2,000, this interval amounts to an infuriating one-second delay between the time you press the shutter button and the instant the picture is actually recorded. Unfortunately, that's more than enough time for you to miss the precise moment your daughter blows out the candles on her birthday cake, your son's first step, and that adorable expression on your cat's face. Fractions of a second are a lifetime in photography (Figure 1-7).

Figure 1-7:
"Did you get me jumping backward over the coffee table? Did you get it? Tell me you got that shot! Tell me you got it…" Every digital photographer has a collection of these missed shots, thanks to shutter lag.

You can reduce or minimize shutter lag in either of two ways. First, of course, you can set the camera's focus and exposure manually, as described in the next two chapters. That way, there's no thinking left for the camera to do when you actually squeeze the shutter button.

Second, you can *prefocus*. This trick involves squeezing the shutter button halfway, ahead of time, forcing the camera to do its calculations. Keep your finger halfway down until the moment of truth. Now, when you finally squeeze it down all the way, you get the shot you wanted with very little delay.

Unfortunately, neither of these techniques works in all situations. Manually focusing and prefocusing both take time and eliminate spontaneity.

Until the electronics of digital cameras improves, the best you can hope for is to buy a model with the smallest shutter lag possible. You won't find this spec in brochures, though; your best bet is to visit one of the camera-review Web sites listed in Appendix C. Many of them list the shutter-lag timings for popular digital cameras.

Burst Mode (RAM Buffer)

When you press the shutter button on a digital camera, the image begins a long tour through the camera's guts. First, the lens projects the image onto an electronic sensor—a *CCD* (Charge-Coupled Device) or *CMOS* (Complementary Metal Oxide Semiconductor). Second, the sensor dumps the image temporarily into the camera's built-in memory (a memory *buffer*). Finally, the camera's circuitry feeds the image from its memory buffer onto the memory card.

You might be wondering about that second step. Why don't digital cameras record the image directly to the memory card?

The answer is simple: You would hate it. It would take forever. You'd only be able to take a new picture every few seconds or so. By stashing shots into a memory buffer as a temporary holding tank (a very fast process) before recording the image on the memory card (a much slower process), the camera frees up its attention so that you can take another photo quickly. The camera catches up later, when you've released the shutter button. (All of this is one reason why digital cameras aren't as responsive as film cameras, which transfer your images directly from lens to film.)

The size of this memory buffer in your digital camera affects your life in a couple of different ways. First, it permits certain cameras to have a *burst mode*, which lets you fire off several shots per second. That's a great feature when you're trying to capture an extremely fleeting scene, such as a great soccer goal, your three-year-old's smile, or Microsoft being humble.

A big memory buffer also permits *movie mode*, described later. It can even help fight shutter lag, because the ability to fire off a burst of five or six frames improves your odds of capturing that perfect moment.

As you shop, you probably won't see the amount of memory in a certain camera advertised. But keeping your eye out for cameras with burst mode (and checking out *how many* frames per second it can capture) is good advice.

Panorama Mode

How many times have you showed a travel picture to a friend and remarked, "It looked a lot bigger in real life"? That's because it *was* bigger, and your camera couldn't capture it all. Capturing a vast landscape with a digital camera is like looking at the Grand Canyon through a paper-towel tube.

Digital camera makers have created an ingenious solution to widen this narrow view of life: panorama mode (Figure 1-8). With it, you can stitch together a series of individual images to create a single, beautiful vista, similar to what you saw when you were standing there in real life. The camera's onscreen display helps align the edge of the last shot with the beginning of the next one.

Figure 1-8:
This image is actually four pictures stitched together using the Panorama Mode.

Software Bundle

When reviewing the software bundle included with a camera you're considering, look for Mac OS X compatibility—not for importing and organizing the pictures (you've got iPhoto for that), but for editing them and stitching together panoramas, if your camera offers that feature.

Don't rule out a good camera if the software isn't perfect; for most purposes, iPhoto may be all the software you ever need. But if you're torn between two cameras, favor the one with Mac OS X software in the box.

Tip: You can keep track of all the latest imaging programs for Mac OS X by checking Apple's Web site: *www.apple.com/downloads/macosx/imaging_3d/.*

Noise Reduction

The longer the exposure to record a scene, the more important *noise reduction* becomes. When you shoot nighttime shots, what should be a jet-black sky exhibits tiny colored specks—*artifacts*—that put a considerable damper on your photo's impact.

The noise reduction feature, if your camera has it, usually kicks in when the shutter speed becomes very slow. The technology varies by manufacturer, but most work like this: When you press the shutter, the camera takes *two* shots—the one that you think you're getting, and a second shot with the shutter completely closed. Since it's the electronics of the camera itself that produces visual noise, both shots theoretically should contain the same colored speckles in the same spots. The camera compares the two shots, concludes that all of the colored specks it finds in the *closed-*shutter shot must be unwanted, and deletes them from the real shot.

Chances are you'll have to dig through the literature or the specs on the manufacturer's Web site to find out whether the camera you're considering has this feature. But if you're a nighttime shooter, it's well worth the time spent investigating.

Tripod Mount

Nobody *likes* to use a tripod with a digital camera. But there are moments when a tripod is necessary for a beautiful artistic shot, such as streaking car lights across a bridge, or almost anything at night.

So take a moment to turn your camera candidate upside down and inspect the socket. Is it plastic or metal? Metal is better. Where is it positioned? Near the center of the base is preferred to way off on one side or another.

The location and composition of the tripod mount isn't going to be a deal breaker, but it's certainly worth the short time it takes to examine while the sales clerk is writing up your order.

Movie Mode

Almost every digital camera claims to capture video; some do it better than others.

Cheaper cameras produce movies that are tiny, low-resolution QuickTime flicks. These mini-movies have their novelty value, and are better than nothing when your intention is to email your newborn baby's first cry to eager relatives across the globe.

But more expensive cameras these days can capture QuickTime flicks at decent size (320 x 240 pixels) and smoothness (15 frames per second), usually complete with soundtrack. More on this topic in Chapter 3.

Just remember that digital movies fill up your memory card like a fire hydrant filling up a thimble. So if you want to use this function, spend the extra dough for a large-capacity memory card.

Price

Sooner or later, you'll have to confront the "P" word. Unfortunately, it's a painful subject in the world of electronic photography. Feature for feature, digital cameras simply cost more than traditional film cameras. Prices are more palatable now than they were a few years ago, but you should still consider your camera a short-term investment, thereby giving it careful consideration.

You can count on the 35mm film camera remaining current and serviceable for at least five years. Whatever digital camera you buy now, however, will be discontinued by its manufacturer *within a year.*

The pace of obsolescence will eventually slow down as the technology levels off. But for now, when you evaluate how much you're willing to spend, keep in mind that this might be a one-year purchase at worst, and a two-year investment at best.

Generally speaking, prices start at $400 for high-quality 3-megapixel cameras, and $600 for "prosumer" cameras in the 4 to 5 megapixel range. (Of course, you can also find extremely professional models that cost $3,000 and up.)

Whatever you do, price-compare before you buy. You'll be astonished at the differences in prices you'll find from store to store. Begin your search at, for example, *www.dealtime.com* (Figure 1-9).

Figure 1-9:
At Dealtime.com (a price-comparison site), start by searching for the specific camera you want. Then sort the results by the quality of the store (that is, by the customer rating). Buy your camera from a store that has been rated with four stars or more, being very careful to watch out for low prices that come with ridiculously inflated "shipping" charges.

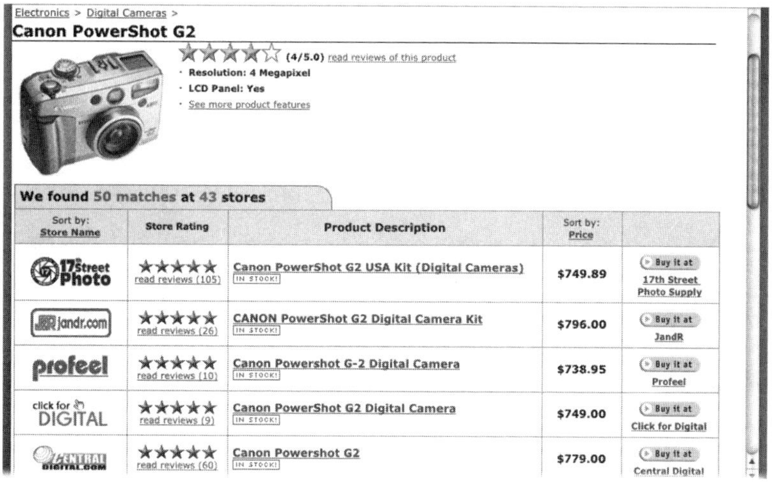

Electronics > Digital Cameras >
Canon PowerShot G2
★★★★☆ (4/5.0) read reviews of this product
· **Resolution: 4 Megapixel**
· **LCD Panel: Yes**
· See more product features

We found 50 matches at 43 stores

Sort by: Store Name	Store Rating	Product Description	Sort by: Price	
17th Street Photo	★★★★★ read reviews (105)	Canon PowerShot G2 USA Kit (Digital Cameras) [IN STOCK!]	$749.89	▸ Buy It at 17th Street Photo Supply
jandr.com	★★★★★ read reviews (26)	CANON PowerShot G2 Digital Camera Kit [IN STOCK!]	$796.00	▸ Buy It at JandR
profeel	★★★★★ read reviews (10)	Canon Powershot G-2 Digital Camera [IN STOCK!]	$738.95	▸ Buy It at Profeel
click for DIGITAL	★★★★★ read reviews (9)	Canon PowerShot G2 Digital Camera [IN STOCK!]	$749.00	▸ Buy It at Click for Digital
CENTRAL DIGITAL.COM	★★★★☆ read reviews (60)	Canon Powershot G2 [IN STOCK!]	$779.00	▸ Buy It at Central Digital

Composing
Brilliant Photos

I f your eyes are bleeding from the technical underbrush of Chapter 1—bells, whistles, megabytes—switch on your right brain. This chapter has little to do with electronics and everything to do with the more artful side of photography: composition.

What follows are a few tips that photographers have been using for years to create good pictures regardless of the camera type. These time-honored secrets can be applied to digital imaging too. Good composition is just as important with a $199 digicam as it is with a $3,000 pro digital SLR—and just as enjoyable.

This chapter offers four tips that will immediately improve your pictures. But first, a few words about composition itself.

Composition

Composition is the arrangement of your picture, the interplay between foreground and background, the way the subject fills the frame, the way the parts of the picture relate to each other, and so on.

Will the shot be clearer, better, or more interesting if you move closer? What about walking around to the other side of the action, or zooming in slightly, or letting tall grass fill the foreground? Would the picture be more interesting if it were framed by horizontal, vertical, or diagonal structures (such as branches, pillars, or a road stretching away)? All of this floats through a veteran photographer's head before the shutter button clicks.

It's easy to think, "Hey, it's a picture, not a painting—I have to shoot what's there." However, the fact is that photography is every bit as creative as painting. You have more control over the composition than you realize.

Note: If the primary thrust of your photographic ambition is to take casual vacation pictures, some of the following suggestions for professional composition may strike you as overkill.

But read them anyway. If you let some of these tips rub off on you, you'll be able to apply them even in everyday snapshot situations. There's no law against casual vacation pictures being *good* casual vacation pictures.

The Rule of Thirds

Most people assume that the center of the frame should contain the most important element of your shot. In fact, 98 percent of all amateur photos feature the subject of the shot in dead center.

Figure 2-1:
Top: When shooting a head and shoulder portrait, frame the shot so that her eyes fall on the upper imaginary line, a third of the way down the frame.

Bottom: When shooting a landscape, put the horizon line on the bottom third line if you want to emphasize the sky or tall objects like mountains, trees, and buildings. Put the horizon on the upper third line to emphasize what's on the ground, such as the people in the shot.

For the most visually interesting shots, however, dead center is actually the *least* compelling location for the subject. Artists and psychologists have found, instead, that following the so-called Rule of Thirds ensures better photos.

Imagine that the photo frame is divided into thirds, both horizontally and vertically, as shown in Figure 2-1. The Rule of Thirds contends that the intersections of these lines are the strongest parts of the frame. Putting the most interesting parts of the image at these four points, in other words, makes better composition.

Save the center square of the frame for tight close-ups—and even then, aim for having the subject's eyes on the upper-third line.

Get Closer

Step one to better pictures: Get closer. Step two: Get closer still.

Move your feet toward the subject, and don't stop moving them until the subject fills the frame (Figure 2-2). Of course, the zoom lens on your camera can help with this process quite a bit.

Figure 2-2:
Top: This otter shot seemed like a great photo at the time it was taken. Once it was uploaded to iPhoto, however, it became something of a disappointment—bland, because the otters were too far away and at an uninteresting angle.

Bottom: By getting (or zooming) closer, however, you get far more interesting results. In this case, the photographer had to apply the time-honored skill of patience, waiting for the sea otters to drift within better range. Sometimes getting closer means waiting for the action to come to you.

Try it with your dog. Take the first picture standing where you normally would stand—probably about five feet away and above Rover's head.

Now prepare to take a second picture—but first crouch down so that you see the world at dog level. Come close enough to the dog so that he can almost lick your camera lens. (But don't let him *do* it; dog slobber is very bad for optics.)

Take the second picture. Load both photos into iPhoto and study them. The first shot probably looks pretty boring compared to the second one.

Clearly, you weren't thinking about *composition* the first time. You were thinking about *taking a picture* of your dog.

The point is, *taking a picture* is usually a mindless act that doesn't result in the most memorable photos. Getting closer to create an interesting *composition* makes for compelling photography.

Tip: Filling the frame with your subject also means that you'll have less uninteresting background to crop out before making prints. As a result, you'll get higher resolution (more pixels) in the printout, which enhances the photo's quality.

Eliminate Busy Backgrounds

Busy backgrounds destroy photographs (Figure 2-3, top). Unless the intent of your image is to confuse and irritate the viewer's eye (headbanger-music CD album cover, anyone?), do what you can to eliminate distracting elements from your picture. You want to make it easy for the viewer to find the key elements of your composition, and enjoy them once they're there.

In other words, don't become so enamored with your subject that you don't notice the telephone wires that seem to run through her skull. Train your eye to examine the subject first, and then survey the surrounding scene.

Here are some problems to look out for—and avoid—in the backgrounds of your shots:

- **All forms of poles.** Telephone poles, fence posts, street signs, and malnourished trees can creep into your photos and ruin them.

- **Linear patterns.** Avoid busy background elements, such as bricks, paneling, fences, and zebra skins.

- **Parts of things.** When people see a "part of a thing" in your picture—for example, the front of a tractor, the leg of a ladder, the rear end of a camel—they can't help wondering what the rest of it looks like, instead of focusing on your subject.

Tip: Get in the habit of scanning all four corners of your frame before clicking the shutter. That way, you'll catch those telephone poles and street signs that you wouldn't normally see until it's too late.

Look for backgrounds that have subtle tones, soft edges, and nondescript elements. Moving your subject forward, away from the background, can help soften the backdrop even more.

Figure 2-3:
Top: Egads! What's this picture about? The people? The boats? Linear elements in the background usually spell doom for people shots.

Bottom: Avoid the clutter and opt for a more soothing background, such as water, sky, or any other subtle element. Your subjects—and audience—will thank you.

Go Low, Go High

Change your camera angle often. This is where a flip screen comes in handy, as described in Chapter 1.

Put the camera on the ground and study the composition. Raise it over your head and see how the world looks from that angle (Figure 2-4). If possible, walk around the subject and examine it from left to right.

Or adopt this technique: When you first approach an interesting subject, take the picture, just to get a safe one in the camera. Then change your angle and take another shot. If you have time, get closer and take a few more. Work the subject for as long as the opportunity presents itself.

More often than not, the "safe" shot will be your least favorite of the series. You'll find the latter frames far more compelling.

Figure 2-4:
Top: To really capture the "feel" of this breakfast nook, raise the angle of the camera, even if it means standing on a chair to do so. Bottom: Try going low, too. "Getting to the bottom of things" provides you with dramatic angles and impressive images. And in this case, it's the only way to capture the whole thing; without stooping down and shooting up, you would have brought home only a photo of a black-painted panel.

The Right Way to Compose

Finally, one last suggestion: Consider the pointers in this chapter as guidelines only. There is no one right way in photography; when you come down to it, the best photos are the ones you *like.*

CHAPTER 3

Beyond the
Simple Snapshot

There you sit, surveying your boxes of old photos. Snapshots of your family. Snapshots on vacation. Snapshots of tourist attractions. But they're all *snap-shots.*

Then the professional photos in some magazine or newspaper hit you. There's the brilliant close-up of a ladybug on a leaf, with the bushes in the background gently out of focus. There's the amazing shot of the soccer player butting the ball with his head, frozen in action so completely that you can see individual flecks of sweat flying from his hair. There's the incredible shot of the city lights at night, with car taillights drawing colorful firefly tracks across the frame.

You can't help but wonder: "How do they *do* that? And why can't I do it too?"

Actually, you probably can. Sure, some of these special shots require special gear, but most of them involve nothing more than good technique—and knowing when to invoke which of your camera's special features. With just a little practice, you can take pictures just as compelling, colorful, and intimate as the shots you see in the magazines.

This chapter is dedicated to laying bare the secrets of professional photographers. May you never take another dull snapshot.

Sports Photography

Everybody's seen those incredible high-speed action photos of athletes frozen in mid-leap. Without these shots (and the swimsuit photos), *Sports Illustrated* would be no thicker than a pamphlet.

Through a combination of careful positioning, focusing, lighting, and shutter-speed adjustments, this kind of photo is absolutely within your reach. As a handy bonus, mastering the frozen-action sports picture also means you've mastered frozen-action water splashes, frozen-action bird-in-flight shots, and frozen-action kid moments.

Tip: Don't get frustrated if, despite learning all of the following techniques, many of your pictures don't come out well. Sports photography produces lots of waste. Pros shoot dozens, sometimes hundreds, of frames just to get one good picture.

In short, a very low good-to-bad ratio is par for the course in this kind of shooting, but what the heck? It isn't costing you anything, and one great shot can make the entire effort worthwhile.

Getting Close to the Action

If your digital camera has a zoom lens at all, it's probably a 3X zoom, meaning that it can magnify the scene three times. Unfortunately, if you're in the stands at the football game, hoping for action shots of an individual player, 3X is not powerful enough. What you really need is one of those enormous, bazooka-like telephoto lenses that protrude three feet in front of the camera.

Figure 3-1:
You might not be able to afford a digital SLR with a $10,000 super telephoto. But if you have a 3-megapixel camera or an even better one, here's a way to "zoom in" on the action. Shoot at your camera's highest resolution—zoomed in as much as you can. Once the picture is in iPhoto, you can "zoom in" even further by cropping the portion of the picture you want to keep (page 125). Thanks to the high resolution of the original photo, you'll still have enough pixels to make a nice print or slide show, and the photo is much more effective this way.

But that doesn't mean you can't still capture good shots. Find a position on the sidelines that puts you as close to the action as possible. Zoom in with your camera and then use the trick shown in Figure 3-1.

If it's a bright, sunny day, the standard "automatic everything" setting of the camera might work just fine. Take a few sample shots, trying to get the action as it's coming at you.

Tip: If you still can't fill the frame with the action you want, consider turning on the camera's *digital zoom*.

As noted in Chapter 1, digital zoom should generally be avoided since it compromises image quality.

Still, at low levels (2X or 3X, for example), the deterioration in image quality might be tolerable. Experimenting with this feature might be worthwhile when covering a spectator sport, for instance.

Fast Shutter Speeds

If the results are blurry because the motion is too fast, you'll have to instruct the camera to use a faster shutter speed.

Unfortunately, the very cheapest, point-and-shoot-only cameras don't offer any such setting—hey, you get what you pay for. But even cameras a slight cut above those basic ones may offer a solution to this problem.

Shutter-priority mode

As noted in Chapter 1, certain more expensive cameras offer manual controls that pay off in precisely such special occasions as this.

In this case, what you want is the feature called *shutter priority.* In this mode—a time-honored feature of traditional film cameras—you tell the camera that the *speed* of the shot is what matters. You want the "film" exposed for only 1/500th of a second, for example.

Understanding what this mode does is slightly technical, but extremely important.

Whenever you take a picture, the amount of light that enters the camera is determined by two things: the *speed* of the shutter opening and closing, and the *size* of the opening of the diaphragm in the lens (the *aperture*).

If you want to freeze the action, you'll want the shutter to open and close very quickly. Of course, that means not as much light is entering the camera. To prevent the picture from being too dark, you want the camera to make the aperture larger for that fraction of a second.

In shutter-priority mode, that's exactly what happens. You say, "I don't care about the aperture—you worry about that, little camera buddy. I just want this picture *fast.*" The camera nods in its little digital way and agrees to open up its aperture wide enough to compensate for your fast shutter speed.

Exactly how you turn on shutter-priority mode differs radically by camera. On some cameras, you have to fiddle around with the menu system (see Figure 3-2); on others, you simply turn the little control knob on the top to a position marked *S* or *TV* (old-time photography lingo for *time value*), as shown in Figure 3-3.

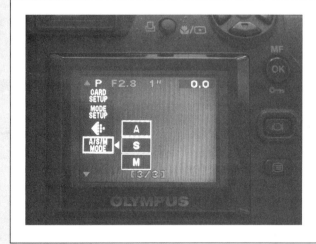

Figure 3-2:
Camera makers often position advanced controls where they're difficult to find—like buried in the onscreen menus, as shown here. On this Olympus, you have three alternative exposure modes: "A" for aperture priority, "S" for shutter priority, and "M" for manual mode. To freeze action, choose "S" for shutter priority. Then set your camera's shutter speed to 1/500th of a second or faster (such as 1/1000th) to freeze the action.

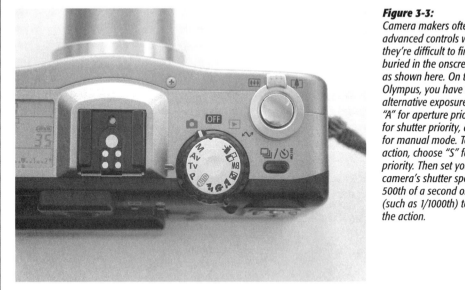

Figure 3-3:
Camera makers often position advanced controls where they're difficult to find—like buried in the onscreen menus, as shown here. On this Olympus, you have three alternative exposure modes: "A" for aperture priority, "S" for shutter priority, and "M" for manual mode. To freeze action, choose "S" for shutter priority. Then set your camera's shutter speed to 1/500th of a second or faster (such as 1/1000th) to freeze the action.

In any case, once you're in this mode, you must use some kind of dial or slider to indicate *how* fast you want the shutter to snap. You might start with 1/500 or 1/1000 of a second and take another series of shots. (The screen may show only "500" or

"1000," but you'll know what it means.) If the result is too dark, slow down the shutter speed to the next notch; you already know that the camera is opening the aperture as wide as it can.

Focusing and Shutter Lag

Whenever you try to photograph something fast, you may run headfirst into a chronic problem of digital cameras called *shutter lag*. That's the time the camera takes to calculate the focus and exposure from the instant you squeeze the shutter button to the instant the shutter actually snaps. It's usually at least one second long. Unfortunately, a delay that long means death to perfect sports photography. You'll miss the critical instant every time.

You have the following two possible solutions:

- **Prefocus.** Suppose you're trying to get a shot of the goalie in a soccer game. Take advantage of the time when he's just standing there doing nothing. Frame the shot on your camera screen.

  Then, as the opposing team comes barreling down the field toward him, press the shutter button just halfway. Half-pressing the shutter makes the camera calculate the exposure and focus *in advance*. Keep the button half-pressed until the moment of truth, when the goalie dives for the ball. *Now* squeeze the shutter the rest of the way. You'll experience less shutter lag, freezing the action closer to the critical moment.

  This is only one example of how *anticipating* the critical moment pays big dividends in sports photography. With a little practice, you can learn to press the shutter button *right before* the big moment, rewarding you with the perfect shot.

- **Use burst mode.** Most digital cameras released in 2001 and later offer something called *burst mode,* in which the camera snaps a series of shots in rapid succession, for as long as you hold down the shutter button. (It's something like the motor drive on a traditional film camera, so often featured in movies in which the main character is a photographer.)

  Most cameras can capture only about two frames per second, but that's still enough to improve the odds that one of your shots will be good. With a little practice, using the burst mode can help you compensate for shutter lag—especially if you anticipate the action.

Light Metering

Ordinarily, a digital camera calculates the amount of light in a scene by averaging all light from all areas of the frame. And ordinarily, that system works perfectly well.

In sports photography, however, the surrounding scene is usually substantially brighter or darker than the athletes, leading to improper exposure of the one thing you really want: the action.

Fortunately, many cameras offer *spot metering.* In this mode, you see little bracket markers (or a square or circle) in the center of your viewing frame (Figure 3-4). You can use these brackets to tell the camera which portion of the scene to pay attention to in calculating the exposure. By turning on this feature for sports shooting, you'll make sure that the athlete is correctly lit, background notwithstanding.

Figure 3-4:
In this picture, the athletes are brighter than the baseball field. If you were to use your camera's normal "averaging" or "evaluative" mode, there's a good chance that the players would be too bright, or overexposed. By using spot metering, you can tell your camera to set the exposure for the smaller area in the center of the frame. Now the subjects of the photo will be correctly exposed!

Portraits

You may have noticed that in most professional photo portraits, the background is softly out of focus. Unless you have the cheapest camera on the planet, you can create a similar great-looking effect yourself.

In photographic terms, a shot with a soft-focus background is said to have a *shallow depth of field.* The term "depth of field" refers to how much of the picture is in focus. When you're photographing your family in front of the Great Wall of China, you'll probably want a *deep* depth of field, so that both the people and the background remain in focus. But in typical headshot-type portraits, you'll want a *shallow* depth of field—and a blurry background. Figure 3-5 should make this more clear.

So how do you control the depth of field? Here are a few ways.

Trick 1: Zoom In

It might not seem logical that you'd want to use your camera's zoom lens (if it has one) for a portrait. After all, you can get as close as you want to the subject just by walking.

But thanks to a quirk of optics, zooming in helps create a shallow depth of field, which is just what you want for portraits.

Trick 2: Move the Background Back

The farther away your model is from the background, the softer the background will appear. If you choose an ivy-covered wall as your backdrop, for example, position your subject 10, 20, or 30 feet away from the wall—the farther, the better.

Trick 3: Choose a Wide Aperture Setting

You may remember from page 37 that two factors determine how much light fills a shot: how long the shutter remains open (the shutter speed) and how much it opens (the aperture).

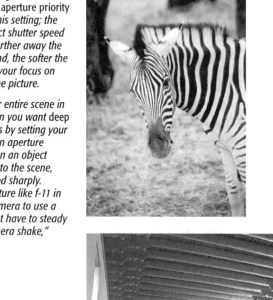

Figure 3-5:

Top: The trick to creating a soft background is to use a large aperture opening, such as f-2.8 or f-4. If your camera has an aperture priority mode, then you can lock in this setting; the camera will handle the correct shutter speed for you. Also, note that the farther away the subject is from the background, the softer the background will appear. Set your focus on the subject's eyes and take the picture.

Bottom: When you want your entire scene in focus, from front to back, then you want deep depth of field. You can do this by setting your aperture to f-8, f-11, or f-16 (in aperture priority mode). If you focus on an object about one third of the way into the scene, everything should be rendered sharply. Unfortunately, using an aperture like f-11 in low light might force your camera to use a slow shutter speed. You might have to steady it with a tripod to avoid "camera shake," which means blurriness.

In sports photography, what you care about most is usually the shutter speed. In portrait photography, what you care about most is the aperture setting—because the size of the aperture controls the depth of field. Low-numbered aperture settings like f-2.8 or f-4 are referred to as *wide aperture settings* by photographers because they let lots of light through the lens. These wide settings also help create soft backgrounds for portraits.

The portrait setting (program)

Many cameras offer a *portrait* mode, often designated on the control dial by the silhouette of a human head (Figure 3-6). Setting the camera to this mode automatically creates a short depth of field, blurring the background.

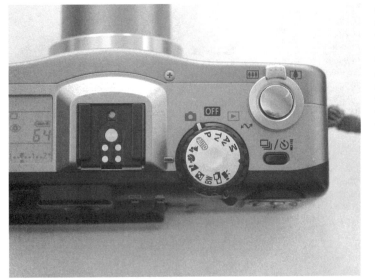

Figure 3-6:
If you don't want to mess with aperture settings, you can use the portrait mode *on your camera, if it has one—indicated here by the P on the mode dial—to help create a soft background. Often, this mode is represented by a silhouette of a human head.*

Aperture-priority mode

More-expensive cameras offer more control over depth of field in the form of an *aperture-priority mode*. It lets you tell the camera: "I want to control how much of this shot is in focus; that is, I want to set the aperture. You, the camera, should worry about the other half of the equation—the shutter speed."

Entering aperture-priority mode (if your camera has it) may be as simple as turning a dial to the A or AV position, or as complicated as having to pull up the camera's onscreen menu system.

(See Figures 3-2 and 3-3 for examples of how you might turn on shutter-priority mode. Aperture-priority mode is very similar, and is usually parked right next to shutter priority.)

In any case, once you've turned on this mode, you adjust the aperture by turning a knob or pressing up/down buttons. On the screen, you'll see the changing *f-stop* numbers, which represent different aperture sizes.

The following table should offer some indication of what you're in for:

f-stop	diameter of aperture	depth of field	background looks
f-2	very large diameter	very shallow	very soft
f-2.8	large diameter	shallow	soft
f-4	medium diameter	moderate	a little out of focus
f-5.6	medium diameter	moderate	a little out of focus
f-8	small diameter	moderately deep	mostly in focus
f-11	small diameter	deep	sharp
f-16	very small diameter	very deep	very sharp

Making the Shot

Position your model so the backdrop is in the distance. Check for telephone poles or anything else that may appear to pierce the model's head. If you can, shoot on a cloudy day, first thing in the morning or late in the afternoon; these are the best situations for outdoor portraits, when the light is softer and more flattering. Otherwise, try to place the model in open shade, like under a tree.

Adjust the flash settings so the flash is forced to go off, which will provide a nice supplemental burst of light. Don't stand more than ten feet away from your subject or your fill flash won't reach.

Finally, zoom in and start shooting. You'll notice that if you're standing within ten feet (so the flash will reach) and zooming in as much as your lens allows (to help soften the background), your model's upper body will fill the frame. That's what you want. Unwittingly, most snap shooters stand too far away from their subjects.

After a few frames, review your work and adjust as necessary. The soft background effect might not be as strong compared to pro images shot with ultra-long telephoto lenses, but you will definitely notice a pleasant difference.

Existing-Light Portraits

Cameras love light, that's for sure. And in general, you'll need the flash for indoor shots.

But not always. Some of the best interior photos are recorded using nothing more than light streaming in from a window. Images that use only ambient light without adding flash are called *existing light* or *natural light* photos.

This technique isn't right for every situation. But when it's appropriate, existing-light photos have these advantages over flash photography:

• **More depth.** The problem with the flash is that it illuminates only about the first ten feet of the scene. Everything beyond that fades to black.

In existing-light photography, on the other hand, your camera reads the lighting for the entire room. Not only is your primary subject exposed properly, but the surrounding setting is too, giving the picture more depth.

- **Less harsh.** The light in an existing-light photo generally comes from a variety of sources: overhead lights, windows, lamps, and reflections off walls and ceilings. All of this adds up to softer, more balanced light than what you get from the laser beam generated by your built-in flash.

- **More expressive.** Too often, flash pictures produce the "deer in the headlights" look from your subjects—if indeed the close-range flash doesn't whitewash them completely. Existing-light pictures tend to be more natural and expressive, and the people you're shooting are more relaxed when they're not being pelted by bursts of light.

An existing-light indoor portrait has a classic feel, because it's reminiscent of those timeless paintings by great artists like Rembrandt.

Keep It Steady

In a natural-light portrait, keep the flash turned off (that's why it's called *natural* light!). The camera's shutter will have to remain open for a relatively long interval to admit enough light for a good picture. As a result, you'll need to keep the camera very steady—which pretty much means you'll need a tripod.

Pocket tripods are great for this type of shooting. They only weigh a few ounces, steady the camera well, and can be used on all kinds of tables, countertops, and so on.

Once the tripod is steady, you face another challenge: taking the picture without jiggling the camera by pushing the shutter button. Even a little camera shake will blur your entire image, creating an out-of-focus appearance.

If a remote control came with the camera, use it. If not, use the camera's self-timer feature, which counts off, say, ten seconds before snapping the picture automatically.

In either case, do what you can to persuade the subject to keep still; during a long exposure like this, fidgety people mean blurry portraits. (Of course, you can use this effect to your advantage, too, if you want to create a moody interior picture with ghostlike subjects.)

The Camera Setup

If you have adjustable "film speed" settings (page 20), then you might want to use the 200 or 400 setting to make your camera more light-sensitive. (On the other hand, if you do have enough light for a decent exposure, then don't increase the film speed, because it'll slightly degrade the image quality.)

How can you tell if you don't have enough light and need to increase the film speed? Review your test shot. If it's too dark or has motion blur, increase the film speed from 100 to 200. Take another test shot. If things are still looking dark, try one more time at 400 speed. And don't forget to open the drapes all the way!

Also consider turning on spot metering (page 40). It permits the camera to make exposure decisions based only on the subject, without being affected by the lighting in the surrounding background.

The Model Setup

You'll need a window, tripod, trusty digital camera, and willing model for this project (Figure 3-7).

Tip: Great painters of the past preferred the light coming through a *north* window for their portraits, especially in the early hours of the day. Try this setting for your existing-light portraits.

Figure 3-7:
When "on the go," you can get great results with a tabletop tripod, or by resting your elbows on a table and slowly squeezing the shutter. Make sure the flash is turned off. If you have a spot meter, you might want to direct it to the subject's face to achieve that perfect exposure.

Turn your model three-quarters toward the light coming in the window. You may want to put the camera on a tripod (page 69) to avoid camera shake.

Now look at the lighting the way the camera would see the scene, not the way you would normally view it (see the box on page 47). If there's a noticeable difference between the brightest area of the model's face and the darkest area, then you may want to add a little of what's called *fill light*.

If you were a serious photographer with actual photographic gear lying around—and maybe you are—you could use a low-power flash as a fill light. Of course, then it would no longer be an *existing*-light portrait.

It's a better idea to find a reflector and position it so that light bounces off it onto the dark side of the model's face. A reflector is a common piece of photographic gear; it's essentially a big white shiny surface on its own pole. If you don't happen to have lighting equipment sitting around the house, but you really want this portrait to look good, just rig a big piece of white cardboard or white foam board to serve as a reflecting surface.

When you think you've balanced the tones, take a picture and review your results. Chances are that the shadow areas look darker to the camera than they do to your eyes. In that case, move the reflector closer to brighten the shadows.

Figure 3-8:
The top image represents how your eyes see the world. You see all of the tones from the dark shadows to the bright highlights, and everything in between. Unfortunately, your camera isn't quite as sophisticated. It generally records only a slice of the tonal range you can see, as represented by the bottom picture. This means that you have to decide what's most important to you: the bright areas or the dark ones? Then let your camera take a meter reading from that area.

White Balance (Color Balance)

Here's a mind-bending example of the way your eyes and your camera see completely different things. It turns out that different kinds of lights—regular incandescent light bulbs, fluorescent office lighting, the sun—cast subtle tinges of color on everything they illuminate. When you shoot non-flash photos indoors or in open shade outside, you'll get a bluish or "cool" cast. If you shoot without a flash under incandescent lighting, then the shots will have a "warmer" tint, mostly yellow and red.

So why haven't you ever noticed these different lighting artifacts? Because your brain compensates almost instantly for these different *color temperatures* (as they're called). To you, light is light.

But to a camera, tints are tints—and you'll see them onscreen and in your printouts. Unfortunately, they can detract from your photos. For example, portraits with warmer casts are generally more pleasing to the eye. But natural light from the window imparts a bluish cast, which isn't good for skin tones.

In the "old" days of traditional film photography, you would have corrected the color temperature by placing a screw-on filter over the lens. On a digital camera, you can change the color temperature by adjusting something called the camera's *white balance* (or *color balance*). Almost every digital camera has this function.

As shown in Figure 3-9, your camera probably has a little knob or menu whose icons represent the following lighting situations:

- The sun icon represents normal daylight conditions in direct light.
- The cloud icon is for overcast days, open shade, and window-illuminated interiors.

UP TO SPEED

The Tale of Two Perceptions

The reason photographic lighting is such a challenge is that you have two different systems operating at once: your eyes and your camera.

Your pupils are super-advanced apertures that constantly adjust to ambient light. Even in extreme conditions, such as when you go from a completely dark theater to the bright lobby, it only takes seconds for your optical system to adjust.

Furthermore, you can look at a scene that contains both deep shadows and super-bright highlights—and see detail in both areas simultaneously. Your eyes, optical nerves, and brain are constantly adjusting to interpret the ever-changing landscape around you.

Too bad your camera can't do the same.

Whereas your eyes can pick up the entire *tonal range* of a scene (the shades from brightest white to darkest black), a camera can pick up detail in only a slice of it. For example, if you're shooting a bright sky filled with clouds and trees casting deep shadows on meadow grass, you have a deci-

sion to make. What parts of this scene are most important to you? The bright sky, the trees, or the deep shadows? On a good day, your camera will be able to record detail in two out of the three (Figure 3-8).

No wonder some of your shots turn out to be disappointments.

With practice, however, you can learn to see the world the way your camera does, to the great benefit of your photos. For example, try setting up a natural-light scene, such as a still life with fruit. Put the camera on a tripod. Study the scene with your eyes, and then photograph it. Compare what the lens records with the image in your head.

Are they the same? Probably not. How are the two images different? Make a few notes about your perceptions as compared to what the camera captured, and then repeat the exercise with a different scene.

When the image in your head begins to match the one on the camera's LCD screen, then you've truly begun to see the world through your camera's lens.

• The light bulb icon is for incandescent lighting.

• The bar icon is for fluorescent lighting.

(If you're used to working with traditional camera filters, the sun is your "Sky 1A" filter, the cloud is your "81B warming" filter, the light bulb is your "80A cooling" filter, and the tube is the "FLD fluorescent correction" filter.)

Tip: When you're using the flash, change your camera's color balance from *auto* to *cloudy*. Electronic flashes tend to produce images that have a *cool cast*. Switching to the cloudy setting on your digital camera warms them up nicely.

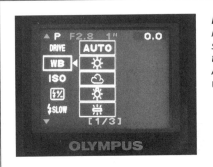

Figure 3-9:
Most digital cameras let you adjust color balance. Sometimes the setting is labeled "WB" (white balance, which is essentially the same thing as color balance). Most of the time, you can leave this setting on Auto. But if the tones start looking too cool or too warm, you might want to override auto and make the adjustment yourself.

Taking the Picture

With time and practice, you'll be able to "calibrate" your eyes so that they see shadows the same way your camera does. You'll spend less and less time testing before the shoot, and more time creating your classic image.

As you've figured out by now, creating a great natural-like portrait means learning to work with light as though it's a paintbrush. It takes time and practice to become proficient at this, but even your first efforts will probably surprise you with their expressiveness.

Tip: Don't be too quick to delete shots from the camera before viewing them on the computer screen. Existing-light shots sometimes contain subtleties that don't appear on tiny LCD screens. You'll be pleasantly surprised by many of the images that may have looked uninteresting when viewed on your camera's two-inch display.

Self-Portraits

Sometimes it's easier to take your own picture than to hand the camera to someone else—especially when you're practicing with your camera.

The preceding discussion about blurring the background applies to pictures you take of yourself, too, of course. But there are a few other considerations.

If you're on vacation, the natural scenery might be all the backdrop you need. If you're shooting a picture to use on a résumé or to post on your Web page, however, find a well-lit room with some open wall space. The blank wall (preferably light-colored) will serve as your backdrop. Natural light coming in from windows is best for this setup.

Find a stool or a low-back chair without arms, and position it about five feet in front of your backdrop. If possible, it should face the brightest window in the room.

Next, you'll need a way to position your camera. A standard tripod is best (page 69), but you can use a pocket tripod on top of a table if necessary. Either way, position the camera about five feet from your stool.

Turn on the flash. Even though the ambient room lighting will often be bright enough to provide overall even illumination, the flash will provide a little burst of front light to smooth out facial blemishes and put a twinkle in your eyes.

The best cameras for self-portraits have a flip screen and a remote control. The flip screen lets you preview how you look in the frame before you shoot the shot, and the remote control lets you actually take the shot while sitting comfortably on your stool.

If you don't have these options, put your camera in self-timer mode. To help you frame the shot while you're not actually on the stool, use a table lamp as a stand-in.

Check your hair and clothing in a mirror, press the shutter button to trigger the self-timer countdown, and then sit on the stool (preferably *after* removing the table lamp).

Once the camera fires, play back the photo on the screen. Did you zoom in close enough? Are you in focus and centered in the frame? How does the lighting look?

Figure 3-10:
Left: Here's a traditional head shot—a staple of unemployed actors, corporate annual reports, and Most Wanted lists. Note the solid background. The camera was on a tripod and the self-timer tripped the shutter.

Right: In this informal self-portrait, the camera was held out at arm's length with the lens pointed back at the photographer.

If you need to add a little light to one side of your face or the other because it's appearing too shadowy, you can construct a homemade reflector out of white cardboard or similar material. Position your reflector as close to you as possible (although not in the photo itself) and angle it so it "bounces" light off the brightest light source onto the area requiring illumination. This will help "lighten up" the dark areas.

Shoot another round. Once you get the basic setup looking good, experiment with different angles and facial expressions. One advantage of taking your own portraits is that you can be more creative. Remember, you can always erase the embarrassing frames—or all of them. Remember, too, that self-portraits don't have to be dull headshots; they can be every bit as interesting as any other photo.

Kid Photography

Children are challenging for all photographers. They're like flash floods: fast, low to the ground, and unpredictable. But with a little patience and perseverance, you can keep up with them and get the shot (Figure 3-11). Here are some tips:

- **Be prepared.** Rule one for capturing great kid pictures is to have your camera handy at all times, charged and with memory-card space to spare. Great kid shots come and go in the blink of an eye. Parents don't have the luxury of keeping their equipment snugly stowed away in a camera bag in the closet.

- **Get down there.** The best kid shots are generally photographed at kid level, and that means getting low. (Flip screens are particularly useful for kid shots, because they let you position the camera down low without you actually having to lie on the ground.)

- **Get close.** Your shots will have much more impact if the subject fills the frame, plus you won't have to do as much cropping later in iPhoto.

- **Prefocus.** Shutter lag will make you miss the shot every time. In many cases, you can defeat it by prefocusing—that is, half-pressing the shutter button when the kid's not doing anything special. Keep your finger on the button until the magical smile appears, then press fully to snap the shot.

- **Force the flash.** Indoors or out, you'll want the flash to fire, since it provides even illumination and helps freeze the action. Switch your camera's flash setting so that it's always on.

- **Make it bright.** See page 62 for a discussion of red-eye, but don't bother using the *red-eye reduction* flash mode on your camera. By the time your camera has finished strobing and stuttering, your kid will be in the next county.

  If red-eye is a problem in your flash photos of kids, make the room as bright as possible, shoot from an angle that isn't dead-on into your kids' eyes, and touch up the red-eye later in iPhoto, if necessary.

- **Fire at will.** Child photography is like shooting a sports event—you'll take lots of bad shots in order to get a few gems. Again, who cares? The duds don't cost you anything. And once you've captured the image of a lifetime, you'll forget about all the outtakes you deleted previously.

Figure 3-11:
If you want great-looking kid shots, you've got to play on their turf. That means down on your hands and knees, or even your tummy.

Theater Performances

Capturing stage performances is difficult even for professional photographers. What makes theater lighting tricky is that the bright main light on the actors is often right in the same frame with a subdued or even darkened background. If you photograph this composition "as is" in automatic mode, then the camera calibrates the exposure, brightening up the image enough to display the dominate dim background. As a result, the spotlighted actors turn into white-hot, irradiated ghosts.

Your built-in flash is useless under these conditions (unless you climb right up onto the stage beside the actors, which is generally frowned upon by the management). The typical range for the camera's flash is about ten feet, after which it's about as useful as a snow-cone machine in Alaska. *Turn your flash off* at theater performances— because it's annoying to the rest of the audience, because it's worthless, and because it's usually forbidden.

To overcome this challenge, use the other tools built into your camera. If you have a *spot meter mode,* then you have a fighting chance. As noted previously, your camera generally gauges the brightness of the scene by averaging the light across the entire frame—a recipe for disaster when you're shooting the stage.

Spot metering, however, lets you designate a particular spot in the scene whose brightness you want the camera to measure. (You indicate what spot that is by positioning a frame marker that appears in the center of the frame.) Point the spot-metering area at the brightly lit actors. The camera then sets the exposure on them instead of on the vast expanse of the dimly lit set (Figure 3-12).

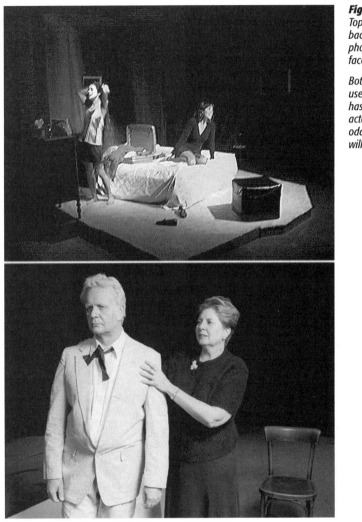

Figure 3-12:
Top: Brightly lit actors and dark backgrounds are a recipe for photographic disaster. The actors' faces have bleached out completely.

Bottom: To overcome this challenge, use your camera's spot meter (if it has one) and direct it toward the actors, not the background. Your odds for an acceptable exposure will increase dramatically.

Not all cameras have a spot-metering mode. But even basic cameras generally offer some kind of *exposure compensation*, an overall brightness control. For theater situations, try lowering the exposure to -1 or -1.5, for example. The objective is to darken the entire scene. The background will be *too* dark, of course, but at least the actors won't be "blown out."

Finally, if you know ahead of time that you want pictures from a particular performance, do what you can to secure a ticket in the first few rows. When it comes to theater shooting, the closer you get, the better.

Tip: Depending on the kind of performance you're trying to photograph, getting the right lighting may be just the tip of the iceberg. Getting *permission* to photograph might be the greater obstacle.

In these cases, consider taking your pictures at the dress rehearsal. (This means you, parents of kids in school plays.) Not only is the management likely to be more permissive, but you'll be able to sit right there in the front row, to the immense benefit of your photos.

Underwater Photography

Water is the mortal enemy of digital cameras. Still, you can buy waterproof enclosures for many camera models, which opens up a whole new world of photographic possibilities.

Sometimes these enclosures are made by the camera manufacturer. Canon, for example, makes clear plastic cases for a number of its digital cameras. For other models, you can often find enclosures for sale at Web sites like *www.ikelite.com* or *www.uwimaging.com.*

The good news is that these enclosures protect the camera at depths down to 100 feet, for example, and provide access to the camera's controls. The bad news is that the underwater housing can cost as much as the camera!

When shooting underwater, force the flash to turn on; it's dark down there. You might also want to play with the color balance adjustment to help offset the bluish tint of the water. If your camera has a dial that lets you call up different lighting presets, try the Cloudy setting to warm up the tones.

Oh, and don't try to change the batteries while you're underwater.

Travel Photography

Digital cameras are perfect vacation companions. Memory cards are easy to pack, there's no film for airport X-rays to wash out, and when the day is done, you can review all of your images on the camera's LCD screen, on your laptop, or on the hotel room TV.

Shooting on the road presents unique photo opportunities that simply aren't available at home—like museums, fjords, and Cinderella's Castle. Here's how to master those moments and add a little spice to your vacation slide show.

Packing up

Digital cameras may be small and compact, but they're often accompanied by just as much accessory junk as film cameras. Here's a checklist to consult before your trip:

• **Batteries.** The laws of photography dictate that you'll run out of juice at the precise moment the perfect shot appears.

If your camera comes with its own proprietary, rechargeable battery, consider buying a second one. Charge both batteries every night, and take them both with you during the day. (Oh, by the way: Pack the charger, too.)

If your camera accepts AA-type batteries instead, you have much more flexibility. Bring your set of NiMH rechargeables, as described as page 15, and their charger. Also pack an emergency set of disposables, like alkaline AA's or Duracell CRV3 lithium disposables, if your camera accepts them.

• **Memory cards.** Nobody has ever said, "Oh, I wish I'd bought a smaller memory card." You'll be grateful for every last megabyte.

As a rough rule of thumb, figure that you'll wind up keeping 36 shots a day (not including the ones that you delete right off the camera). If you have a 3-megapixel camera, a 64 MB card might be enough for one day of shooting. If you brought a laptop on the trip, you can rush back to the hotel room each night and offload the pictures into iPhoto, freeing up the card for the next day's shooting.

If you don't plan to take the laptop along, buy a much bigger memory card (or several). If you're on the road for a week with that hypothetical 3-megapixel camera, you'll need at least 448 megabytes to hold those 36 pictures a day. It's generally cheaper to buy two 256 MB cards than one 512 MB card, but shop around to get the best deal possible (*www.shopper.com,* for example).

• **Camera bag.** If your camera didn't come with a case, get one for it. Not only will it protect your camera (even if it's a compact model with a self-closing lens cover), but it will keep all of your batteries, cards, and cables together.

Tip: If you can find a camera bag that doesn't *look* like a camera bag, it's less likely to be ripped off. An insulated beverage bag can do nicely, for example.

• **Tripod.** Nobody likes to lug a tripod across Europe—or across town, for that matter. But if you're a serious photographer, or aspire to be one, you'll occasionally need a way to steady your camera.

A miniature tabletop tripod like the UltraPod 2 is an ideal compromise. It weighs only four ounces, costs $22, and provides solid support for your camera in a variety of situations. A quick search at *www.google.com* should help you find a good mail-order company that carries it.

• **Weatherproofing.** Keep a couple plastic bags tucked in your carrying case for use in bad weather. Digital cameras hate water, but some of nature's most dramatic shows occur at the beginning and end of storms.

• **Lens cloth.** Microfiber lens cloths are light, inexpensive (about $5), and easy to pack—and they're the best way to keep your optics sparkling clean. They look like a regular soft cloth, but they actually have thousands of micro fibers that "grab" smudges off your lens and whisk them away.

- **Small flashlight.** Don't risk losing a great night shot just because you can't read your camera's controls. Pack a small flashlight to help you work in dim lighting situations.

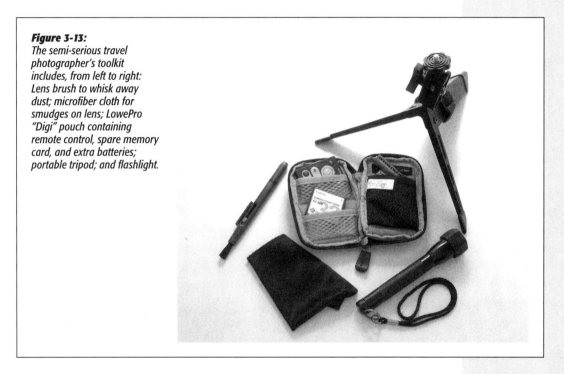

Figure 3-13:
The semi-serious travel photographer's toolkit includes, from left to right: Lens brush to whisk away dust; microfiber cloth for smudges on lens; LowePro "Digi" pouch containing remote control, spare memory card, and extra batteries; portable tripod; and flashlight.

The Museum Challenge

Many museums permit photography, provided you keep the flash off and don't use a full-size tripod. Digital cameras are particularly well suited to these assignments.

Once you're in, here are some techniques to consider:

- You might want to increase the "film speed" setting to 200 or 400 to better handle the dimmer interior lighting. (See page 20.)

- Museums often use halogen light bulbs to illuminate the artwork, which could lend a red or yellow cast to your photos.

    If your particular camera automatically adjusts its color balance nicely, then no problem. But if your sample shots look too "warm" (reddish or yellowish), consider switching the camera's white-balance control to the incandescent setting (usually denoted by a light bulb icon on the control dial).

    If that doesn't improve the pictures, adjust the camera's white balance as described on page 46 (if your camera offers this feature).

• How do you take a picture of what's in a glass display case without getting nasty reflections?

The trick is to put the front of your lens barrel right against the glass. You'll probably have to zoom out all the way to frame the shot properly.

• Finally, hold the camera steady when shooting in museums. Because of the low lighting, your camera will probably choose a slow shutter speed, which introduces the possibility that the camera will shake, introducing blur. The steadier you hold your camera, the sharper your shots will be.

Portraits on the Road

In standard headshots, you generally want to frame the subject as tightly as possible. But when you're traveling, you want to include the background so it might suggest your location.

Unfortunately, many travelers include *too much* information about the location (see Figure 3-14). In reality, sometimes you need two shots to convey one message.

Figure 3-14:

Left: If you take a portrait when your subject is standing in front of the entire tower, your travel companion appears to be the size of a microbe. Instead, start by taking an establishing shot *of the monument—the "postcard picture" that shows the entire structure.*

Right: Then move closer to the tower and shoot the portrait of your partner in front of an element of the structure. When you show your pictures to people at home, first show the establishing shot, then show the portrait with an element of the location. It's a very effective technique.

Get Creative

Picture taking should be fun while on vacation. You won't be graded on your shots; it's not a term paper to be turned in at the end of the week. So enjoy the process of shooting as much as the trip itself.

Digital cameras encourage playfulness. You can try something silly, look at it on the LCD screen, and—if it's too incriminating—erase it before anyone else discovers just *how* amateur an amateur photographer you really are. The bottom line: Taking pictures should be *part of your vacation.*

So here are a few ideas for you to try the next time you're exploring the world:

- **Get in the picture.** Almost every digicam comes with a self-timer. Position the camera so that you have an interesting background, trip the timer, and get in the shot. It's really fun if you're with a group, too.

- **Try the close-up mode.** Almost every digital camera model offers a *macro* (super-close-up) mode that lets you get within inches of your subject. The world is a very different place at this magnification. Let your imagination run wild. Everything is a potential shot, from local currency to flower petals.

- **Vary the shots.** The standard shot of your travel companions standing posed in front of the Grand Canyon is fine, but that's only the beginning. The so-called "little shots," such as your son staring out the train window, or your friend buying flowers from a street vendor, are often more compelling than the typical "stand in front of a building and smile" photo.

- **The city lights from your balcony at sunset.** There's a magic moment every day at twilight when the city lights come on right before the sun sets. Grab your camera, park it on a wall or windowsill for stability, and take a few shots.

- **Shoot from the passenger-side window.** Ask your travel companion to take the wheel as you drive along. Sitting on the passenger side of the car, roll down the window and look for interesting pictures. Don't worry about the background blurring and other little glitches, because they're often what make the pictures compelling.

UP TO SPEED

Cautions on the Road

Camera-toting tourists are prime targets for thieves—and digital cameras make delicious loot. When you're on the road, keep in mind the following tips, which are designed to help you bring home more than just memories:

- Consider packing your camera gear in a backpack or a fanny pack instead of a traditional camera bag. That way, you're not walking through the streets of India with a bag that screams, "I'm an expensive camera—steal me!"

- To prevent damage, carry your camera bag onto the plane instead of checking it with the luggage.

- Secure the camera strap to your body when touring.

- Be wary when handing your camera to strangers for group shots. They may run away with it. Use the camera's self-timer to take pictures of yourselves—or at least use your best judgment in summing up passersby.

- Keep an eye on your equipment as you go through airport security. The best plan is to have your travel mate go through security first, then send through both of your equipment, then you go through. That way you always have someone close to your stuff.

- Don't leave your camera lying around your hotel room. If you leave it behind, put it in the room's safe.

- **Signs and placards instead of notes**. Museums, monuments, and national parks are all loaded with informative signs and placards. Instead of taking notes and lugging brochures, take pictures of these tidbits of information. When you put together your trip slide show in iPhoto, these will make spectacular introductory shots for each segment.

- **Shooting through shop windows**. Storefront displays say so much about the local culture. But taking pictures through glass can be tricky, thanks to unwanted reflections. As when shooting glass display cases in museums, the trick is to zoom out, and then get the front of the lens barrel as close to the window as possible. The closer you are, the fewer reflections you'll have in your picture.

Now that you're armed with lots of ideas and techniques, you're probably getting the itch to take a vacation. When you go, don't forget your camera, a few memory cards, and plenty of battery power.

Outdoor Portraits

Everybody knows what the camera's built-in flash is for, right? It goes off automatically when there's not enough light.

Unfortunately, everybody also knows how ornery and feeble these flashes are. If you're too close to the subject, the flash blows out the picture, turning your best friend into a ghost face that looks like it was photographed during a nuclear test. If you're farther than about eight feet away, the flash is too weak to do anything useful at all.

Figure 3-15:
Left: The camera is reading the background, the lawn, the reflections…everything except what you really care about: the person in the foreground. As a result, your subject is underexposed and too dark.

Right: Forcing the flash on solves the problem nicely.

No matter what kind of camera you have, however, you'll take your best pictures when *you* decide to use the flash, not when the camera decides. Believe it or not, the camera's automatic mode is wrong about half the time.

Outdoor portraits represent a perfect example. If you leave the flash setting to "auto" when you shoot outdoors, you can guess what will happen: The camera will conclude that there's plenty of light and won't bother to fire the flash.

The camera has correctly concluded that there's enough light *in the entire frame*. But it's not smart enough to recognize that the person you're photographing is, in fact, in shadow (Figure 3-15).

The solution in this situation is to *force* the flash on—a very common trick. Provided you're close enough to the subject, the flash will provide enough *fill light* to balance the subject's exposure with that of the surrounding background. (If you're using your on-camera flash, stand within about eight feet of the subject so you can get enough flash for a proper exposure.)

This kind of fill flash will dramatically improve your outdoor portraits. Not only will it eliminate the silhouette effect when your subject is standing in front of a bright background, but frontal light is very flattering. It softens smile lines and wrinkles, and it puts a nice twinkle in the subject's eyes.

How do you take your flash off auto mode? Most cameras offer a couple different flash settings. Look for the icon that represents a lightning bolt with an arrow tip on the end—the universal icon for electronic flash. Generally, if you push the button next to this icon, it cycles through the flash modes on your camera. These usually include *auto flash* (no icon), *red-eye reduction* (eyeball icon), *no flash* (universal "circle with a diagonal line through it" icon) and *flash on*, or *forced flash* (stand-alone lightning bolt icon). For your outdoor portraits, cycle through the icons until you get to the forced-flash mode.

Tip: If you're that rare digital photographer who owns an external flash attachment, use *it* in these situations. The more powerful strobe illuminates the subject better and provides a more flexible working distance.

It's also the only way to go if your subject wears glasses. If the flash is on a dedicated cord, you can raise it a couple feet above the camera to minimize the reflection of the flash in the glasses.

Rim Lighting

Once you've experimented with fill flash, try this variation that pros use to create striking portraits: *rim lighting*.

Position the subject with her back to the sun (preferably when it's high in the sky and not shining directly into your camera lens). Now set your camera to fire the flash (the lightning bolt, not the automatic setting). If the sun is shining into the lens, block it using your hand or a lens shade.

The first thing you'll notice is that the sun creates a *rim light* around the subject's hair (Figure 3-16). You'll also notice that her eyes are more relaxed and open. In one swift move, you've made your subject more comfortable and improved your chances for a dramatic portrait.

Figure 3-16:
Remember how you were always told to have the sun at your back when taking a picture. That's not the best advice for portraits. In fact, you want the sun on the model's back to create a rim-light *effect. Notice how her hair and her shoulder are highlighted? Remember to turn on your fill flash so the model's face isn't underexposed. If your camera accepts filters, try a softening filter* on rim light shots; the effect can be quite pleasing.

If you were to shoot the picture right now, without the fill flash, the result would be the classic *backlit photo*. In other words, the background would be nicely exposed— but the subject would be shadowy or even silhouetted. You would join the throngs who, on a daily basis, ruin golden opportunities for great photographs.

Once again, the solution is to force the flash, creating a nice fill light.

Now take a few pictures and review your work onscreen. If your model is too bright, move back a few steps and try again. If she's too dark, move a little closer.

When it works, rim lighting creates portraits that you'll be very proud of. It's not the right technique for every situation, but sometimes it produces jaw-dropping results.

Tip: If your camera accepts filters, try a *softening filter* for your rim-lighting shots. It can reduce facial wrinkles and create a nice glow around the subject's head.

Open Shade

Working in open shade, like the shadow of a tree, produces less dramatic portraits than rim lighting, but very pleasing ones nonetheless.

The open shade eliminates harsh shadows around the face and keeps the subject from squinting. Here again, forcing the flash on your digital camera is a great idea. Look for a subtle background without distracting elements.

The beauty of this technique is that you capture an evenly lit, relaxed subject with a perfectly exposed background. You won't even notice that it was shot in the shade.

Indoor Flash

Over the years, you've probably seen plenty of indoor flash pictures that have a pitch-black background and an overexposed, practically nuked subject.

Many factors conspire to produce these stark, unflattering shots, but one of the major contributors is, once again, your camera thinking on its own. You're letting *it* decide when to turn on the flash and which shutter speed to use.

First of all, you don't always need the flash. Indoor photography offers many opportunities for stunning "existing light" portraits and moody interior shots, as described earlier. And when you do have to turn on the flash, you can make certain adjustments to preserve the ambiance of the room so that your background doesn't fall into a black hole.

Slow-Synchro Interiors

There are two reasons why your flash shots often have a pitch-black background. The first problem is that the light from a typical digital camera's flash reaches only about eight to ten feet. Anything beyond this range, and you've got yourself an inadvertent existing-light photo.

If your camera has a *manual mode* that allows you to dictate both the aperture (f-stop) and shutter speed, you can easily overcome these problems. Once in manual mode, try this combination as a starting point for flash photography indoors:

- Set your film speed to 100 (page 20).

- Set the aperture (f-stop) to f-5.6.

- Set the shutter speed to 1/15 of a second.

- Use the forced-flash mode. (*Don't* use the red-eye reduction feature.)

Now hold the camera as steady as possible. (At these slow shutter speeds, your shots are more vulnerable to camera shake, and therefore to blurriness. Your flash will help freeze everything in its range—but the background, not illuminated by the flash, may blur if the camera isn't steady.)

Take a shot. As you review the picture, you'll see that it looks much different than what you're accustomed to. Specifically, it has more room ambiance and background detail.

Figure 3-17:
Tired of having your flash subjects lost in a black hole of darkness? Try using what photographers call "slow-synchro flash." Set your camera's shutter speed and aperture manually to control the exposure of the background. The camera's flash will ensure the subjects are exposed properly.

How to Really Get Rid of Red-Eye

For years now, camera manufacturers have been inflicting a torturous device on their customers known as *red-eye reduction mode*. It's a series of bright, strobing flashes that's not only annoying to the people you're photographing, but it doesn't even work.

What causes red-eye? In a dimly lit room, the subject's pupil dilates, revealing more of the retina. On cameras on which the flash is close to the camera lens (as it almost always is), the light from the flash shines through the dilated pupil, bounces off the retina, and reflects as a red circle directly back into the lens. (The same thing happens to animals, too, except that the color is sometimes green instead of red.)

The solution is to move the flash away from the camera lens. That way, the reflection from the retina doesn't bounce directly back at the camera. But on a camera that fits in your pocket, it's a little tough to achieve much separation of flash and lens.

Since camera makers couldn't move the flash away, they went to Plan B: firing the flash a few times *before* the shutter snaps, in theory contracting the subjects' pupils, thereby revealing less retina. Guess what? It doesn't really work. Its main accomplishment is to delay the shot just long enough for your subjects to quit smiling.

You have three ways out of red-eye. If you can turn up the lights, do it. If you have that rare camera that accepts an external, detachable flash, use it. And if none of that works, remember that iPhoto has its own red-eye-removal tool (page 130).

If your camera doesn't have a manual mode, all is not lost. Almost every consumer model has a setting called *nighttime* or *slow-synchro* mode. This setting is often indicated by a "stars over a mountain" icon. The intention of this mode is to shoot portraits at twilight, as described in the next section. But you can also use nighttime mode indoors to "open up" the background (Figure 3-17). Granted, you don't have as much control with this setting as you do with manual mode, but you might be pleasantly surprised with the results.

Twilight Portraits

Twilight is a magic time for photographers. The setting sun bathes the landscape in a warm glow, providing a beautiful backdrop for portraits. This is an ideal time to shoot any type of shot.

First, you'll need a tripod or some other means to steady the camera. There's far less light during this time of day, and therefore the shutter slows down considerably.

Now inspect your camera's flash options. Look for an option called either *slow-synchro* or *nighttime* flash—a setting that synchronizes your flash with the very slow shutter. Look for a "stars and mountain" or "stars and person" icon.

Now position your model in front of the most beautiful part of the landscape and take the picture.

When you push the button, the camera opens the shutter long enough to compensate for the dim twilight lighting, capturing all of the rich, saturated colors. The flash, meanwhile, throttles down, emitting just enough light to illuminate the subject from the front.

The result can be an incredibly striking image that will make your travel pictures the talk of the office. It's a great technique when shooting somebody standing in front of lighted monuments and buildings at night, sunsets over the ocean, and festive nighttime lighting.

Tip: If your subject is rendered too bright (overexposed by the flash), move back a few feet, zoom in, and try again. Conversely, if your subject is too dark (underexposed by the flash), move in a couple of feet.

Landscape and Nature

Unlike portraiture, where *you* have to arrange the lights and the models, landscape photography demands a different discipline: patience. Nature calls the shots here. Your job is to be prepared and in position.

Shoot with Sweet Light

Photographers generally covet the first and last two hours of the day for shooting (which half explains why they're always getting up at 5 in the morning). The lower angle of the sun, and the slightly denser atmosphere through which it passes, create rich, saturated tones as well as what photographers call "sweet light."

It's a far cry from the midday sun, which creates much harsher shadows and much more severe highlights. Landscape shooting is more difficult when the sun is high overhead on a bright, cloudless day.

Layer Your Lights and Darks

Ansel Adams, probably the most famous American landscape photographer, looked for scenes in sweet light that had alternating light and dark areas. As you view one of these pictures from the bottom of the frame to the top, you might see light falling on the foreground, then a shadow cast by a tree, then a pool of light behind the tree, followed by more shadows from a hill, and finally an illuminated sky at the top of the composition.

A lighting situation like this creates more depth in your pictures (and, yes, lets you "shoot like Ansel").

Highlight a Foreground Object with Flash

Sometimes you can lend nature a helping hand by turning on your flash to illuminate an object in the immediate foreground. Remember, just because your eyes can see detail in the dark area at the bottom of the frame doesn't mean that your camera can. Look for an interesting object—a bush, perhaps. Move the camera close to it and zoom out. Then turn on the flash and shoot. The effect can be stunning.

Sunsets

Your camera usually does a good job of exposing the sky during sunset, even in automatic mode. Keep the flash turned off and shoot at will.

Tip: Keep an eye on your shutter speed (if your camera shows it). If it goes below 1/30th of a second, you may need a tripod or some other steady surface to prevent camera shake. Activate the self-timer or remote control to avoid jiggling the camera when you press the shutter.

The biggest mistake people make when shooting sunsets has nothing to do with the sky—it's the *ground* that ruins the shots. Your eyes can make out much more detail in the shadowy ground than your camera will. Therefore, it's not worth trying to split the frame in half, composing it with the sky above and the ground below. The bottom half of your photo will just be a murky black blob in the final image.

Instead, fill your composition with 90 percent sky and 10 percent ground or water. This arrangement may feel funny—at least until you look at your prints and see how much more dynamic they are with this composition.

Tip: Many photographers make the mistake of leaving the scene right after the sun dips below the horizon. Hang around for another 10 minutes or so; sometimes there's a truly amazing after-burst of light.

Weddings

Weddings dominate special event photography, not to mention being the primary income source for a huge percentage of professional photographers.

If you can shoot an entire wedding, then you're prepared for any other event that comes your way. For example, graduations are just weddings without the reception. Birthday parties are weddings without the ceremony (there's even cake!).

If you're a guest, one critical element of successful photography at a wedding is not interfering with the *hired* photographer's shots. Introduce yourself to the photographer and ask if it's OK to take a couple of shots right after the pro has finished each setup. You'll generally receive permission—and the opportunity to capture the highlights of the day.

POWER USERS' CLINIC

Built-In Flash Vs. External Flash

A few high-end digital cameras offer serious photographers a wonderful feature: a place to plug in an external flash attachment.

For example, an external flash moves the light source away from the lens, which reduces red-eye (page 62), especially if the flash is on its own separate bracket rather than a hot shoe right on the camera. The external flash enables your camera's battery to last longer, too, because it has its own batteries. You'll be grateful during long events like weddings.

The most versatile way to attach an external flash is with a standard hot shoe right on top of the camera, as shown here. You can either connect the flash directly, or you can use a "dedicated" flash cord that allows you to move the flash away from the camera, but still retain "communication" between the two.

Some cameras just aren't big enough to accommodate a hot shoe. To circumvent this problem, some camera makers have engineered a system that uses a tiny socket on the camera that connects to the flash via a proprietary cord and bracket. This system isn't the height of versatility, but it does allow you the flexibility of an external flash on a very compact camera.

A wedding is one primary example of a situation where you'll find this useful. When you're not the primary photographer, you won't get the prime shooting locations during big events (like the cake cutting). Therefore, you'll need all the flash power possible to get the shots even when you're out of position like this—another advantage of an external flash unit.

Finally, a detached flash attachment gives you more flexibility, because you can use it to bounce light off the wall or ceiling to provide fill lighting for certain shots.

A good external flash with a dedicated cord costs at least $200, and, of course, only the more expensive digital cameras can accommodate them. But as you become more serious with your photographic pastime, you'll find that external flashes help you capture shots that on-camera flashes just can't get.

Tip: As a digital photographer, you can bring a new dimension to the celebration that most pros don't even offer: immediacy. If you like, you can hook up your camera to a TV to play the pictures back while the reception is still going on. Or, thanks to iPhoto, you can have shots on the Web before the pro even gets his film to the lab. Put your favorites together and add a little music; suddenly you have a QuickTime movie for downloading.

Shots to Look For

In part, your success at shooting a wedding depends on your ability to anticipate the action. If you've been to any weddings recently, you probably know that you can expect classic photo ops like these:

- **Before the wedding.** Bride making final dress adjustments, alone in dress, with mother, with maid of honor, with bridesmaids, and so on. The groom with his best man, with his ushers, with his family.

- **During the ceremony.** The groom waiting at the altar, his parents being seated, the bride's mother being seated, the processional, the bride coming down the aisle, the vows, the ring ceremony, the kiss, the bride and groom coming back down the aisle. Oh, and of course the obligatory adorable shots of the flower girl and ring-bearer boy walking down the aisle looking dazed.

- **Directly after the ceremony.** The wedding party at the altar, the bride and groom with family, the bride and groom with officiate, close-up of the bride and grooms' hands on the ring pillow.

- **During the reception.** Guests signing the guest book, the bride dancing with groom/father/father-in-law, the groom dancing with mother/mother-in-law, the cake table, the cake cutting, the cake feeding, the toasts, the bouquet tossing, the decorated getaway car.

Tip: One of the advantages you might have over the hired photographer is that you'll *know* people at the wedding. In theory at least, you'll therefore have the opportunity to take candid, relaxed pictures of the guests—a sure bride-and-groom pleaser.

That's the checklist for a professional photographer, of course. If you're one of the guests, use that list only for inspiration. Wedding days provide dozens of opportunities for memorable pictures. If you get only a fraction of them, you'll still have plenty to share at the end of the day.

Photographing Objects

Most people usually photograph people and places. Every now and then, however, you'll need to photograph *things:* stuff you plan to sell on eBay, illustrations for a report, your personal belongings (for insurance purposes), and so on.

The *macro* (close-up) mode of your digital camera makes it easy to shoot objects. All you need to do is set up and light your shot; the camera will do the rest.

The Home Studio

The trick to lighting any object professionally, whether it's a painting or a teapot, is to position *two* lights, each at a 45-degree angle to the plane of the subject.

At a hardware store, buy a couple of lamps. Sometimes called shop lights, they have clamps and ball joints to lock the lamp at a certain angle.

Note: Buy lamps that accommodate regular light bulbs—not the high-powered halogen models that melt everything within 50 yards.

Regular 100-watt "soft light" bulbs will work fine. While you're at the hardware store, look for some white *butcher paper* or some other paper that will give you a seamless background at least six feet long and four feet wide. (Camera stores also sell paper backdrops for about $30 a roll.)

Now you're ready to set up your temporary photo studio. Slide a table against the wall, then hang your butcher paper about three feet above the table. Tape it to the top surface of the table, making sure that it has a gentle curve as it goes from vertical to horizontal. Place the item that you want to photograph in the center of the table, about a foot in front of the paper curve.

Next, it's time to set up your lights. You can use chair backs to clamp your lights, which should be pointing directly at your subject at a 45-degree angle, about three feet away from the subject, pointing slightly downward.

Note: Some photographers eschew the two-light setup, preferring a bit of shadow on one side of the object. For this effect, use only one light; on the opposite side, create a reflective surface like a white piece of cardboard, aluminum foil, or white foam board. Make sure that the reflector bounces the light toward the object's non-illuminated side.

Now your subject object is evenly lit, with a minimum of glare and harsh shadows. Even though this homemade product rig might not look beautiful, the shots you create with it can be very appealing.

Some other tips:

- Adjust your camera's white balance for the type of light you're using (page 46). Uncorrected incandescent lights produce an overly warm (reddish) cast; flash tends to produce images a bit on the cool (bluish) side.

- A tripod will help keep the camera in precise position.

- If your camera has a manual-focus mode, use it to lock in the focus on the object's area that is most important to you.

- Once your camera is positioned and focused, you may find its remote control or self-timer mode convenient, so you won't have to constantly bend over during the course of a long shoot.

You're ready to shoot.

Natural Lighting for Objects

Of course, you won't always be at home with a bunch of lights and roll paper at your disposal. Many of your object shots will be more spontaneous, impromptu affairs, or you may decide that a home studio isn't your cup of tea. In these cases, let nature provide the lighting.

In taking natural-light shots like this, the trick is to keep your subject out of direct sunlight, which would create harsh contrast and "hot spots" on the object's surface. Instead, work in open shade, preferably in the morning or late afternoon hours when the light is the "sweetest." A north-facing window is perfect for this type of shooting.

Once again, pay close attention to the background. You might have to get creative in setting up the shot so that it has a continuous background without any distracting edges.

Finally, set the white balance controls (page 46) to the "cloudy" setting in order to offset the blue cast created by open shade.

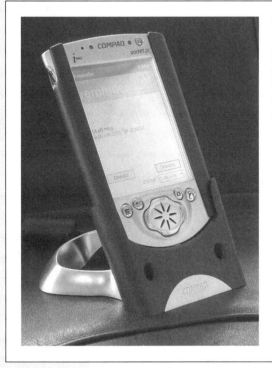

Figure 3-18:
You don't need to build a home studio to produce great product shots. This picture was created by setting a table next to a north-facing window. A piece of white cardboard was used as a reflector to "bounce" some light back into the shadow side of the object. The background: a legal-sized, leather notepad cover angled in an "L" shape to give the shot an "executive" look.

Nighttime Photography

Because photography is the art and science of capturing light, you wouldn't think that nighttime would present many photo opportunities. But in fact, nighttime pictures can be the most spectacular ones in your portfolio. City lights, river lights, sky lights, and even car lights can stand out like bright colors on a black canvas.

Unfortunately, you can't even think about this kind of photography without a tripod. Sure, you can practice the following techniques by bracing the camera against a wall—but you'll find the job infinitely easier with a true tripod (page 69).

Trailing Car Lights

You've seen this shot on postcards and in magazines: neon bands of light streaking across the frame, with a nicely lit bridge or building in the background. The trick to these shots is to keep the shutter open long enough for the cars to pass all the way from one side of the frame to the other.

When using film cameras, photographers rely on something called the camera's "B" setting, in combination with a *cable release* (a shutter button on the end of a cord). The "B" setting (short for *bulb*) keeps the shutter open for as long as you hold down the release. Many a photographer has stood out in the cold, thumbs pressing down on icy cable releases, softly counting: "One thousand one, one thousand two, one thousand three…"

Your digital camera probably doesn't have a "B" setting (although a few do have bulb modes). But you can capture these dramatic shots if your camera offers a shutter priority mode (often marked by the letter "S" or "TV" on the control dial; see Figures 3-2 and 3-3). In this mode, you can tell the camera to keep the shutter open for a long time indeed—for car-taillight photos, four seconds or more.

BUYERS' GUIDE

How to Buy a Tripod

A tripod has two parts: the legs and the *pan head*. The camera attaches to the pan head, and the legs support the head.

You can buy a tripod with any of three pan head types. *Friction heads* are the simplest, least expensive, and most popular with still photographers. *Fluid heads* are desirable if you'll also be using your tripod for a camcorder, as they smooth out panning and tilting. (This means you, iMovie fans.) They're more expensive than friction heads, but are well worth the money if you're after a professional look to your footage. Finally, *geared heads* are big, heavy, expensive, and difficult to use.

The tripod's legs may be made of metal, wood, or composite. Metal is light and inexpensive, but easier to damage by accident (thin metal is easily bent). Wood and composite legs are much more expensive; they're designed for heavier professional broadcast and film equipment. The bottoms of the legs have rubber feet, which is great for use indoors and on solid floors.

Good tripods also have *spreaders* that prevent the legs from spreading apart and causing the entire apparatus to crash to the ground. If your tripod doesn't have spreaders, put the tripod on a piece of carpet, which prevents the legs from slipping apart.

Tip: When preparing for nighttime shooting, pack a pocket flashlight so you can see the camera's controls in the dark.

Figure 3-19:
Don't wait until complete darkness for this type of shot, or your sky will go completely black. Twilight is the best time to shoot streaming car lights.

Try to find a vantage point high enough to provide a good overview of the scene. A nicely lit building, bridge, or monument in the background provides a nice contrast to erratic lights created by the cars passing through the scene.

Put your camera on a tripod or some other steady surface, and set it in shutter-priority mode. After you've composed your shot, set the shutter for four seconds. The camera will control the aperture automatically. Use your remote control, if you have one, or your camera's self-timer mode.

When you see cars coming into the scene, trip the shutter. Review the results on the LCD screen. If the streaks aren't long enough, then add a couple seconds to the shutter setting; if the streaks are too long, subtract a second or two.

With a little trial and error, you can capture beautiful, dramatic taillight shots just like the postcards you've seen for years.

Nighttime Portraits

Nighttime portraits can be extremely interesting, especially when your subject is in front of a lit monument or building.

Put your camera on a tripod or steady surface as you compose the background. The key to this shot will be opening the aperture very wide, to admit as much light as possible. You can do this in one of two ways.

Aperture-priority mode

If you can put your camera into *aperture-priority mode*, as described on page 42, set the aperture to f-2.8 or f-4.

Take a shot of just the background and review it onscreen. If it looks good, turn on your flash (fill flash mode) and position your subject within ten feet of the camera. Ask your subject to stand still until you give the OK to move. When you take the picture, the flash will fire very briefly, but the shutter will stay open for another second or two to soak in enough light to pick up the background.

Review the results on the camera. If your subject is too bright, move the camera farther away. Move closer if the subject is too dark.

POWER USERS' CLINIC

Star Trails

If you *really* want to impress your friends with your budding photographic skills, try capturing *star trails*. Surely you've seen these dramatic shots: one star, located in the center of the frame, remains a point of light, but all the other stars in the universe seem to carve concentric circle segments around it, as though the galaxy were spinning dizzily.

That one fixed star, in case you were wondering, is the North Star. It remains steady as all the other stars seem to travel in a circular path around it, thanks to the rotation of the earth.

Find some place dark with a clean horizon line. If you want the ground in the shot at all, compose the frame so that the sky fills 90 percent of it, and the ground occupies the bottom 10 percent.

The setup for this shot is the same as with the car light trails, except that you'll have to keep the shutter open much longer—at least fifteen seconds for very short trails as in the example here, or (if your camera can handle it) up to fifteen minutes for dramatic star trails. (The photo here, showing the Pleiades constellation [sometimes referred to as the Seven Sisters] was captured with a shutter speed of just a few seconds. The stars are already beginning to "trail.")

The longer the exposure, the longer the star trails, so push your camera to the limit. If the trails aren't bright enough, then increase your camera's light sensitivity by changing the film speed (page 20) to 200 or 400.

Nighttime-flash mode

If your camera doesn't have an aperture-priority mode, it might have a *nighttime-flash* mode. It's pretty much the same idea—it opens the aperture very wide—except that you can't control precisely *how* wide. The camera will attempt to properly expose the background while providing just enough additional flash for your model.

Try it. If your model is too bright or too dark, move closer or farther.

Time-Lapse Photography

Time-lapse photography is an effective way to depict a subject changing from one state of being to another: a butterfly emerging from a cocoon, the unfurling of a rose bud, and so on. Obviously, the result you want is a movie, not a still picture—but that's just fine with you. You've got a Mac, and the Mac has QuickTime.

The idea is that you'll take a picture at regular intervals—once an hour, for example. At the end of eighteen hours, you'll have eighteen images that you can upload to iPhoto for processing. (You'll also be very tired, but that's another story.)

You'll then be able to use the Export to QuickTime function of iPhoto 1.1 or later, which will turn your still frames into a live-action movie, at the frame rate you specify. Chapter 11 details this process.

When setting up for a time-lapse shoot, keep these things in mind.

- Put your camera on a tripod. You want every shot to have precisely the same angle, distance, and composition.

- Make sure the background is plain. You don't want a lot of changing background activity in your sequence of shots, since it will distract from the main subject.

- You may want to keep the camera plugged into a wall jack (an AC adapter is an extra purchase with most camera models). Trying to change the batteries once the time-lapse process has begun is sure to alter the camera's original positioning.

- Focus manually, if your camera allows it, to ensure sharpness in every frame.

- Try not to use the flash. Close-range flash shooting generally blows your subject into blinding white.

- Experiment with exposure intervals. Try one shot every fifteen minutes for one project, and then repeat the project again using 30-minute intervals. With a little trial and error, you'll find the perfect setting for your subject.

Once you've captured your sequence of shots, upload them to iPhoto. Chapter 11 has the full details about creating QuickTime movies of your slide shows. For time-lapse movies, the process is just as described there, with a few additional suggestions. They include:

- Don't crop individual photos. You want them to line up with each other in the finished movie.

- Put all of the pictures into a new album.

- In the iPhoto→Preferences dialog box, choose a duration for each frame along the lines of .25, .50, or 1.0 seconds.

Digital Movies

Movie making probably wasn't what you had in mind when you bought a digital *still* camera. Even so, most cameras offer this feature, and it can come in handy now and then.

Movie mode lets you capture 30 seconds or so of QuickTime video, often with sound, and save it to your memory card right alongside your still pictures. Of course, 30 seconds might not sound very long, but hey—that's the standard length of TV commercials, and don't some of them seem to last an eternity?

Once you've transferred the movie to your Mac, you can play it, email it to people, or post it on a Web page.

Note: iPhoto doesn't do movies. In other words, you must transfer the movie file to your Mac using whatever transfer software came with the camera. Most recent models simplify this process: When you plug their USB cable into the Mac, the camera's memory card appears on the Mac OS X desktop as though it's an external disk drive. You can just double-click it to open it. Inside, you'll find several folders: one that contains your still photos, and another that contains the movies.

If your camera doesn't appear on the desktop as a disk, you'll have to buy a USB memory-card reader, as described on page 85.

These movies have modest dimensions (typically 320 x 240), so it's best to keep your expectations low. Even so, life is filled with situations when a few frames of Quick-Time are better that no movies at all.

Just keep these pointers in mind:

- **Remember your memory.** Digital movies, even these low-quality ones, fill up your memory card in seconds. This is 128 MB card territory. Remember, you're shooting twelve or fifteen little pictures *per second.*

- **Steady the camera.** If you don't have a tripod, put the camera strap around your neck, pull the camera outward so the strap is taut, and only then begin filming. Using the strap to steady the camera results in less shaky movies.

- **Give it up in darkness.** The flash doesn't work for movies, so look for the best lighting possible before composing your shot.

Tip: If you've upgraded your copy of QuickTime to QuickTime Pro (by paying $30 and visiting the Apple Web site), you can combine several short movies into one longer one. Open movie B; choose Edit→Select All; choose Edit→Copy.

Now open movie A. Scroll to the very end, and then choose Edit→Paste.

Infrared Black-and-White Photography

Black-and-white photography no longer dominates the print world as it did during the heyday of *Life* magazine, but it's still popular. Black-and-white shots impart a special artistic feeling that's often lacking in color shots.

Unfortunately, many of the tricks used by expert black-and-white artists aren't readily available to casual photographers employing digital means without a visit to high-end image editors like Photoshop. There is, however, a powerful black-and-white alternative that doesn't require an advanced degree in photo editing: *infrared* photography.

Infrared photography deals with the spectrum of light that you can't see but your digital camera can. It's an option only if your camera accepts filters—and if you're willing to buy an *infrared* filter, which eliminates the visible spectrum and captures only the infrared rays.

The first thing you'll notice in infrared photography is that the blue sky goes dark and that most trees turn very light. Glare is minimized, as you can see by the road in the before-and-after examples shown here.

The most popular filter for digicam infrared photography is the Hoya R72. If your camera accepts filters, then go to the camera store, attach the R72, and look at a brightly-lit scene on the LCD screen. You'll know right away if your camera is suitable for this kind of photography.

Cameras that work well with infrared include the Nikon CoolPix 800 and 950, Canon G1 and S10, Olympus C-3000 series, and Kodak DC 260. Many others will also work. In an attempt to improve overall picture quality, some camera makers add internal filtering—but unfortunately this only disables their infrared capability. The Canon G2 and the Nikon CoolPix 990 exhibit this problem, for example, even though both their predecessors worked well for infrared black and white.

If you're lucky enough to have a camera that can capture infrared images and accept filters, then get your hands on a Hoya R72 and go have some fun. You can create some astonishing pictures that will attract lots of attention.

Part Two:
iPhoto Basics

2

Camera Meets Mac

The Ansel Adams part of your job is over. Your digital camera is brimming with photos. You've snapped the perfect graduation portrait, captured that jaw-dropping sunset over the Pacific, or compiled an unforgettable photo essay of your two-year-old attempting to eat a bowl of spaghetti. It's time to use your Mac to gather, organize, and tweak all these photos so that you can share them with the rest of the world.

This is the core of this book—compiling, organizing, and adjusting your pictures using iPhoto and then transforming this random collection of digital photos into a professional-looking slide show, set of prints, movie, Web page, poster, email, desktop picture set, or bound book.

But before you actually start organizing and publishing these pictures using iPhoto, you need to transfer them from your camera (or its memory card) to the Mac itself. This chapter shows you how to get pictures from camera to computer and introduces you to iPhoto itself.

iPhoto: The Application

iPhoto approaches digital photo management as a five-step process, with each step corresponding to one of the following major areas of the program:

- **Import.** Working with iPhoto begins with feeding your digital pictures—either from a digital camera or from files on a disk—into the program. During the import process, iPhoto duplicates your pictures and stores them in its own Photo Library. If iPhoto automatically recognizes your camera or memory-card reader model, importing is literally a one-click process. This is the part of iPhoto covered in this chapter.

- **Organize**. This step is about sorting and categorizing your chaotic jumble of pictures so that you can easily find them and arrange them into logical groups. You can add searchable keywords like Vacation or Kids to pictures to make them easier to find. You can change the order of images, and group them into discrete "folders" called albums. Instead of having 4,300 randomly named digital photos scattered about on your three hard drives, you end up with a set of neatly categorized and immediately accessible photo collections. Chapter 5 covers every one of iPhoto's organization tools.

- **Edit**. This is where you fine-tune your photos to make them look as good as possible. iPhoto provides the basic tools you need for rotating, resizing, cropping, or brightening your pictures. More significant image adjustments—adjusting color balance, sharpening, editing out an ex-spouse—require another image-editing program. Editing your photos is the focus of Chapter 6.

- **Book.** iPhoto comes with a built-in page-layout program dedicated to a single purpose: helping you design a linen-covered, acid-free, hardback book of your photos. After you choose a book style, such as Story Book or Portfolio, iPhoto steps you through the process of laying out the photos on each page, complete with titles, captions, and page numbers. When you're done, you can either print out the book yourself, or have it professionally printed and bound using the Order Book feature described in Chapter 10.

- **Share**. When it comes to displaying your pictures, the Share mode is where most of the action is. In this part of iPhoto, you'll find nine different ways of publishing your albums onscreen and on paper. In addition to simply printing pictures out on your own computer printer (in a variety of interesting layouts and book styles), you can display images as an onscreen slide show, turn the slide show into a QuickTime movie, order professional-quality prints or a hardback book (based on the design you came up with using the Order Book feature described in the previous paragraph), email them, apply one to your desktop as a backdrop, select a batch to become your Mac OS X screen saver, or post them on your iTools Web site. If you've already got your own Web site, you can export a collection of photos as a series of ready-to-post Web pages. Chapters 7 through 12 explain how to undertake each of these self-publishing tasks.

Note: Although much of this book is focused on using digital cameras, remember this: You *don't* have to shoot digital photos in order to use iPhoto. You can just as easily use it to organize and publish pictures you've shot with a traditional film camera and digitized using a scanner. Importing scanned photos is covered later in this chapter on page 87.

Getting iPhoto

If you bought your Mac after January 2002, you probably already have iPhoto, since it's included free on all current Mac models. You'll find it in the Applications folder that lives at the root level of your hard drive. Just double-click the iPhoto icon and you'll be up and running.

Tip: You can press Shift-⌘-A, choose Go→Applications, or click the Applications icon in the toolbar along the top of any Finder window to jump straight to the Applications folder. Once you've found the iPhoto icon, drag it to the Dock so its icon is parked there permanently for easy access.

Apple released iPhoto 1.1.1 in April 2002, adding a slew of important new features. If you've got an older Mac that didn't come with iPhoto (or if you've got a copy of the older iPhoto 1.0 and need to replace it), you can download the most current version for free from Apple's Web site, *www.apple.com/iphoto/download*. (Apple doesn't want money for iPhoto, but you will have to surrender your name and email address on the download page.) And if you're dialing up with a modem, be ready for a bit of a wait, as the iPhoto installer package is nearly 20 MB.

Once you've downloaded it, you end up with a file called iPhoto 1.1.1.dmg on your desktop. This is a *disk image* file—a common single-file format for packaging up and distributing Mac software. When you double-click the file, a fake "disk" icon called iPhoto appears on your desktop. Open this virtual disk and double-click the iPhoto.pkg file to kick off the easy installation process. You'll need about 118 MB of space to install iPhoto.

When the installation is complete, double-click the iPhoto icon to launch the program and view the program's main window, the basic elements of which are shown in Figure 4-1.

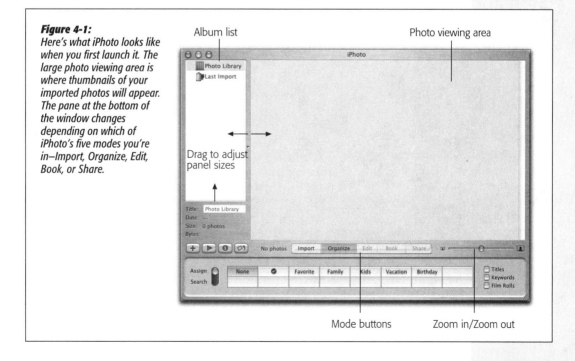

Figure 4-1:
Here's what iPhoto looks like when you first launch it. The large photo viewing area is where thumbnails of your imported photos will appear. The pane at the bottom of the window changes depending on which of iPhoto's five modes you're in—Import, Organize, Edit, Book, or Share.

Album list

Photo viewing area

Drag to adjust panel sizes

Mode buttons   Zoom in/Zoom out

Upgrading to iPhoto 1.1.1

Compared to its predecessor, iPhoto 1.1.1 is a significant upgrade, since it adds several features that were conspicuously absent from iPhoto 1.0. Among other new features, iPhoto 1.1.1 lets you email photos, preserve their original file names, and find photos by searching their Comments boxes.

If you haven't started using iPhoto yet, get the 1.1.1 upgrade. Don't even waste time with the copy of iPhoto 1.0 that may be preinstalled on your Mac.

If you've already been using iPhoto 1.0, perform the upgrade by all means—but proceed with caution. When you upgrade to 1.1.1, iPhoto has to update your iPhoto library (the program's built-in database that tracks your photos) to a new format that's incompatible with iPhoto 1.0. As a precaution, back up the whole folder called iPhoto Library, located in your Home folder→Pictures folder, before running the 1.1.1 installer. (This folder may be huge, since it contains copies of all the photos you've imported into iPhoto.)

Now, if anything should go wrong with the conversion process (there have been some reports of this), you'll still have a clean, uncorrupted copy of your iPhoto Library files. Ordinarily, though, the upgrade process is seamless: iPhoto 1.1.1 will completely replace your old version, and the photos, comments, titles, and albums you set up in Photo 1.0 will be perfectly preserved and accessible using 1.1.1.

UP TO SPEED

The Installer Password

When you run the iPhoto installer, your efforts are almost immediately interrupted by a message telling you that you need an "Administrator password" to install the program.

Not to worry. The iPhoto installer is just checking to make sure that you, as the administrator of your Mac, truly have permission to load new software on it. (If you're new to Mac OS X, get used to it; well-written programs often ask you to establish your authority to install new programs.)

To enter the password, click the lock icon in the lower-left corner of the Authorization screen of the installer. You'll be prompted for the name and password of an Administrator account for your Mac.

If you're not sure which user account is the administrator's, choose →System Preferences. Click the Users icon to view a list of people with *accounts* on your Mac. Those who have been designated as administrators are clearly marked.

You don't actually have to log in as an administrator to install the software; you just need to know an administrator's name and password. In other words, if you are not yourself an administrator, you can call one over to the machine and ask him to type in his information so you can proceed with the installation.

What you need to run iPhoto

According to Apple, iPhoto needs a Mac that has a USB port with a 400-MHz G3 processor or better, at least 256 MB of memory, and Mac OS X version 10.1.2 or later.

The USB port makes it possible to connect a camera or memory-card reader for direct importing of the photos. Technically, you don't need a USB port, since you can always import photos from the hard drive or a CD, as described later in this chapter.

As for processor speed and RAM: iPhoto may be among the most memory-dependent programs on your Mac. It *loves* memory. Memory is even more important to iPhoto than your Mac's processor speed. It makes the difference between tolerable speed and sluggishness, or between a 2,000-photo collection and a 10,000-photo collection.

You can run iPhoto on a slower Mac with less memory, but the speed may not be what you'd hope for, especially as more photos join your collection.

Getting Your Pictures into iPhoto

With iPhoto installed and ready to run, it's time for you to import your own pictures into the program—a process that's remarkably easy, especially if your photos are going directly from your digital camera or memory card into iPhoto.

Of course, if you've been taking digital photos for some time, you probably have a lot of photo files already crammed into folders on your hard drive or on Zip disks or

---

FREQUENTLY ASKED QUESTION

Is My Camera iPhoto-Friendly?

How can I tell if my digital camera is compatible with iPhoto?

The official answer is: Check Apple's compatibility list. Go to *www.apple.com/iphoto/compatibility*, where you'll find a list of every camera, memory-card reader, and printer that works with iPhoto. The list already includes dozens of camera models from Canon, Fuji, Hewlett-Packard, Kodak, Nikon, Olympus, Sony, Minolta and others.

If you're camera *isn't* on the list, however, don't despair; the list is by no means all-inclusive. Almost any camera released *after* iPhoto works with iPhoto, whether or not it appears on the list. In short, the list includes only camera models that Apple's engineers have personally tested—not every camera on earth that works with iPhoto.

If you have an older model that *truly* doesn't work with iPhoto, still all is not lost. You can always move photos from camera to computer yourself, using whatever software came with the camera—and then *drag* them into iPhoto.

Alternatively, you can buy a memory-card reader that *is* iPhoto-compatible (under $30) and load images into your Mac by putting the camera's memory card into it. (Some professionals prefer this method anyway, because it saves the camera's battery power.)

In other words, as long as your digital photos end up in one of the dozen or so file formats that iPhoto understands, you can use iPhoto—regardless of the make and model of your camera.

CDs. If you shoot pictures with a traditional film camera and use a scanner to digitize them, you've probably got piles of JPEG or TIFF images stashed away on disks already, waiting to be cataloged using iPhoto.

This section explains how to transfer files from each of these sources into iPhoto itself.

Connecting with a USB Camera

Virtually every modern digital camera can connect to a Mac using the USB (Universal Serial Bus) port. If your Mac has more than one USB jack, you can use any of them when connecting your digital camera.

Plugging a USB-compatible camera into your Mac is the easiest way to transfer pictures from your camera into iPhoto. The whole process practically happens by itself.

1. **With your camera turned off, plug it into one of your Mac's USB jacks.**

   To make this camera-to-Mac USB connection, you need what is usually called an "A-to-B" USB cable; your camera probably came with one. The "A" end—the part you plug into your camera—has a small, six-sided, flat-bottomed plug. The Mac ("B") end of the cable has a larger, flatter, rectangular plug. Make sure both ends of the cable are plugged in firmly.

   iPhoto doesn't have to be running when you make this connection. The program will launch itself and spring into action as soon as you switch on the camera.

   Note: If this is the first time you've ever run iPhoto, it will ask if you *always* want it to run when you plug in the camera. (Mac OS X comes set to open the older Image Capture program instead; iPhoto is asking to take over from now on.) If you value your time, say yes.

   ---

2. **Turn on the camera.**

   If iPhoto is running, it will immediately detect that there are new photos available for download and subsequently stand ready to import them. If iPhoto isn't running, your Mac is smart enough to detect the presence of the connected camera and launch iPhoto for you.

   Note: There's no danger in plugging your camera in while it's turned on; it's just that the Mac might not detect the presence of certain camera models until it has been turned on while plugged into the USB port. If, for some reason, iPhoto doesn't "see" your camera after you connect it and turn it on, try turning the camera off, then on again, while it's plugged in.

   You can tell if iPhoto is ready to do its job by checking out the information area at the bottom panel, as shown in Figure 4-2. You should see the name of your camera listed, along with a status line indicating how many pictures iPhoto has detected on the camera, ready to be imported. (The number may be somewhat larger than you expect if you forgot to erase your last batch of photos.)

3. **Turn on the "Erase contents after transfer" checkbox, if you like.**

Think about this one for a moment. It's the one big decision you have to make when importing your photos. If you turn on "Erase contents after transfer," iPhoto will automatically erase all photos from your camera's memory card once they're safely on the Mac.

The advantage of using this option is that your camera's memory card is instantly and effortlessly wiped clean, making it ready for you to fill with more pictures. This self-cleaning feature also eliminates the possibility that you'll accidentally import the *same* pictures into iPhoto the next time you hook up your camera, resulting in a load of duplicates.

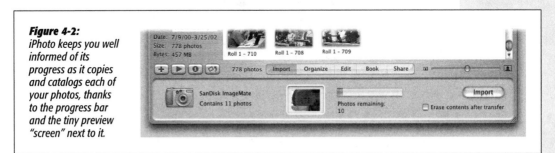

Figure 4-2:
iPhoto keeps you well informed of its progress as it copies and catalogs each of your photos, thanks to the progress bar and the tiny preview "screen" next to it.

On the other hand, this auto-erasing scheme may sound a bit risky. Do you really want your Mac to zap a whole camera full of files into oblivion before you've even confirmed that they've been safely copied to their new location?

Of course, iPhoto isn't supposed to delete your pictures until *after* it has successfully copied them all to the iPhoto Library. However, it's not beyond the realm of possibility that a hard disk could fail during an iPhoto import, or that a file could get corrupted when copied, thereby becoming unopenable. If you want to play it safe, leave the "Erase contents after transfer" option turned off.

Then, after you've confirmed that each photo has been copied into the iPhoto Library folder, you can switch to the Finder, open the "disk" icon that represents the memory card there, drag the photos into the Trash, and delete them once and for all. (You can also use the camera's own card-erasing features, of course.)

4. **Click the Import button.**

This is the big moment: iPhoto swings into action, copying each photo from your camera to your hard drive, as shown in Figure 4-2. (If you chose to use the auto-erase feature, you'll see a final "Are you sure…?" dialog box.)

Tip: Want to import only *some* of the pictures on your camera? You can do it using the workaround described on page 261.

The program also creates a *thumbnail* of each picture—a tiny, low-resolution version of each photo that appears, like a slide on a slide sorter, in the main iPhoto window.

When the process is over, your freshly imported photos will be on display in the main iPhoto window, awaiting your organizational talents.

5. **Switch to the Finder.**

   If iPhoto is the only program running, a quick way to jump back to the desktop is to press ⌘-H. That's the keyboard shortcut for Hide iPhoto. It makes iPhoto's window disappear, so that you're right back at the desktop.

   There you should see a "disk" icon that represents your camera's memory card. It probably has some cryptic name.

Tip: This is how less-fortunate computer owners get their pictures off the camera, by the way. They open this disk icon and drag the pictures manually to the hard drive.

That's a trick worth remembering. Opening this "disk" icon is the only way to *selectively* delete photos from the card. (If you do that, though, eject and reinsert the card before importing into iPhoto, to avoid thoroughly confusing the software.) This trick also offers you the chance to copy photos back *onto* your camera—just drag them onto the memory-card "disk" icon in the Finder.

---

6. **Drag the camera memory-card "disk" icon from the desktop to the Trash, turn off the camera, and then unplug it.**

   This is the official Apple-blessed procedure for disconnecting your camera. If you just yank the USB cord out of the Mac (or the camera) or turn off the camera, the Mac doesn't take it kindly (see Figure 4-3).

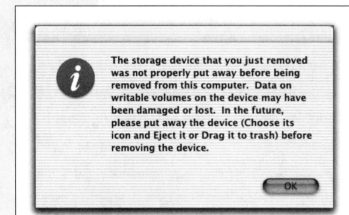

The storage device that you just removed was not properly put away before being removed from this computer. Data on writable volumes on the device may have been damaged or lost. In the future, please put away the device (Choose its icon and Eject it or Drag it to trash) before removing the device.

OK

Figure 4-3:
This is the kind of scary message you might see if you disconnect your camera from your Mac without first either dragging its icon to the Trash or selecting it and choosing File→Eject. Despite the sternly worded message in this dialog box, nothing on your camera's memory card is likely to be lost or damaged.

Connecting with a USB Card Reader

If your camera happens to be an older model without a USB cable connector, you still may be able to take advantage of iPhoto's automated file-importing features. The secret is to use an inexpensive USB *memory-card reader* to transfer photos from the camera's memory card to iPhoto. iPhoto recognizes several different card readers, from ImageMate, Sony, SmartDisk, LaCie, and so on. Most of these card readers, which look like tiny disk drives, are under $40; several can read more than one kind of memory card.

Tip: iPhoto may not be able to recognize your *camcorder,* even if it's the kind that can take still pictures. See page 260 for troubleshooting tips on this topic.

Connecting with a USB-compatible memory-card reader is almost identical to connecting a camera. Here's how:

1. **Pop a memory card out of your camera and insert it into the reader.**

   Of course, the card reader should already be plugged into one of the Mac's USB jacks.

   As when you connect a camera, iPhoto acknowledges the presence of the memory-card reader in its status panel and reports the number of images on the card. As described above, you can turn on the "Erase contents after transfer" checkbox if you want iPhoto to automatically clear the memory card after copying the files to your Mac.

2. **Click the Import button.**

UP TO SPEED

JPEG and TIFF

Most digital cameras capture photos in a graphics file format called JPEG. That's the world's most popular file format for photos, because even though it's compressed to take up a *lot* less disk space, the visual quality is still very high.

Some cameras offer you the chance to leave your photos *uncompressed* on the camera, in what's called TIFF format. These files are huge—you'll be lucky if you can fit *one* TIFF file on the memory card that came with the camera—but retain 100 percent of the picture's original quality. (You'd be hard-pressed to detect the quality loss in a JPEG file, but technically speaking, there is some.)

iPhoto recognizes both kinds of files when you import them. (For that matter, iPhoto can also import graphics files in BMP, GIF, MacPaint, PICT, PNG, Photoshop, SGI, Targa, and FlashPix formats, as described later in this chapter.)

Note, however, that the instant you *edit* a TIFF-format photo (Chapter 6), iPhoto converts it into JPEG.

If you plan to order prints from iPhoto, or a hardback book (Chapter 10), that's just fine; JPEG files are required for those purposes. But if you took that once-in-a-lifetime, priceless shot as a TIFF file, don't do any editing (even rotating) in iPhoto if you hope to maintain its perfect, pristine quality.

It's worth noting that many people prefer using this card-reader setup over making a direct camera-to-Mac hookup, even if they do have a USB-equipped, iPhoto-compatible camera. First, the card-reader route saves camera battery power; second, it's just less of a hassle to pull a memory card out of your camera and slip it into your always-plugged-in card reader than it is to constantly plug and unplug camera cables.

3. **Switch to the Finder. Drag the memory card's icon from the desktop to the Trash when you're done, and then remove the card from the reader.**

Put it back into the camera, so it's ready for more action.

Importing Photos from Non-USB Cameras

If your camera doesn't have a USB connection (and you don't have a memory-card reader), you're still not out of luck.

First copy the photos from your camera or memory card onto your hard drive (or other disk) using whatever software or hardware came with your camera. Then bring them into iPhoto using one of these two methods:

- Drag the files directly into the main iPhoto window, which automatically starts the import process. You can also drop an entire *folder* of images into iPhoto to import the contents of the whole folder, as shown in Figure 4-4.

Tip: Take the time to name your folders intelligently before dragging them into iPhoto, because the program retains their names. If you drag a folder directly into the main photo area, you get a new *film roll* named for the folder (page 93); if you drag the folder into the album list at the left side of the screen, you get a new *album* named for the folder. (Folders *inside* folders, too, become new film rolls and albums.)

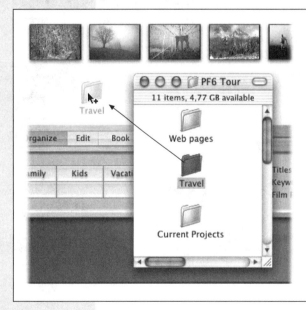

Figure 4-4:
When you drop a folder into iPhoto, the program automatically scans all the folders inside it, looking for pictures to catalog. It creates a new film roll *(Chapter 5) for each folder it finds. iPhoto ignores irrelevant files and stores only the pictures that are in a format it can read.*

- Choose File→Import (or press ⌘-I) in iPhoto and select a file or folder in the Open dialog box (Figure 4-5).

Tip: If your camera or memory card "mounts" on the Mac desktop like any other removable disk, you can simply drag the photo icons from this "disk" icon directly into iPhoto.

Figure 4-5:
When the Import Photos dialog box appears, navigate to and select any graphics files you want to bring into iPhoto. You can ⌘-click individual graphics to select more than one simultaneously, as shown here. You can also click one, then Shift-click another one, to highlight both files and everything in the list in between.

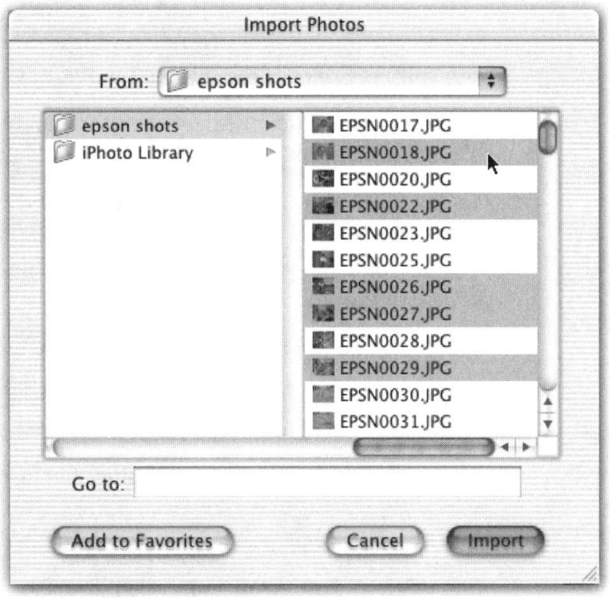

Importing Existing Graphics Files

If you've already got digital photos—or any other kinds of graphics files—stored somewhere on your computer, the easiest way to import them into iPhoto is simply to drag their icons into the main iPhoto window (as described just a few paragraphs earlier), or by using the File→Import command (see Figure 4-5).

You can also select and import files from CD-ROMs, DVDs, Jaz, or Zip disks, or other disks on the network. If your photos are on a Kodak Photo CD, you can insert the CD (with iPhoto already running) and then click the Import button on the Import pane—just as if you were importing photos from a connected camera. As always, iPhoto makes fresh copies of the files you import, storing them in one centralized photo repository (the iPhoto Library folder) on your hard drive. The program also creates thumbnail versions of each image for display in the main iPhoto window.

Note: Through this process and all other importing processes, remember this: iPhoto *never moves* files, whether from a memory card or disk. It only copies them.

The File Format Factor

iPhoto can't import pictures unless it understands their file format. For the most part, this isn't a problem; almost every digital camera saves photos as either *JPEG* or *TIFF* files—and iPhoto handles both of these widely used formats beautifully.

Beware, though, that some of the better digital cameras include an option for saving images in a nonstandard file format that's unique to the camera manufacturer. Kodak, Olympus, and Nikon cameras, for example, can all save images in a *RAW* format that iPhoto can't read. If you hope to bring your photos into iPhoto, set your camera to save photos as JPEGs or TIFFs instead, or use the camera company's software to convert RAW files to something iPhoto will find more palatable.

Of course, iPhoto also lets you load pictures that have been saved in a number of other file formats, too—including a few unusual ones. They include:

- **GIF** is the most common format used for nonphoto graphics on Web pages. The borders, backgrounds, and logos you typically encounter on Web sites are usually GIF files—as well as 98 percent of those blinking, flashing banner ads that drive you insane.

- **PNG** and **FlashPix** are also used in Web design, though not nearly as much as JPEG and GIF. They often display more complex graphic elements.

- **BMP** is a popular graphics file format on Windows PCs.

- **PICT** was the original graphics file format of the Macintosh prior to Mac OS X. When you take a screen shot in Mac OS 9, paste a picture from the Clipboard, or copy an image from the Scrapbook, you're using a PICT file.

- **Photoshop** refers to Adobe Photoshop, the world's most popular image-editing and photo-retouching program. iPhoto can even recognize and import *layered* Photoshop files—those in which different image adjustments or graphic elements are stored in different layers, sandwiched together.

WORKAROUND WORKSHOP

Import vs. Import

There's plenty about iPhoto that is remarkably straightforward and intuitive—but not the Import command.

There are, in fact, two Import commands: One is a menu command (File→Import) and the other is a big pulsating button in the lower-right corner of the Import screen. They don't do the same thing, however.

The Import *button* is strictly for importing photos from iPhoto-compatible digital cameras and memory-card readers. In fact, if iPhoto doesn't detect the presence of a cam-

era, card reader, or Kodak Photo CD, the Import button is dimmed out and can't do a thing.

The Import command in the File menu is only for importing digital photos already on disk. Use this command to import photos stored on your hard drive, CDs, Jaz disks, and other disks.

You can effectively ignore the File→Import command, though, since simply dropping the files or folders you want to import into the main iPhoto window accomplishes exactly the same thing.

- **MacPaint** is the ancient file format of MacPaint, Apple's very first graphics program from the mid-1980s. No, you probably won't be working with any MacPaint 2.0 files in iPhoto. But isn't it nice to know that if one of these old, black-and-white, 8 x 10 pictures, generated on a vintage Mac SE, happens to slip through a wormhole in the fabric of time and land on your desk, you'll be ready?

- **SGI** and **Targa** are specialized graphics formats used on high-end Silicon Graphics workstations and Truevision video-editing systems.

- **PDF** files are Portable Document Format files, the kind that open up in Acrobat Reader so that you can read a user manual, brochure, or Read Me file that you downloaded or received on a CD. Apple doesn't publicize the fact that iPhoto can import PDF files, maybe because iPhoto displays only the first page of multipage documents. (Most of the PDFs you come across aren't photos; they're usually multipage documents filled with both text and graphics.)

Note: Most digital photos you work with are probably JPEG files—but they're not always *called* JPEG files. You may also see JPEG referred to as *JFIF* (JPEG File Interchange Format). Bottom line: The terms JPEG, JFIF, and JPEG JFIF all mean the same thing.

If you try to import a file that iPhoto doesn't understand, you see the message shown in Figure 4-6.

Figure 4-6:
Here's iPhoto's way of telling you that you just tried to feed it a file that it can't digest: an EPS file, Adobe Illustrator drawing, QuickTime movie, or PowerPoint file, for example.

Unreadable Photo

The file cannot be imported. It is either not a photo, or a damaged one.

OK

A First Look

Once you've imported a batch of pictures into iPhoto, you can click the Last Import icon near the upper-left corner of the window to survey the new arrivals en masse. Rotate the pictures that need rotating (page 132), and then click the triangular Play button beneath the album list for an immediate slide show of your latest pictures (Chapter 7). If you're like most people, this is the first opportunity you have to see, at full size, the masterpieces you and your camera came up with.

Click the mouse to end the slide show.

Where iPhoto Keeps Your Files

Having dumped your vast collection of digital photos—from a camera, memory card, hard disk, or anywhere else—into iPhoto, you may find yourself wondering: Where's iPhoto putting all those files, anyway?

Technically, you don't really need to know the answer. You can preview, open, edit, rotate, copy, export, and print all your photos right in iPhoto, without actually opening a folder or double-clicking a single JPEG file.

Even so, it's worthwhile to know where iPhoto keeps your pictures on the hard drive. Armed with this information, you can keep those valuable files backed up and avoid accidentally throwing them away six months from now when you're cleaning up your hard drive.

A Trip to the Library

Whenever you import pictures into iPhoto, the program makes *copies* of your photos, always leaving your original files untouched.

- When you import from a camera, iPhoto leaves the photos right where they are on its memory card (unless you use the "Erase" option).

- When you import from the hard drive, iPhoto leaves the originals in whichever folders they're in. As a result, transferring photos from your hard drive into iPhoto *more than doubles* the amount of disk space they take up. In other words, importing 1 GB of photos will require an additional 1 GB of disk space, because you'll end up with two copies of each file—the original and iPhoto's copy of the photo. In addition, iPhoto creates a separate thumbnail version of each picture, consuming about another 10 K to 20 K per photo.

iPhoto stores its copies of your pictures in a special folder called iPhoto Library, which you can find in your Home→Pictures folder. (To find your Home folder, choose Go→Home.) If the short name you use to log into Mac OS X is *mozart*, the full path to your iPhoto Library folder from the main hard drive window would be Macintosh HD→Users→mozart→Pictures→iPhoto Library.

Tip: You should regularly back up this iPhoto Library folder to another disk (or burn it to a CD, if it fits). It contains all the photos you import into iPhoto—essentially, your entire photography collection. Chapter 13 offers much more on this file-management topic.

What all those numbers mean

Within the iPhoto Library, you'll find a set of mysteriously numbered files and folders. At first glance, this setup may look bizarre, but there's a method to iPhoto's madness, of course. It turns out that iPhoto meticulously arranges your photos within these numbered folders according to the *creation dates* of the originals, as explained in Figure 4-7.

Other folders in the iPhoto Library

In addition to the numbered folders, you'll find several other items nested in the iPhoto Library folder. You can just ignore most of the following:

- **Albums folder**. The Albums folder doesn't contain any pictures. The files it holds contain information about which photos are included in the *albums* you create within iPhoto. Photo Albums, which are like folders for organizing photos in iPhoto, are described in Chapter 5.

- **Data folder**. This folder contains iPhoto's for-internal-use-only documents. They store information about your iPhoto Library, such as which keywords you've used. Inside each Data folder, numbered files correspond to each of the photos in your library. These text files are where iPhoto stores the image dimensions, file size, and modification date for each photo.

- **Thumbs folder**. Each numbered folder containing pictures also contains a Thumbs folder. Here, iPhoto stores the small thumbnail versions of the pictures in your iPhoto Library—the "slides" that actually appear in the iPhoto window.

  Even though there's one thumbnail image for each photo you've imported into iPhoto, the two files (the photo and its thumbnail) are named differently. The photo bears its original file name, but the thumbnail files are given a numeric sequence—234.jpg, 235.jpg, and so on—based on the order in which they were imported. This file-naming convention is strictly for iPhoto's internal use; you never *see* these numeric file names in iPhoto.

- **Originals folder**. Some photo folders may contain an Originals folder. It doesn't appear until you use one of iPhoto's editing tools (Chapter 6) to touch up a photo. The Originals folder is the key to one of iPhoto's most remarkable features: the Revert to Original command.

Figure 4-7:
Behold the mysteries of the iPhoto Library. Once you know the secret, this seemingly cryptic folder structure actually makes sense, with all the photos in the library organized by their creation date. At the top level are the year folders—2002, 2001, and so on. Within those folders are subfolders for each month (01 for January, 02 for February), and nested within those are subfolders labeled for each day of each month. So, a photo that was originally saved on March 26, 2002 is stored in iPhoto Library→2002→03→26.

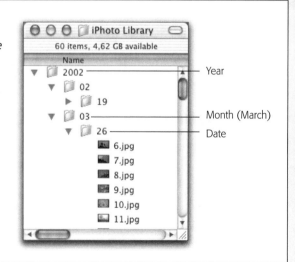

Before it applies any potentially destructive operations to your photos—such as cropping, red-eye removal, brightening, black-and-white conversion—iPhoto *duplicates* the files and stuffs pristine, unedited copies of them in the Originals folder. If you later decide to scrap your changes to a photo using the Revert to Original command, iPhoto moves the unedited file back into its original location, returning your photo to its originally imported state.

Note: Don't confuse the files in the Originals folders with your *true* originals—the files on your hard drive, camera, or memory card that you first imported into iPhoto. As mentioned earlier, iPhoto *never* touches those originals; they're left exactly where they were when you imported them.

Look, don't touch

While it's enlightening to wander through the iPhoto Library to see how iPhoto keeps itself organized, never rename or move any of the folders or files in it. Making such changes will confuse iPhoto to the point where it will either be unable to display some of your photos or just crash.

The rest of the story

Now that you've had a glimpse of iPhoto's secret folder stash, you're ready to put that information to work. In Chapter 13, you can find out how to manage *multiple* iPhoto libraries, back up your library folder, combine the photo collections of two Macs, and much more.

POWER USERS' CLINIC

Return of the Original File Name

Certain Mac fans, vocal on the Internet, were shocked—shocked!—by the way iPhoto 1.0 totally ignored the names of your original photos. If you imported a picture called anniversary2001.jpg, it ended up being called something like "Roll 23–40" in the iPhoto window, while on disk the corresponding file in the iPhoto Library folder got branded with a descriptive name like 743.jpg. The original name, which is the only one that had any meaning in the first place, was nowhere to be seen.

Fortunately, Apple promptly fixed this "feature" in iPhoto 1.1.1. iPhoto still uses its own internal numbering scheme to keep track of thumbnails and organize its folder structure, but your original file names are preserved when you import photos. Those are the names you actually see displayed in the main iPhoto window.

CHAPTER 5

The Digital Shoebox

If you've imported your photos into iPhoto using any of the methods described in the previous chapter, you should now see a neatly arranged grid of thumbnails in iPhoto's main photo viewing area. You're looking at what iPhoto refers to as your *Photo Library*—your entire photo collection, including every last picture you've ever imported. This is the digital equivalent of that old shoebox you've had stuffed in the closet for the last ten years, brimming with snapshots, waiting to be sorted and sifted, often never to be seen again.

You're not really organized yet, but at least all your photos are in one place. Your journey out of chaos has begun. From here, you can sort your photos, give them titles, group them into smaller sub-collections (called *albums*) and tag them with keywords so you'll be able to find them quickly. This chapter helps you tackle each of those organizing tasks as painlessly as possible.

Working with Your Photos

Even before you start naming your photos, assigning them keywords, or organizing them into albums, iPhoto imposes an order of its own on your digital shoebox. For example, instead of just lumping all your photos together in one indivisible clump in the photo viewing area, it automatically groups them into neatly date-stamped batches called *film rolls*.

Each time you import a new set of photos into iPhoto—whether from your hard drive, a camera, or a memory card—that batch of imported photos constitutes one film roll. Of course, there's no real film in digital photography, and your pictures aren't on a "roll" of anything. But if you think about it, the metaphor makes sense:

For just as in traditional photography, where each batch of photos you shoot is captured on a discrete roll of film, in iPhoto, each separate batch of photos you download into the program gets classified as its own film roll. (This means that if you bring all your existing digital photos into iPhoto from one folder *in one download*, you end up with one giant film roll containing all your images.)

Tip: As noted in Chapter 4, if you drag a folder of photos into iPhoto, the name of the folder becomes the name of the film roll, so it pays to bring photos into iPhoto from intelligently named folders. In fact, if you import a series of nested folders containing photos, each individual folder of images gets grouped together as its own separately named film roll. (By contrast, if you drag a group of individual files into iPhoto, the group gets a generic label like "Roll 45.")

How iPhoto sorts your photos

iPhoto starts out sorting your Photo Library by film roll, meaning that the most recently imported batch of photos appears at the bottom of the window. Here are the two ways you can change this sort order:

- To change the sort order to reflect the *creation* date of the photos (rather than the date they were imported), choose Edit→Arrange Photos→By Date (or press Shift-⌘-D). To return to film roll-based sorting, choose Edit→Arrange Photos→By Film Roll (Shift-⌘-F).

- Whether you choose to sort photos by film roll or date, you can reverse the sort order so that the most recent items appear at the *top* of the iPhoto window instead of the bottom—an idea that can save you a lot of scrolling through thumbnails. Choose iPhoto→Preferences, turn on "Most recent at top," and click OK.

Displaying film rolls

The Film Roll checkbox in the lower-right corner of the iPhoto window hides or shows the horizontal film-roll dividers between batches of photos, as shown in Figure 5-1. Turning on the Film Roll checkbox also *sorts* your photos by film roll, if they weren't already sorted that way. (The Film Roll checkbox is dimmed except when the Photo Library icon is selected at the top of the album list.)

FREQUENTLY ASKED QUESTION

Your Own Personal Sorting Order

I don't want my photos sorted by creation date or *import date—I want to put them in my* own *order. I tried using Edit→Arrange Photos→Manually, but the command is dimmed out! Did Apple accidentally forget to turn this on?*

No, the command works—but only in a *photo album*, not in the main Photo Library. If you create a new photo album (as explained later in this chapter) and fill it with photos, you can then drag them into any order you want.

You'll probably come to find this arrangement so convenient that you'll leave it turned on permanently. As your Photo Library becomes ever more massive, these handy groupings become excellent visual and mnemonic aids to help you locate a certain photo, months or years after the fact.

As your Photo Library expands, furthermore, you may need to rely on these film-roll groupings just for your sanity: By collapsing the "flippy triangles" next to the photo groups you're not looking at (Figure 5-1), you speed up iPhoto considerably. Otherwise, iPhoto may grind almost to a halt as it tries to scroll through ever more photos. (Even so, about 10,000 pictures is its realistic limit, even on a fast machine with boxcars of RAM. At that point, consider swapping your libraries in and out as needed, as described on page 245.)

Tip: Click the little roll-of-film icon in the film row divider line to simultaneously select all the photos in a film roll.

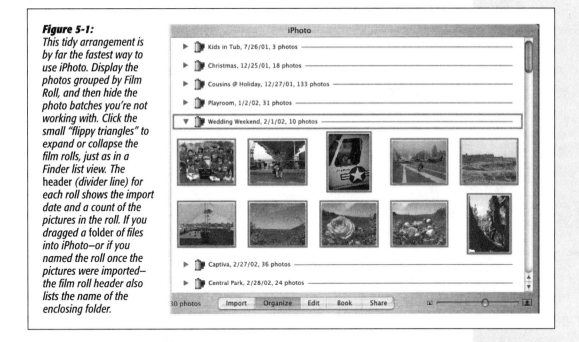

Figure 5-1:
This tidy arrangement is by far the fastest way to use iPhoto. Display the photos grouped by Film Roll, and then hide the photo batches you're not working with. Click the small "flippy triangles" to expand or collapse the film rolls, just as in a Finder list view. The header *(divider line) for each roll shows the import date and a count of the pictures in the roll. If you dragged a* folder *of files into iPhoto—or if you named the roll once the pictures were imported— the film roll header also lists the name of the enclosing folder.*

Even if you opt not to display the film roll divider lines in the photo viewing area, you can still sort the pictures in your Photo Library by film roll. Just choose Edit→Arrange Photos→By Film Roll. You won't be able to see where one film roll ends and the next begins, but the photos will be in the right order.

Renaming and dating film rolls
iPhoto ordinarily labels each film roll with either a roll number (if you imported individual files from a camera or disk) or a folder name (if you imported a folder of

photos). In either case, you can easily change the name of the film roll to something more descriptive.

To edit the name of a roll, click the little roll-of-film icon in the film roll divider line. Now the Title text box at the lower-left edge of the window identifies the roll's current name. Just type a new name into this box—ideally, something that helps you remember the batch of photos at a glance. Press Enter when you're finished.

Using this same technique, you can also change the *date* that appears in the film roll header. This date usually identifies when you imported the photos, but for most purposes, that date is relatively irrelevant. What you probably care more about is the day or month that the photos were actually *taken.*

Once again, start by clicking the roll-of-film icon in the film roll divider. This time, type a new date in the Date text box on the Info pane. You can type the date in a variety of formats—*4 September 2002, September 4, 2002,* and *4/9/02* all work—but you must use a complete date, including day, month, and year. If you don't, iPhoto will take a guess, filling in the missing information for you—and sometimes getting it wrong.

(When you press Return or Enter, the batch of photos in that roll may jump to a new position as iPhoto sorts them by date.)

The last imported film roll

Most of the time, you'll probably work with the photos that you just downloaded from your camera. Conveniently, iPhoto always keeps track of your most recently added film roll, so you can view its contents without having to do a lot of browsing, sorting, or scrolling.

That's the purpose of the roll-of-film icon called Last Import in the Album pane. With one click, iPhoto displays only your most recent photos, hiding all the others. This Last Import feature can save you a lot of time as your Photo Library grows.

If, at any time, you want to return to the grand overview of all of your pictures, just click the Photo Library icon at the top of the Album pane.

Scrolling Through Your Photos

Browsing, selecting, and opening photos in iPhoto is straightforward. Here's everything you need to know:

- Use the vertical scroll bar, or your Page Up and Page Down keys, to navigate through your thumbnails.

Tip: If your photos scroll by too fast for you to find the ones you want, try using iPhoto's Slow Scroll mode. Hold down the Option key while dragging the scroll box in the scroll bar. You get a much slower, smoother scroll, making it easier to navigate to a specific row of thumbnails.

- Scrolling can take awhile if you have a lot of images in your Photo Library, especially if you haven't collapsed the film rolls you're not using, as described earlier. But you can use this standard Mac OS X trick for faster navigation: Instead of dragging the scroll box or clicking the scroll bar arrows, *Option-click* the portion of the scroll bar that corresponds to the location you want to view in your Photo Library. If you want to jump to the bottom of the Photo Library, Option-click near the bottom of the scroll bar. To find photos in the middle of your collection, Option-click the middle portion of the scroll bar, and so on.

Note: By turning on "Scroll to here" in the General panel of your System Preferences, you can make this the standard behavior for Mac OS X scroll bars—that is, you won't need the Option key.

- To create the most expansive photo viewing area possible, you can temporarily hide the Album pane anchored to the left side of the window. To do so, drag the divider bar (between the Album pane and the main photo viewing area) all the way to the left edge of the window. You've just hidden the Album pane.

  To open that panel again (to open a Photo Album, for example), just grab the left edge of the iPhoto window and drag it back to the right.

Selecting Photos

To highlight a single picture in preparation for printing, opening, duplicating, or deleting, click the icon once with the mouse.

That much may seem obvious. But many first-time Mac users have no idea how to manipulate *more* than one icon at a time—an essential survival skill.

To highlight multiple photos in preparation for deleting, moving, duplicating, printing, and so on, use one of these techniques:

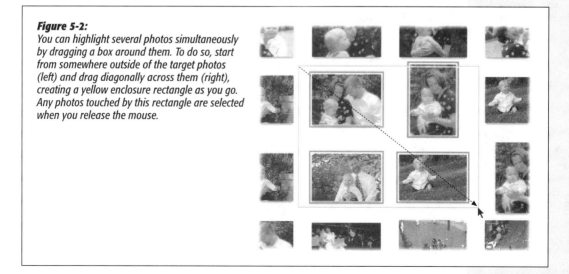

Figure 5-2:
You can highlight several photos simultaneously by dragging a box around them. To do so, start from somewhere outside of the target photos (left) and drag diagonally across them (right), creating a yellow enclosure rectangle as you go. Any photos touched by this rectangle are selected when you release the mouse.

- **To highlight all the photos.** To select all the pictures in the set you're viewing, press ⌘-A (the equivalent of the Edit→Select All command).

- **To highlight several photos by dragging.** You can drag diagonally to highlight a group of nearby photos, as shown in Figure 5-2. You don't even have to enclose the thumbnails completely, as your cursor can touch any part of any icon to highlight it. In fact, if you keep dragging past the edge of the window, iPhoto scrolls the window automatically.

Tip: If you include a particular icon in your diagonally dragged group by mistake, ⌘-click it to remove it from the selected cluster.

- **To highlight consecutive photos.** Click the first thumbnail you want to highlight, and then Shift-click the last one. All the files in between are automatically selected, along with the two photos you clicked (Figure 5-3, top). This trick mirrors the way Shift-clicking works in a word processor as well as many other kinds of programs.

- **To highlight random photos.** If you want to highlight only, for example, the first, third, and seventh photos in a window, start by clicking icon No. 1. Then ⌘-click

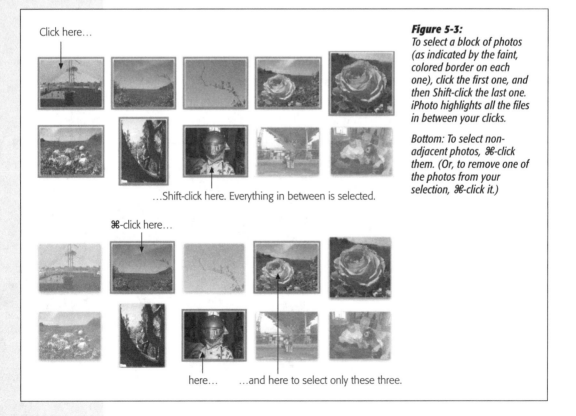

Click here…

…Shift-click here. Everything in between is selected.

⌘-click here…

here…   …and here to select only these three.

Figure 5-3:
To select a block of photos (as indicated by the faint, colored border on each one), click the first one, and then Shift-click the last one. iPhoto highlights all the files in between your clicks.

Bottom: To select non-adjacent photos, ⌘-click them. (Or, to remove one of the photos from your selection, ⌘-click it.)

each of the others. Each thumbnail sprouts a colored border to indicate that you've selected it (Figure 5-3, bottom).

If you're highlighting a long string of photos and then click one by mistake, you don't have to start over. Instead, just ⌘-click it again and the dark highlighting disappears. (If you do want to start over from the beginning, just deselect all selected photos by clicking any empty part of the window.)

The ⌘-key trick is especially handy if you want to select *almost* all the photos in a window. Press ⌘-A to select everything in the folder, then ⌘-click any unwanted photos to deselect them.

Once you've highlighted multiple photos, you can manipulate them all at once. For example, you can drag them en masse out of the window and onto your desktop—a quick way to export them. (Actually, drag them onto a *folder* in the Finder to avoid spraying their icons all over your desktop.) Or you can drag them into an album at the left side of the iPhoto window. Just drag any *one* of the highlighted photos; all other highlighted thumbnails go along for the ride.

Additionally, when multiple photos are selected, the commands in the File and Edit menus—such as Duplicate, Print, and Revert To Original—apply to all of them simultaneously.

Opening Photos

iPhoto wouldn't be a terribly useful program if it let you view only postage-stamp versions of your photos (unless, of course, your photos happen to *be* pictures of postage stamps). Fortunately, iPhoto lets you open photos at full size, zoom up on

---

UP TO SPEED

The Five Faces of iPhoto

iPhoto operates in five different modes—Import, Organize, Edit, Book, and Share. In the previous chapter, you worked in Import mode, bringing your raw digital photos from camera, disk, card, or hard drive into iPhoto's library.

In this chapter, you'll be working in Organize mode, which provides access to iPhoto's keyword tools. When working in iPhoto, it's important that you're in the right mode for the task at hand—otherwise you may not have access to the iPhoto features that you need.

Here's how to tell what mode the program is in:

- Look at the five mode buttons in the middle of

the iPhoto window. The highlighted button indicates the current mode.

- Look at the bottom pane of the iPhoto window, which changes with each mode. When you're in Import mode, for example, the bottom pane displays information about the files you're importing. In Organize mode, the pane contains the controls you'll use to assign keywords to your pictures.

The five mode buttons let you switch from mode to mode at any time. If you're not in Organize mode and you need to be, just click the Organize button to switch over.

---

details, and even conduct some basic editing to make them look better. (Editing photos is covered blow-by-blow in the next chapter.)

The easiest way to open a photo is simply to double-click a thumbnail. Unless you've changed iPhoto's settings, the photo opens in the main iPhoto window, scaled to fit into the viewing area.

This is certainly the way most people start out opening pictures using iPhoto, and there's nothing technically wrong with this method. But it does have several drawbacks, such as:

- You can have only one picture open at a time this way.

- Pictures opened this way are always scaled to fit within the iPhoto window, even if that means scaling them *upward,* over 100 percent of their actual size. As a result, smaller pictures wind up pixellated and distorted as they're stretched to fill the whole window.

  Worse, at this point, there's no way to zoom *out.* You can zoom in further, but you can't reduce the magnification.

- You have no way of knowing if your photo *has* been scaled to fit in the window, since iPhoto doesn't display the magnification level it's using. You can't tell if you're looking at a small photo displayed at 100 percent, or a gigantic photo that's been scaled down to 26 percent.

- Opening a photo this way catapults you directly into iPhoto's *Edit mode,* hiding all your other thumbnails and transforming the lower panel in the iPhoto window into the Edit pane, with its various cropping, red-eye removal, and color-changing tools. That's great if you're ready to start editing photos. But if you opened the picture simply because you wanted to see it at full size, you must now click the Organize button (just under the photo viewing area) to return to *Organize mode,* so you can view other photos, access keywords, sort photos, and so on.

The better way to open photos

You can avoid all of the problems listed above by using iPhoto's much smarter, but less obvious, method of opening photos: Open each picture *in its own window.*

There are two ways to do this:

- Hold down the Option key when double-clicking a thumbnail.

- Go to iPhoto→Preferences and change the photo-opening setting. Under the heading, "Double-clicking photos opens them in," select Separate Window. Then click OK.

  When a photo opens in its own window, all kinds of control and flexibility await you. First of all, you can scale it up *or* down simply by making the window larger or smaller (drag its lower-right corner). You can close an open photo from the keyboard by pressing ⌘-W. And best of all, you can open multiple pictures and look at them side by side, as shown in Figure 5-4.

Another way to zoom

As mentioned above, one way to change the magnification level of a photo opened in its own window is to change the size of the window itself. Enlarge the window to zoom in, shrink it to zoom out.

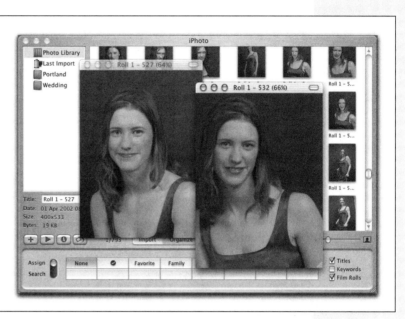

Figure 5-4:
Several advantages of opening photos in their own windows are illustrated here. Specifically, not only can you look at multiple full-size images at the same time—a critical feature when comparing a series of similar shots—but you can also keep your other thumbnails in view, allowing you to easily open additional photos without closing the ones you already have open. Also, notice how iPhoto tells you, in the title bar, which magnification level it's using to display each photo.

But you can only make a window so big by dragging its corner before you run out of screen, or so tiny before it just can't be shrunk any further. Therefore, to take advantage of iPhoto's full zoom range (5 to 400 percent), you need to use the Zoom buttons.

Zoom buttons? Where? They're on iPhoto's *Edit toolbar*, which may be hidden. If you don't see it, make sure you've opened a photo into its own window, and then click the capsule-shaped button in the upper-right corner of the window. You'll find the Zoom buttons on the left side of the toolbar, as shown in Figure 5-5. (There's much more about using and customizing the Edit toolbar in the next chapter.)

These buttons enable you to use iPhoto's full zooming power, regardless of the size of your monitor or the size of your photos.

Info and Titles

Just below the Album pane, on the left side of the iPhoto window, you'll find a display of basic information about all of the photos in your collection. The specific kind of information displayed in this Info pane changes, depending on what you've selected in the photo viewing area.

Tip: If you don't see the photo information described here, you may have the Info pane hidden. Click the littl  button in the main iPhoto window to reveal the info. Click twice to reveal the Comments field described below.

- When a single photo is selected, iPhoto displays that picture's creation date, dimensions (in pixels), and file size.

Tip: When you have a single photo selected, you can actually *change* its creation date by editing the Info pane's Date field. You can switch the date from the day the digital file was created to the day the photo was actually taken, for example. (We trust you won't use this feature for nefarious ends, such as "proving" to the jury that you were actually in Disney World on the day of the office robbery.)

Figure 5-5:
Once you've revealed the Edit toolbar, you can increase or reduce the magnification of photos by using the Zoom buttons on the left. The increments of magnification become progressively smaller with each button-click as you zoom out, and progressively larger as you zoom in. You can also drag the lower-right corner to make the window bigger (the photo zooms automatically to fill it).

One interesting phenomenon: Using the Zoom buttons disables iPhoto's zoom-by-changing-the-window-size feature (until you close the photo window and reopen it).

- When multiple photos are selected, you see the *range* of creation dates of the selected items, plus the total number of photos selected, and the total amount of disk space those selected photos occupy.

- When no photos are selected, the Info area displays the total number of pictures in your Photo Library, the grand total file size of your entire library, and a range of creation dates taking in *all* your photos. This last statistic is really pretty cool, in that it amounts to a running stopwatch that measures the span of your interest in digital photography (as of the iPhoto era, anyway).

Tip: The file size info can be extremely useful when creating backups, copying photos to another disk, or burning CDs. One glance at the Info panel—with no photos selected—tells you exactly how much disk space you'll need to fit your entire collection.

It would be awfully convenient to search for specific pictures in iPhoto using this information—finding all photos taken during 2002 that are smaller than 500 K, for example—but, alas, no such search tools are available. (The only way to search for photos is by keywords, titles, or comments, described later in this chapter.)

For each photo in your collection, iPhoto displays two other important chunks of information, both of which you can directly edit right in the Info pane: the Title and Comments.

Adding titles to photos

Every photo that you import into iPhoto receives a title, a unique name that's used to identify the picture within iPhoto. When importing files from your hard drive, iPhoto assigns titles based on those files' names. But if you're loading photos directly from your digital camera, the names of your files (and, therefore, the titles of the photos in iPhoto) are probably useless numeric tags like CRS000321.JPG, CRS000322.JPG, CRS000323.JPG, and so on.

By all means, change these titles to something more descriptive and meaningful! Just select a thumbnail, click in the Title field (just under the Album pane) and type in a new title, as shown in Figure 5-6.

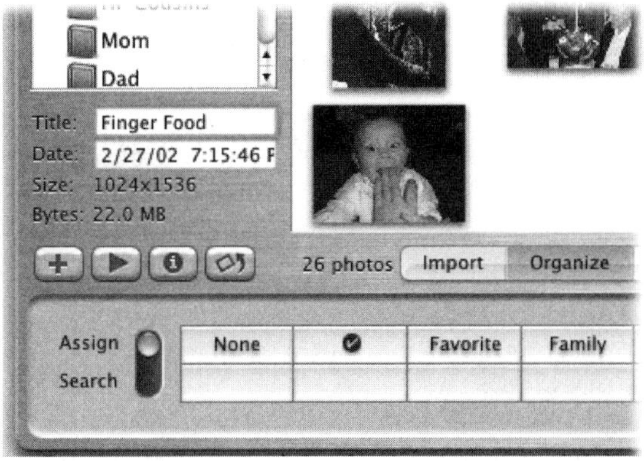

Figure 5-6:
You can make the title as long as you want—but it's smart to keep it short (about ten characters or so). This way, you can see all or most of the title in the Title field (or under the thumbnails themselves, if you turn on the Title checkbox, as explained later in this chapter).

Creating meaningful titles isn't just useful for keeping track of photos within iPhoto. Later, when you publish your digital albums online (Chapter 9) or in print (Chapter 10), iPhoto will use these names to create the titles that appear on the Web pages and book pages.

Tip: If you don't have the patience to rename your photos one by one, you can at least give them semi-helpful names, en masse, by highlighting them and then using the Edit→Set Title To command. This is especially helpful if they came in from the camera with names like SRSC238503.JPG.

Your submenu options include Empty (which deletes all names), Roll Info (which gives them names like "Florida - 93"), File Name (which names them after their actual, behind-the-scenes icons in the Finder), and Date/Time. This last option produces a dialog box where you can specify how you like your dates and times written out: short ("6/26/02"), long ("Wednesday, June 26, 2002 1:25 PM"), or whatever.

The Info Window

The small Info pane in the main iPhoto window displays only the most basic information about your photos: title, date, and size. For more detailed information, use the Show Info command. It opens the Photo Info window, where iPhoto displays a surprisingly broad dossier of details about your photo: the make and model of the digital camera used to take it, for example, and even exposure details like the f-stop, shutter speed, and flash settings.

To open the Photo Info window (Figure 5-7), select a thumbnail, and then choose File→Show Info (or press ⌘-I). (If more than one photo is selected, you'll get only a bunch of dashes in the info window.)

The Photo Info window contains two panels: the Photo panel and the Exposure panel. The Photo panel contains information about the image file itself: when the file was originally created, when it was first imported into iPhoto, and when it was last modified. If the image was shot with a digital camera (as opposed to being scanned in or imported from disk), the make and model of the camera appears at the bottom of the window. Switch to the Exposure panel, shown in Figure 5-7, for details about the specific camera settings that were used to take the picture.

MEMORY LANE

iPhoto 1.0: One Photo, Three Names

One of the most confusing aspects of using the original iPhoto1.0 was its Byzantine photo-naming scheme. By the time you downloaded a digital photo from your camera, brought it into iPhoto, and assigned it a title, the same picture had at least three different names.

First, there was the name of your original file—the one that was on your hard drive or camera before you imported it into iPhoto. iPhoto stuffed this name into a text file buried deep within the iPhoto Library folder, then otherwise ignored it.

Then there was the name that iPhoto gave to its own copy of your photo. This file, located in the iPhoto Library folder,

had a numeric name, such as 533.jpg. You never saw this name displayed anywhere; it was just iPhoto's own internal numbering scheme for tracking your photos.

Finally, there was the photo's title—the name you actually saw displayed underneath each thumbnail in the iPhoto window. iPhoto assigned this title using yet *another* numeric naming scheme, resulting in lovely titles like "Roll 84–964."

For many people, the revamped naming scheme in iPhoto 1.1.1 was one of the new version's most attractive new features. The program now preserves original file names when importing photos.

Tip: Comparing the details on the Exposure panel with the advice in Chapters 2 and 3 can be eye-opening. For example, if you put your camera into its automatic mode and take a few pictures, this is a great way to find out what shutter and lighting settings the camera used—and to learn from it.

How on earth does iPhoto know so much about how your photos were taken? It simply extracts this data from the photos themselves. Most digital cameras embed a wealth of image, camera, lens, and exposure information in the photo files they create, using an industry-standard data format called *EXIF* (short for Exchangeable Image Format). iPhoto automatically scans photos for EXIF data as it imports them.

Note: Some cameras do a better job than others at embedding this EXIF data in photo files. iPhoto can only extract this information if was properly stored by the camera when the digital photo was created. Of course, most (if not all) of this information will be missing altogether if your photos didn't come from a digital camera.

Figure 5-7:
The Photo Info window reports nitty-gritty details about your photos by reading the EXIF tags that your digital camera secretly embeds in your files. At a glance, you can tell that this photo was shot with a flash, at a shutter speed of 1/200, and with an f-stop setting of 2.0. Tracking this information can be useful in determining which settings on your camera produce the best-quality digital photos.

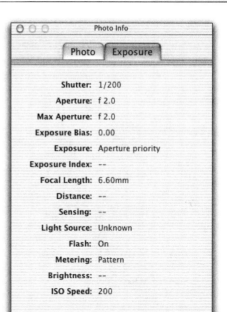

Comments

Sometimes you need more than a one- or two-word title to describe the contents of a photo. If you want to add a lengthier description, you can type it in the Comments field in the Info pane. (If you don't see the Comments field, click the ⓘ button to bring it into view.) Even if you don't write full-blown captions for your pictures, you can use the Comments field to store little details such as the names, places, dates, and events associated with your photos.

The best thing about adding comments in iPhoto 1.1.1 is that they're searchable. After you've entered all this free-form data, you can use it to quickly locate a photo using iPhoto's search command.

Adding comments to photos

To add a comment to a photo, select it, and then click in the Comments field. Keep the following in mind as you squirrel away all those bits and scraps of photo information:

- You don't have to *type* to enter data into the Comments field. You can paste information in using the standard Paste command, or even drag selected text from another program (such as Microsoft Word) right into the field.

- If you feel the need to be verbose, go for it. After all, you can store thousands of words in the Comments field. Careful, though: The field has no scroll bars, so there's a limit as to how much of what you paste or type you'll actually be able to see.

Note: You can't even scroll the Comments box by pressing the arrow keys until the insertion point bumps the top or bottom edge of the box, forcing it to scroll. Even dragging with the mouse all the way to the top or bottom of the box doesn't work. If you've got a lot to say, your best bet is to make the box taller and the whole Album pane wider, as described next.

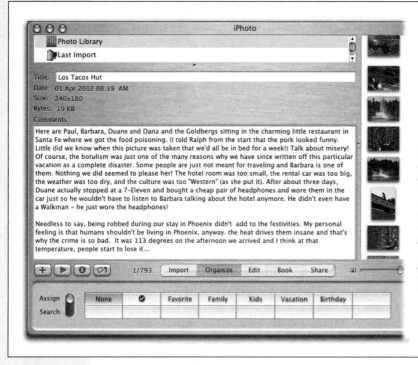

Figure 5-8:
Got a picture that's worth a thousand words? Not a problem— the Comments field can handle it. But you'll have to make iPhoto's Info pane pretty large to see everything you've written. By dragging the bars dividing the Info pane, Album pane, and photo viewing area, you can adjust the amount of space each takes up in the iPhoto window. In this example, the Info pane dominates the view, with the Album pane and photo viewing area squished to the edges.

- You can resize the Comments box by making the Info pane larger, as shown in Figure 5-8. Grab the divider bar above the Title field and drag upward to heighten the Info panel (and shorten the Album pane correspondingly). You can also drag the bar between the Album pane and the photo viewing area to the right, to widen the Info pane.

- Although it doesn't gain you much, you can also type your comments into the wider, shorter box shown in Figure 5-9. To make this space appear, follow the steps at the bottom of the page. Then set the "Assign/Search" switch to Assign.

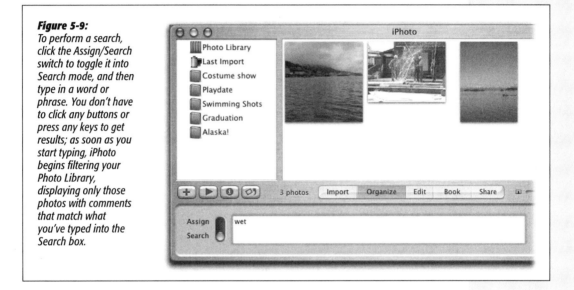

Figure 5-9:
To perform a search, click the Assign/Search switch to toggle it into Search mode, and then type in a word or phrase. You don't have to click any buttons or press any keys to get results; as soon as you start typing, iPhoto begins filtering your Photo Library, displaying only those photos with comments that match what you've typed into the Search box.

- You can't add comments when multiple photos are selected; you must select each photo individually to add comments to it.

- If no photos, or several photos, are selected, the notes you type into the Comments box get attached to the current *album,* rather than to the pictures.

Searching for photos using comments

To perform a search on the Comments field, first inspect the Assign/Search panel in the bottom pane of the iPhoto window. If it shows *keywords* (None, Favorite, Family, and so on), you need to make a quick detour like this:

1. **Choose iPhoto→Preferences.**

   The Preferences dialog box appears.

2. **Where it says "Assign/Search uses," click Comments, and then close the Preferences dialog box.**

   You've just changed the design of iPhoto's bottom panel by eliminating the keywords. In their place is an expanded Comments box, which you'll use for searching. (Later, should you want to assign or search for keywords [page 114], you'll have to switch this preference back again.)

To perform the search itself, see Figure 5-9.

Searching for photos by title or keyword

You can also search for photos that contain certain text in their names—a handy little trick that pays off every time Aunt Enid drops by and suggests, "Hey, let's see your pictures of *me!*"

Just set up a Comments search as described in the previous paragraphs—but turn on the Titles checkbox at the lower-right corner of the screen. If you turn on the Keywords checkbox too, iPhoto will simultaneously round up photos containing the text you specify in their keywords (page 114), too.

Comments as captions

While the Comments field is useful for storing little scraps of background information about your photos, you can also use it to store the *captions* that you want to appear with your photos when you publish them. In fact, some of the book layouts included with iPhoto's book-creation tools (Chapter 10) automatically use the text in the Comments field to generate a caption for each photo.

On the other hand, you don't *have* to use the Comments-box text as your captions. You can always add different captions when you're actually editing the book.

Deleting Photos

As every photographer knows—make that every *good* photographer—not every photo is a keeper. At some point, you'll probably want to delete some of the photos you've imported into iPhoto.

Just remember that deleting a photo from the *Photo Library* is permanent and irreversible. (Note that deleting one from an *album* is different, as described in the box below.)

FREQUENTLY ASKED QUESTION

Undeletable Photos?

iPhoto won't delete photos of my sister. I thought I got rid of a bunch of horrendous pictures the other day—they were really unflattering!—and then found them again when browsing through my Photo Library. Why aren't they staying deleted?

You probably deleted the pictures from a photo *album* (one of the folders in the list at the left side) instead of the

Photo Library itself (the first icon in the list). When you remove a photo from an album, it removes only a *reference* to that picture from the album, leaving the photo itself untouched in the Photo Library.

If the pictures of your sister are really that bad, click the Photo Library icon in the Album pane and *then* delete the photos. That'll get rid of them once and for all.

To send a picture to the great Fotomat in the sky, select a thumbnail (or several) in the Photo Library and perform one of the following:

- Choose Edit→Cut, or press ⌘-X.

- Choose Edit→Clear.

- Press the Delete key.

iPhoto displays an alert message, warning you that the selected photos will be permanently deleted. Whatever pictures you delete this way also disappear from any albums you've created (more on albums later in this chapter). Deleting a photo completely removes it from iPhoto.

Even after you click OK in the alert dialog box, iPhoto gives you *one last chance* to undo the damage. You can choose Edit→Undo Remove Photo From Album (or press ⌘-Z) to restore your photo. If you move on to perform another action in iPhoto, the Undo option vanishes, and your picture is permanently gone. (Of course, if you imported the photo from a file on disk or haven't deleted it from your camera, you can still recover the original file and reimport it.)

Albums

No matter how nicely you title, sort, and arrange photos in your digital shoebox, it's still a *shoebox* at this point, with all your photos piled together in one vast collection. To really get organized and present your photos to others, you need to arrange your photos into *albums*.

In iPhoto terminology, an album is a subset of pictures from your Photo Library. It's a collection of photos with a common theme that you group together for easy access and viewing. It's represented by a little album-book icon in the album list at the left side of the screen. (If you've used playlists in iTunes, or folders full of aliases at the desktop, you'll recognize the concept.)

While your Photo Library as a whole might contain thousands of photos from a hodgepodge of unrelated family events, trips, special occasions, and time periods, a photo album has a focus: Family Trip to Duluth, Steve & Sarah's Wedding, Herb's Knee Surgery, and so on.

As you probably know, mounting snapshots in a *real* photo album is a pain—that's why so many of us still have stacks of Kodak prints stuffed in envelopes and shoeboxes. But with iPhoto, you don't need mounting corners, rubber cement, double-sided tape, or scissors to create a photo album. You just drag and drop thumbnails where you want them. In the digital world, there's absolutely no excuse for leaving your photos in hopeless disarray.

Technically, you're not required to group your digital photos in albums with iPhoto, but consider the following advantages of doing so:

- It makes finding photos much faster. By opening only the relevant photo album, you can avoid scrolling through thousands of thumbnails in the Photo Library to find a picture you want—a factor that takes on added importance as your photo collection expands.

- Only in a photo album can you drag your photos into a different order. To change the order of photos displayed in a slide show or an iPhoto hardbound book, for example, you need to start with a photo album (see Chapters 7 and 10).

Creating an Album

There are two ways to create an iPhoto album: by clicking or by dragging.

The clicking method

Set up a new photo album in iPhoto using any of the following methods:

- Choose File→New Album, or press ⌘-N.

- Click the + button in the iPhoto window, below the album list.

A dialog box appears, prompting you to name the new album; type in a descriptive name (*Summer in Aruba, Yellowstone 2002, Edna in Paris,* or whatever). Then, click OK, and watch as a new photo album icon appears in the Album pane (Figure 5-10).

The dragging method

You can also drag photos into the album list to create a new album. They can come from almost anywhere:

Figure 5-10:
There's no limit to the number of albums you can add, so make as many as you need to logically organize all the photos in your Photo Library. New albums are always added to the end of the list, but you can change the order in which they appear by dragging them up or down in the list.

- Drag a thumbnail (or, more likely, a batch of them) from the photo viewing area directly into an empty portion of the Album pane. The program creates a new album called Album-1 (or whatever it's up to).

- Drag a *film roll* icon from your Photo Library "album" into an empty portion of the Album pane. Again, you get a new, generically named album.

  If there *is* no empty space in the Album pane, by the way, then you can't use either of these techniques. You'll have to use one of the clicking methods described above.

- Drag a bunch of graphics files from the *Finder* (the desktop behind iPhoto) directly into the Album pane. In one step, iPhoto imports the photos, creates a new album, names it after the folder you dragged in, and puts the newly imported photos into that album.

Tip: To rename an existing photo album, double-click its name or icon in the Album pane. A renaming rectangle appears around the album's name, with text highlighted and ready to be edited.

Figure 5-11:
When selecting multiple photos in iPhoto, a little red numeric badge appears next to the pointer telling you exactly how many items you've got selected. In this example, 46 pictures are being dragged en masse into a photo album.

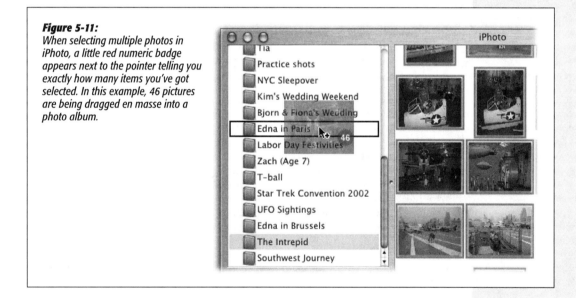

Adding photos to an album

To add photos to an album, just drag them onto the album's icon. Figure 5-11 depicts how you can select multiple photos (using any of the selection techniques described on page 97) and drop them into an album in one batch.

The single most important thing to understand about adding photos to an album is this: Putting photos in an album doesn't really *move or copy* them. It makes no difference where the thumbnails start out—whether it's the Photo Library or another album. You're just creating *references*, or pointers, back to the photos in your master

Photo Library. This feature works a lot like Macintosh aliases; in fact, behind the scenes, iPhoto actually does create aliases of the photos you're dragging. (It stashes them in the appropriate album folders within the iPhoto Library folder.)

What this means is that you don't have to commit a picture to just one album when organizing. One photo can appear in as many different albums as you want. So, if you've got a great shot of Grandma in Hawaii and you can't decide whether to drop the photo into the Hawaiian Vacation album or the Grandma & Grandpa album, the answer is easy: Put it in both. iPhoto just creates two references to the same original photo in your Photo Library.

Tip: You can drag photos directly from the Finder onto a photo album icon in the Album list, forcing iPhoto to file it there in the process of importing.

Viewing a photo album

To view the contents of an album, click its name or icon in the Album list. All the photos included in the selected album appear in the photo viewing area; the other photos in your Photo Library are hidden.

Remember, adding photos to albums doesn't remove them from the Photo Library itself, which is your master collection. So if you lose track of which album contains a particular photo, just click the Photo Library icon at the top of the Album pane to return to the overview of your entire photo collection.

Tip: You can put your albums into any order. Just drag them up or down in the Album pane.

Moving photos between albums

There are two ways to transfer photos from one photo album to another.

- To *move* a photo between albums, select it and then choose Edit→Cut (or press ⌘-X), removing the photo from the album. Click the destination photo album's name or icon, and then choose Edit→Paste (or press ⌘-V). The photo is now a part of the second album.

- To *copy* a photo into another album, just drag it onto the icon of the destination album in the Album pane. That photo is now a part of both albums.

Removing photos from an album

If you change your mind about how you've got your photos organized and want to remove a photo from an album, open the album and select the photo you want to remove. Then do one of the following:

- Choose Edit→Cut, or press ⌘-X.

- Choose Edit→Clear.

- Press the Delete key or the Del (forward-delete) key.

The thumbnail disappears from the album, but it's not really gone from iPhoto. It's still in your Photo Library.

Note: When removing a photo from an album, make sure you're viewing the contents of a *photo album* in the photo viewing area and not the main Photo Library. Deleting a photo from the Photo Library really does delete it for good. (iPhoto will warn you to that effect.)

Figure 5-12:
Arrange photos in any order you want by dragging them to a new location within a photo album. In this example, two selected photos from the top left corner are being dragged to a new location in the next row. The "2" indicates the number of items that are being moved, while the black vertical bar indicates where iPhoto will insert the photos when the mouse button is released.

Duplicating a photo

You can't drag the same photo into an album twice. When you try, the thumbnail simply leaps stubbornly back into its original location, as though to say, "Nyah, nyah, you can't drag the same photo into an album twice."

It's often useful to have two copies of a picture, though. As you'll discover in Chapter 8, a photo whose dimensions are appropriate for a slide show or desktop picture (that is, a 4:3 proportion) are inappropriate for ordering prints (4 x 6, 8 x 10, or whatever). To use the same photo for both purposes, you really need to crop them independently.

In this case, the old adding-to-album trick isn't going to help you. This time, you truly must duplicate the file, consuming more hard drive space behind the scenes. To do that, highlight the photo and choose File→Duplicate (⌘-D). iPhoto switches briefly into Import mode, copies the file, and then returns to your previous mode. The copy appears next to the original, bearing the same name plus the word "copy."

Note: If you duplicated the photo in an album, you'll see the duplicate both there and in the Photo Library, but not in any other albums. If you duplicated it in the Photo Library, that's the only place you'll see it duplicated.

Putting Photos in Order

If you plan to turn your photo album into an onscreen slide show, a series of Web pages, or a printed book, you'll have to tinker with the order of the pictures, arranging them in the most logical and compelling sequence. Photos in the main Photo Library are locked into a strict sort order—by either creation date or film roll—but once they're dragged into a photo album, you can shuffle them manually into a new sequence.

To custom-sort photos in an album, simply drag and drop, as shown in Figure 5-12.

Duplicating an Album

It stands to reason that if you have several favorite photos, you might want to use them in more than one of iPhoto's presentations (in a slide show and a book, for example). That's why it's often convenient to duplicate an album: so that you can create two different sequences for the photos inside.

Just highlight an album and then choose File→Duplicate. iPhoto does the duplicating in a flash—after all, it's just duplicating a bunch of tiny aliases. Now you're free to rearrange the order of the photos inside, to add or delete photos, and so on, completely independent of the original album.

Deleting an Album

To delete an album, select its icon in the Album pane, and then choose Edit→Clear or press the Delete key. iPhoto asks you to confirm your intention.

Deleting an album doesn't delete any photos, just the references to those photos. Even if you delete *all* your photo albums, your entire Photo Library, containing all your photos, remains intact.

Using Keywords

Keywords are descriptive words—such as *family*, *vacation*, or *kids*—that you can use to label and categorize your photos, regardless of which photo album they're in.

The beauty of keywords in iPhoto is that, like the Comments field described earlier in this chapter, they're searchable. Want to comb through all the photos in your library to find every close-up taken of your children during summer vacation? Instead of browsing through multiple photo albums, just perform an iPhoto search for photos containing the keywords *kids*, *vacation, close-up* and *summer*. You'll have the results in a couple of seconds.

iPhoto's keyword feature isn't especially powerful. You're limited to fourteen keywords, and the keyword tools themselves rank among Apple's clunkiest. But a well-chosen set of keywords applied consistently throughout your Photo Library can be extremely useful when it comes to keeping track of your pictures.

Figure 5-13:
The second photo here has been assigned three keywords. You can tell which ones–Family, Kids, and Portrait–because their buttons are highlighted. To remove a keyword after assigning it, just click it again to turn it off. If you want to remove all the keywords assigned to a photo, click the None button in the upper-left corner of the keyword button.

Editing Keywords

iPhoto's keywords appear in two rows of buttons along the bottom pane of the window when you're in Organize mode. Apple starts you off with five sample keywords: Favorite, Family, Vacation, Kids, and Birthday. You can add another nine keywords of your own in the remaining blank buttons, or edit the original five and come up with fourteen of your own words.

(If you don't see any keywords in the bottom pane of the iPhoto window—and you're definitely in Organize mode—you may have to reset the Assign/Search panel to display Keywords instead of Comments. Choose iPhoto→Preferences, then use the radio buttons to change the Assign/Search option from Comments to Keywords.)

To enter keyword-editing mode, choose Edit→Edit Keywords, or press ⌘-K. Once you're in editing mode, you can click in any of the blank keyword buttons to type in a new keyword, or double-click an existing keyword to edit it.

Tip: When in keyword-editing mode, press the Tab key to move from keyword to keyword.

It may take some time to develop a really good master set of keywords. The idea is to assign labels that are general enough to apply across your entire photo collection, but specific enough to be meaningful when conducting searches.

Here's a general rule of thumb: Use *albums* to group pictures of specific events—a wedding, family vacation, or beach party, for example. Use *keywords* to focus on general characteristics that are likely to appear through your entire photo collection—words like Family, Friends, Travel, Home, Work, and Vacation. See Figure 5-14 to survey photo keywords at a glance.

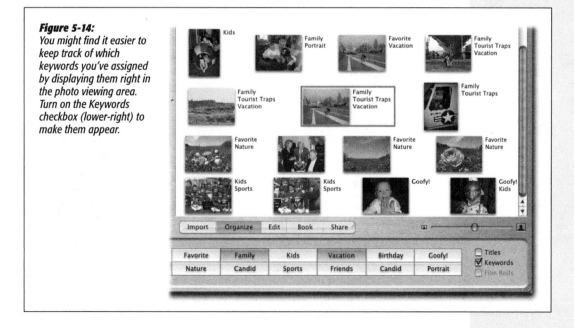

Figure 5-14:
You might find it easier to keep track of which keywords you've assigned by displaying them right in the photo viewing area. Turn on the Keywords checkbox (lower-right) to make them appear.

Suppose your photo collection includes a bunch of photos that you shot during a once-in-a-lifetime trip to Rome last summer. You might be tempted to assign *Rome* as a keyword. Don't do it, because you probably won't use *Rome* on anything other than that one set of photos. It would be smarter to create a photo album called *Trip to Rome* to hold all those Rome pictures. Use your keywords to tag the same pictures with descriptors like Travel or Family. It also might be useful to apply keywords that describe attributes of the photos themselves, such as Close-up, Landscape, Portrait, and Scenic.

Note: You can change keywords after you've started using them, but the results can be messy. If you already applied the keyword "Fishing" to a batch of photos, but later decide to replace the word "Fishing" with "Romantic" in your keyword list, all the photos that had been keyworded "Fishing" automatically inherit the keyword "Romantic." Depending on you and your interests, this may not be what you intended.

When you're done editing your keywords, click the Done button on the left end of the keyword grid, or choose Edit→Done Editing Keywords, or press ⌘-K again.

Assigning Keywords

In order to use keywords to perform searches, you must first assign them to your photos. Here's how the process works:

1. **Make sure the Keyword switch (just to the left of the keyword buttons) is set to Assign instead of Search.**

   If it's not, click the word Assign to toggle the switch.

WORKAROUND WORKSHOP

Beating the Search/Assign Bug

If you're serious about managing photos with keywords, beware: iPhoto's keyword search feature has a tiny bug that may drive you insane.

Here's the problem: You perform a keyword search and find 25 matches out of your collection of 835 photos. At this point, you'd like to browse through those 25 photos, and tag the best twelve with a checkmark so you can find them later. So you select the twelve winners, flip the Keyword switch from Search to Assign and…you lose your search results! Suddenly you find yourself looking at 835 thumbnails again, and must start from scratch.

That's the bug: Whenever you flip the Keyword switch from Search to Assign mode, iPhoto blows away your previous search results.

Fortunately, there's a workaround. After receiving your search results, press ⌘-N to create a new photo album. Name the album (something like Found or Results) and then drag the photos found by your keyword search into the new album, which is going to serve as a temporary holding bin for your search results. Click the album name in the Album pane to open the newly created album.

Now you can flip the Keyword switch from Search to Assign. The photos you found in the previous search will still be visible, since you've grouped them together in their own private photo album. You can apply a checkmark to selected photos, or assign other keywords as needed.

When you're done, just select the album (in the Album pane) and delete it. Deleting the album itself has no effect on the photos, which will retain the checkmarks or any additional keywords you've assigned to them.

2. **Select a photo, or several, in the photo viewing area.**

   You can assign keywords when viewing thumbnails in the main Photo Library, or in a specific photo album. Use any of the selection techniques described on page 97.

3. **Click the keywords that you would like to assign to the selected photo(s).**

   You can click as many of the keyword buttons as you want, thereby assigning multiple keywords, as shown in Figure 5-13.

Tip: If you don't see the keyword buttons in the bottom pane of the iPhoto window, it's because you're no longer in Organize mode. Click the Organize button just under the photo viewing area to snap iPhoto back into Organize mode and display the keywords.

The Checkmark Button

You may have noticed that there's one keyword button that's different from the others. For one thing, it's not a word, but a symbol—a small checkmark. The other difference is that you can't edit this button; it's always a checkmark.

This button works just like the other keyword buttons. But instead of assigning a particular keyword to photos, it tags them with a small checkmark symbol, as shown in Figure 5-15. It's only a marker, a flag—but you'll find it extremely useful for temporary organizational tasks.

For example, you might want to cull only the best images from a photo album for use in a printed book or slide show. As you browse through the images, use the checkmark button to flag each of the shots you want. Later, you can use the Search function to round up all of the images you flagged, so that you can drag them all into an album en masse.

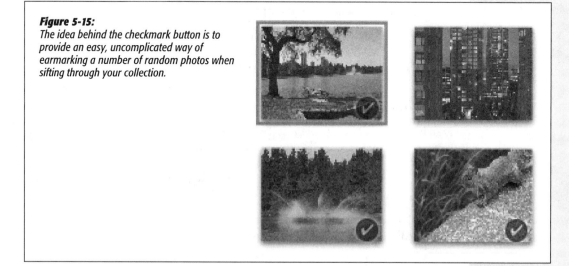

Figure 5-15:
The idea behind the checkmark button is to provide an easy, uncomplicated way of earmarking a number of random photos when sifting through your collection.

You remove checkmarks from photos just as you remove keywords: With the Keyword switch in Assign mode, select a checkmarked photo and click the checkmark button again to turn it off—or click the None keyword button.

Searching by Keyword

Whether you tag photos with the checkmark symbol or a series of keywords, the big payoff for your diligent keywording arrives when you need to get your hands on a specific set of photos, because iPhoto lets you *search* for them.

To perform a keyword search, first make sure the Keyword switch is set to Search, and not Assign. (If it's not, click the word Search to toggle the switch.) Then click a keyword button. iPhoto immediately rounds up all photos labeled with that keyword, displays them in the photo viewing area, and hides all others. Here are the important points to remember when using iPhoto's keyword searches:

- To search for photos that match multiple keywords, just click additional keyword buttons to add them to the search.

Note: When you use multiple keywords, iPhoto finds only the photos that match *all* of those criteria. In other words, if you select *Friends*, *Candid*, and *Vacation* in a keyword search, iPhoto displays only those photos that contain *all three* keywords.

If you want to find photos tagged with the word Friends *or* Candid *or* Vacation, you'll have to perform those searches individually, using a single keyword each time.

- You can confine your search to a single album just by selecting it before searching. Similarly, clicking the Photo Library in the list before searching means that you want to search your entire photo collection.
- When you're in Search mode, the top left keyword button turns into a Show All button. Click it to restore the view to the full Photo Library or the whole album you had visible before you performed the search.
- After your search, you may wonder how to bring all your *other* photos back to the screen. Either click Show All, click another album, or re-click each selected Keyword button until none are turned on.

Customizing the Shoebox

Freshly installed, iPhoto looks just the way you see it in Figure 5-3, with each of your pictures displayed as a small thumbnail against a plain white background. This view makes it easy to browse through photos and work with iPhoto's various tools. But hey, this is *your* digital shoebox. With a little tweaking and fine-tuning, you can completely customize the way iPhoto displays your photos.

Start with a visit to iPhoto→Preferences (⌘-Y), where you can tinker with the background color and other photo viewing options.

Changing the View

The controls in the Photo section of the Preferences window let you make some basic changes to the look of your library (see Figure 5-16). For example:

- **Add a frame or shadow.** The factory setting, Shadow, puts a soft black drop shadow behind each thumbnail in the photo viewing pane, a subtle touch that gives your Photo Library an elegantly 3-D look. If you find the shadow distracting, however, just switch to the Frame radio button to delete them. Now you get a thin gray border around each picture instead.

- **Change the background color.** Next to the Frame radio button, a slider control lets you adjust the background color of the photo viewing pane. Actually, the term "color" is a bit of an overstatement, since your palette of color choices includes white, black, or any shade of gray in between.

- **Alignment.** Turn on the "Align to grid" checkbox if you want thumbnails to snap into evenly spaced rows and columns, even if your collection includes thumbnails of varying sizes and orientations, as shown in Figure 5-16.

Note: If you turn on the Titles or Keywords checkboxes at the lower-right corner of the iPhoto window, all bets are off. iPhoto displays these text tidbits to the right of the thumbnails, throwing them out of alignment regardless of your grid settings.

Figure 5-16:
The "Align to grid" option in iPhoto's preferences is quite insignificant if all your photos are the same size and are all in one orientation. But with a variety of horizontal and vertical images, as shown here, photos stay in strict rows and columns (right) despite their size and shape differences. The window on the left shows an "unaligned" version of the same thumbnails.

Using the Size Control Slider

You can make the thumbnails in iPhoto grow or shrink using the Size Control slider (on the left side of the iPhoto window, just under the photo viewing area). Drag the slider all the way to the left and you get micro-thumbnails so small that you can fit 200 or more of them in the iPhoto window. Drag all the way to the right and you end up with such large thumbnails that you can only see one picture at a time.

Tip: You don't have to *drag* the Size Control slider; just click anywhere along the controller bar to make the slider jump to a new setting. Using this technique, you can instantly change the size of thumbnails from large to small, for example, by clicking once on the left end of the controller.

By the way, you might notice that this Size Control slider performs two different functions, depending on what mode iPhoto is in. When in Organize mode, it controls the size of thumbnails; in Edit or Book mode, it zooms in and out of an individual image.

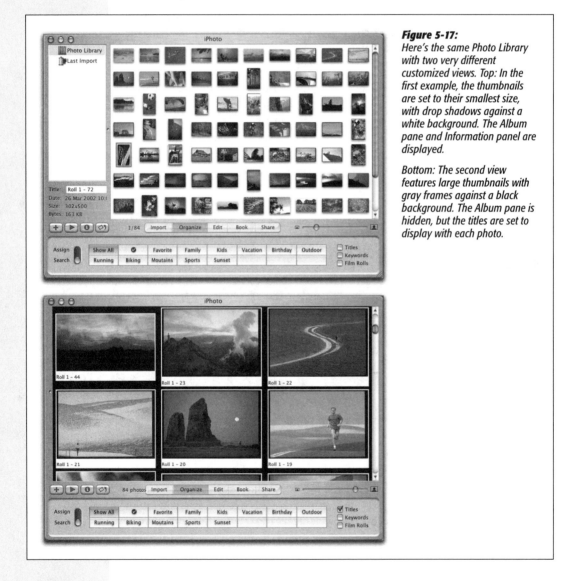

Figure 5-17:
Here's the same Photo Library with two very different customized views. Top: In the first example, the thumbnails are set to their smallest size, with drop shadows against a white background. The Album pane and Information panel are displayed.

Bottom: The second view features large thumbnails with gray frames against a black background. The Album pane is hidden, but the titles are set to display with each photo.

Tip: You may want to adopt a conservative dragging approach when using the size slider, because iPhoto may respond slowly in enlarging or shrinking the photos. Drag in small movements so the program can keep pace with you.

Showing/Hiding Keywords, Titles, and Film Roll Info

If you want to display thumbnails along with the titles and keywords you assign your pictures using iPhoto, turn on the Titles and Keywords checkboxes in the lower-right corner of the iPhoto window. Titles appear under each thumbnail; keywords appear to the right of each picture (see Figure 5-17).

As with most of iPhoto, your formatting options are limited. You can't control the font, style, color, or size of this text. Your only choice is either to display the title and keywords or to keep them hidden.

CHAPTER 6

Editing Your Shots

Fresh from the camera, digital snapshots often need a little bit of help. A photo may be too dark or too light. The colors may be too bluish or too yellowish. The focus may be a little blurry, or the composition may not be quite right.

Fortunately, one of the great things about digital photography is that you can fine-tune images in ways that, in the world of traditional photography, would require a fully equipped darkroom, several bottles of smelly chemicals, and an X-Acto knife.

iPhoto isn't a full-blown photo-editing program like Adobe Photoshop. But it does include a handful of tools that you can use to improve your digital photos. This chapter shows you how to use each of the tools in iPhoto's digital darkroom to spruce up your photos—and how to edit your photos in other programs if more radical image enhancement is needed.

Editing in iPhoto

You can't retouch photos, paint additional elements in, mask out unwanted backgrounds, or apply any special effects filters in iPhoto, as you can with editing programs like Photoshop and GraphicConverter. Instead, iPhoto is designed to handle four basic photo fix-up tasks. They are:

- **Cropping**. The cropping tool lets you cut away the outer portions of a photo to improve its composition or to make it the right size for a printout or Web page.

- **Brightness/Contrast**. Use these sliders to punch up washed-out colors and make photos look more vibrant. These adjustments allow you to tone down bright, overexposed images or lighten up those that look too dark and shadowy.

- **Red-Eye.** This filter gets rid of one very common photo glitch—those red dots that sometimes appear in a person's eyes as the result of flash photography.

- **Black & White.** Turn your color photos into moody black-and-white art shots.

For anything beyond these simple touch-up tasks, you need to open your photos in a more powerful editing program—which you can easily do right from within iPhoto, as explained later in this chapter.

Using the Editing Tools

All iPhoto editing is done in a special editing mode, which you can open up by any of the following methods:

- With a photo selected, click the Edit button in the middle of the main iPhoto window. iPhoto's editing tools appear in the lower pane.

- Double-click a thumbnail. If you have iPhoto set to open photos right in the main window (which is the factory setting), iPhoto jumps into Edit mode. The tools appear, once again, at the bottom of the window.

- If you've instructed iPhoto to open a photo in a separate window when you double-click its thumbnail (as suggested on page 100), the Edit tools appear in a toolbar, as shown in Figure 6-1. (If the toolbar isn't visible, click the capsule-shaped button in the upper-right corner of the window to make it appear, or choose Window→Show Toolbar.)

Tip: You can zoom in or out in either editing mode (in-window or separate-window). Once you've done so, you can ⌘-drag inside the photo area to scroll in any direction. That's more direct than fussing with two independent scroll bars.

Figure 6-1:
A >> symbol at the right end of the toolbar means that the window is too narrow to display all the tools. To see them, make the window wider, or just click the >> to access the tools via a pop-up menu.

Cropping

iPhoto's cropping tool is a digital paper cutter. It lets you neatly shave off unnecessary portions of a photo, leaving behind only the part of the picture you really want.

You'd be surprised at how many photographs can benefit from selective cropping. For example:

- Eliminate parts of a photo you just don't want. This is a great way to chop your brother's ex-girlfriend out of an otherwise perfect family portrait, for example (provided she was standing at the end of the lineup).

- Improve a photo's composition. Trimming a photo allows you to adjust where your subject matter appears within the frame of the picture. If you inspect the professionally shot photos in magazines or books, for example, you'll discover that many pros favor tight cropping around the subject, especially in portraits.

- Get rid of wasted space. Huge expanses of background sky that add nothing to a photo can be eliminated, keeping the focus on your subject.

- Fit a photo to a specific size. If you're going to place your photos in a book layout (Chapter 10) or turn them into standard size prints (Chapter 8), you may need to adjust their proportions. That's because there's a substantial discrepancy between the *aspect ratio* (length-to-width proportions) of your camera's photos and that of film cameras—a difference that will come back to haunt you if you order prints. See the following discussion for details.

How to Crop a Photo

Here are the steps for cropping a photo:

1. **Open the photo in Edit mode.**

   You can use any of the methods mentioned earlier in this chapter.

2. **Make a selection from the Constrain pop-up menu, if you like (Figure 6-2).**

   When this pop-up menu is set to None, you can draw a cropping rectangle of any size and proportion, in essence going freehand.

   When you choose one of the other ten options in the pop-up menu, however, iPhoto *constrains* the rectangle you draw to preset proportions. It prevents you from coloring outside the lines, so to speak. (You can choose a Constrain option either before you drag or after, in which case iPhoto reshapes the cropping area to match your selection.)

   This feature is especially important if you plan to order prints of your photos (Chapter 8). When you attempt to do so, you'll notice that you can order prints only in standard photo sizes: 4 x 6, 5 x 7, 8 x 10, and so on. Most digital cameras, however, produce photos whose proportions are 4 to 3 (width-to-height). That's great for onscreen slide shows, DVD's, and iPhoto *books* (Chapter 10), because your Mac screen, television, and iPhoto book layouts use 4 to 3 ratios, too—but that doesn't divide evenly into standard *print* sizes.

   That's why the Constrain pop-up menu offers you a list of canned choices like 4 x 6, 5 x 7, and so on. Constraining your cropping using one of these preset sizes guarantees that your cropped photos will fit perfectly into Kodak prints. (If you don't constrain your cropping this way, you may wind up with unintended white margins at the sides of the finished prints.)

Other crop-to-fit options in the Constrain menu let you crop photos for use as a desktop picture (1024 x 768 pixels, or whatever dimensions your screen has) or to fit into one of the book layouts available in iPhoto's Book mode (4 to 3 proportions), as described in Chapter 10. The menu contains both landscape (horizontal) and portrait (vertical) versions of each standard photo size.

Note, by the way, that even though the Constrain menu ensures the right *proportions*, it doesn't in any way guarantee that the total *size* of the final photos is adequate.

If you have a "1024 x 768 (Display)" option, for example, your photos won't necessarily wind up at 1024 by 768pixels in size when you crop them. It means only that the proportions of the cropped image will be correct for filling your computer display when the photo is shown in full-screen mode (such as during a slide show). See the the "When Cropping Problems Crop Up" box on the facing page for more about properly sizing your photos.

Tip: Opening a photo into its own separate editing window (by Option-double-clicking its thumbnail) triggers a bonus feature: two boxes in the toolbar labeled Custom. Into these text boxes, you can type any proportions you want: 4 x 7, 15 x 32, or whatever your eccentric design needs happen to call for. Press Tab to jump from box to box, and Return or Enter when you're finished typing.

---

3. **Position the mouse pointer (which appears as a crosshair) at one corner of your photo. Drag diagonally across the portion of the picture that you want to *keep*.**

   As you drag out a rectangle across your photo, the portions *outside* of the selection—the part of the photo that iPhoto will eventually trim away—get dimmed out (Figure 6-2).

Tip: Even if you've turned on one of the Constrain options in step 2, you can override the constraining by pressing ⌘ as you drag.

   Don't worry about getting your selection perfect. iPhoto doesn't actually trim the photo until you click the Crop button.

4. **Adjust the cropping, if necessary.**

   If the shape and size of your selection area is OK, but you want to adjust which part of the image is selected, you can move the selection area without redrawing it. Position your mouse over the selection so that the pointer turns into a hand icon. Then drag the existing rectangle where you want it.

   You can even change the *shape* of the selection rectangle after you've released the mouse button, thanks to an invisible quarter-inch "handle" that surrounds the cropping area. Move your cursor close to any edge or corner so that it changes from the + shape to an arrow. Now you can drag the edge or corner to reshape the rectangle (see Figure 6-2).

Tip: If you're using one of the Constrain options, you can rotate the selection (from horizontal to vertical, or vice versa)—a handy feature if you decide that a portrait orientation might be superior to landscape mode, or vice versa. Here's the trick: While pressing the Option key, move the cursor into the invisible "handle zone"(close to the edges of the selection) and tug in any direction. The selection rectangle crisply turns 90 degrees.

If you get cold feet, you can cancel the operation by clicking once anywhere outside the cropping rectangle (to remain in Edit mode) or by double-clicking anywhere on the photo (to return to Organize mode). Or, if the photo is open in its own window, just close the window.

Note: Despite its elaborate control over the *relative* dimensions of your cropping rectangle, iPhoto offers no preview at all as to what its *actual* size in pixels will be. If the actual size is important to you, you have no choice but to perform your cropping in another program, like GraphicConverter or Photoshop. (See page 135 for instructions on flipping into a different program for editing.)

5. **When the cropping rectangle is set just the way you want, click the Crop button.**

   If throwing away all those cropped-out pixels makes you nervous, relax. When you click the Crop button, iPhoto, behind the scenes, makes a duplicate of the original photo before doing the deed—a handy safety net for the day you decide to revert back to the uncropped version, months or years later.

   If you realize immediately that you've made a cropping mistake, you can choose Edit→Undo Crop Photo to restore your original.

UP TO SPEED

When Cropping Problems Crop Up

Remember that cropping always *shrinks* your photos. Take away too many pixels, and your photo may end up too small to print or display properly—that is, with a resolution that's too low.

Here's an example: You start with a 1600 x 1200 pixel photo. Ordinarily, that's large enough to be professionally printed as a high-quality, standard 8 x 10 portrait.

Then you go in and crop the shot. Now the composition is perfect, but your photo only measures 800 x 640 pixels. You've tossed out nearly a million-and-a-half pixels.

The photo no longer has a high enough *resolution* (pixels per inch) to produce a high-quality 8 x 10. The printer is forced to blow up the photo to fill the specified paper size, producing visible, jaggy-edged pixels in the printout. The 800 x 640 pixel version of your photo would make a great 4 x 5 print (if that were even a standard size print)—but pushing the print's size up further noticeably degrades the quality.

Therein lies a great advantage of using a high-resolution digital camera (3 or 4 megapixels, for example). Because each shot starts out with such a high resolution, you can afford to shave away a few million pixels and still have enough left over for high-resolution prints.

Moral of the story: Know your photo's size and intended use—and don't crop out more photo than you can spare.

If you have regrets *weeks* later, on the other hand, select the photo and choose File→Revert to Original. iPhoto dutifully reinstates the original photo that it had backed up behind the scenes.

Note: When you crop a photo, you're cropping the photo in *all albums* in which it appears (Chapter 5). If you want a photo to appear cropped in one album but not in another, you must first duplicate it (highlight it and then choose File→Duplicate), and then edit each version separately.

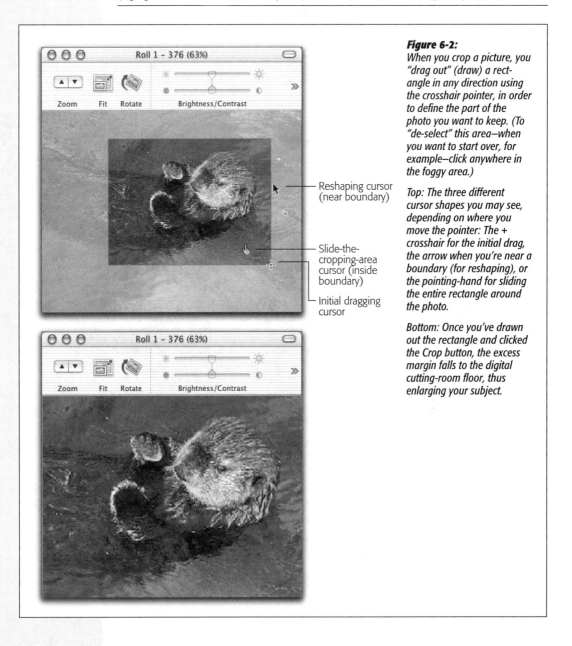

Figure 6-2:
When you crop a picture, you "drag out" (draw) a rectangle in any direction using the crosshair pointer, in order to define the part of the photo you want to keep. (To "de-select" this area—when you want to start over, for example—click anywhere in the foggy area.)

Top: The three different cursor shapes you may see, depending on where you move the pointer: The + crosshair for the initial drag, the arrow when you're near a boundary (for reshaping), or the pointing-hand for sliding the entire rectangle around the photo.

Bottom: Once you've drawn out the rectangle and clicked the Crop button, the excess margin falls to the digital cutting-room floor, thus enlarging your subject.

Labels in figure:
— Reshaping cursor (near boundary)
— Slide-the-cropping-area cursor (inside boundary)
— Initial dragging cursor

Brightness/Contrast

No software can save a photo that was taken with very poor lighting, of course, but
a little time spent with the Brightness and Contrast sliders (which debuted in iPhoto
1.1.1) can make many photos look much more vivid, with deeper, more saturated
colors.

Using the Sliders

These controls are extremely easy to use. Just drag each slider to the left or right to
decrease or increase the overall brightness and contrast of a photo (see Figure 6-3).
The results are displayed instantly right on the image itself, so you can experiment
freely to find the settings that make your photo look best.

Figure 6-3:
*These sliders allow you to make incremental
adjustments in brightness and contrast, but they
can be a little sluggish on large photos. You can
save some time by clicking anywhere along a
slider bar to make the controller jump directly to
that point. Click the sun or circle icon at the ends
of the sliders to crank the brightness or contrast
all the way up or down.*

The brightness and contrast controls can also rescue shots that were either too light
or too dark when they were taken. Again, you can't add details that simply aren't
there, but brightening a dark shadowy image, or deepening the contrast on a washed-
out image, can coax out elements that were barely visible in the original photo.

Tip: When your adjustments are subtle, it's sometimes hard to tell how much you've really improved a
photo without comparing the results directly to the original, unedited one. Here's an undocumented
feature: Just hold down the Control key to see the original, unedited photo. By pressing and releasing
Control, you can toggle back and forth as much as you want, comparing the two versions before deciding
to keep the changes permanently.

As long as you remain in Edit mode, you can back out of your changes no matter
how many of them you've made. For example, if you've adjusted the Brightness and
Contrast sliders, you can remove those changes using the Edit→Undo Brightness/
Contrast command (⌘-Z).

In fact, you can remove these changes even after you've performed other editing
functions too, like cropping or rotating the photo. The only catch is that you must

back out of the changes one at a time. In other words, if you change the contrast on a photo, then crop it, and then rotate it, you'll have to use the Undo command three times in succession—first to unrotate, then to uncrop, and finally, to undo the contrast setting.

But once you leave Edit mode—either by closing the photo's window or by double-clicking it, thereby returning to Organize mode—you lose the ability to undo your edits. At that point, the only way to restore your photo is to choose the File→Revert to Original, which removes all the edits you've made to the photo since importing it.

Red-Eye

You snap a near-perfect family portrait. The focus is sharp, the composition is balanced, everyone's relaxed and smiling. And then you notice it: Uncle Mitch, standing dead center in the picture, looks like a vampire bat. His eyes are glowing red, as though illuminated by the evil within.

You've been victimized by *red-eye,* a common problem in flash photography. That creepy possessed-by-aliens look has ruined many an otherwise great photo.

Red-eye is actually light reflected back from the inside of your subject's eyes. The bright light of your camera's flash passes through the pupil of each eye, illuminating the blood-red retinal tissue at the back of the eye, which is reflected back into the camera lens. Red-eye problems worsen when you shoot pictures in a dim room, because your subject's pupils are dilated wider, allowing even more light from the flash to illuminate the retina.

Page 62 offers advice on how to avoid red-eye to begin with. But if it's too late for that, and people's eyes are already glowing evilly, iPhoto's Red-Eye tool lets you alleviate red-eye problems by digitally removing the offending red pixels. Here's how:

1. **Open your photo in Edit mode.**

   Change the zoom setting, if necessary, so that you have a close-up view of the eye that has the red-eye problem.

2. **Use the crosshair pointer to select the face (by dragging a box across it).**

   The more face that is selected, the better the tool does, since it distinguishes red from almost-red by comparing the eyes with the facial tones. So grab a generous number of pixels, including the eyes.

3. **Click the Red-Eye button.**

   (The Red-Eye button is dimmed until you've actually selected a portion of the photo. If you're editing in a separate window, as shown in Figure 6-4, you may have to use the >> menu at the right end of the toolbar to find the Red-Eye command.)

iPhoto neutralizes the red pixels, painting the pupils solid black.

Of course, this means that everybody winds up looking like they have *black* eyes instead of red ones—but at least they look a little less like the walking undead.

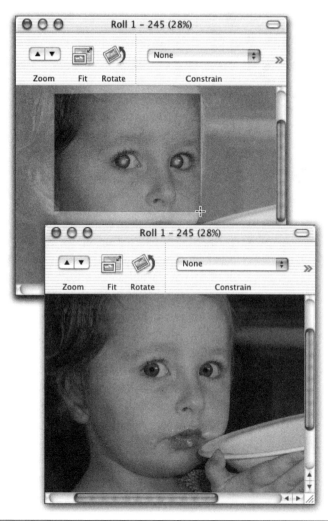

Figure 6-4:
Top: Anything even slightly red in your photo gets blackened out by iPhoto's Red-Eye tool. Select a good chunk of the face as you can, omitting anything else that's visibly red (lips, clothing, furniture, and so on).

Bottom: Truth be told, the Red-Eye tool doesn't know an eyeball from a pinkie toe; it just turns any red pixels black, regardless of what body part they're associated with. Friends and family members look more attractive—and less like Star Trek *characters—after you touch up their phosphorescent red eyes with iPhoto.*

Black & White

The Black & White tool doesn't correct anything; it simply drains the color from your photos, converting them into moody grayscale images—a great technique if you're going for that Ansel Adams look.

Open a photo in Edit mode, and then click the Black & White button. That's all there is to it. If you change your mind, you can use File→Undo to restore the color immediately, or choose File→Revert to Original at any point to return to your original file.

Tip: The Black & White button is labeled "B & W" on the editing Toolbar.

Rotating Photos

iPhoto imports all photos in landscape orientation (wider than they are tall). The program has no way of knowing if you turned the camera 90 degrees when you took your pictures. Once you've imported the photos, just select the ones that are supposed to be vertically oriented and rotate them into position.

Of course, you don't have to be in Edit mode to rotate photos. As noted on page 89, you can select thumbnail images when you're in Organize mode, and then use one of the following methods to turn them right-side up:

- Choose Edit→Rotate→Counter-Clockwise (or Clockwise).

- Click the Rotate button in the main iPhoto window, just under the Info pane (it's the rightmost of the four buttons on the pane)—or, if you've opened the picture into its own window, click the Rotate icon on its toolbar. Option-click this button or icon to reverse the direction of the rotation.

- Press ⌘-R to rotate selected photos counter-clockwise, or Shift-⌘-R to rotate them clockwise.

Tip: After importing a batch of photos, you can save a lot of time and mousing if you select *all* the thumbnails that need rotating first. Then use one of the rotation commands above to fix all the selected photos in one fell swoop.

Incidentally, clicking Rotate (or pressing ⌘-R) generally rotates photos counter-clockwise, and Option-clicking (Shift-⌘-R) generally rotates them clockwise. But you can swap these directions by choosing iPhoto→Preferences and changing the "Rotate photos" setting in the Preferences dialog box.

Note: When you rotate an image saved in GIF format in iPhoto, the resulting rotated picture is saved as a JPEG file. The original GIF is stored unchanged in an Originals folder in the iPhoto Library (see Chapter 4).

Customizing the Toolbar

Like the toolbar in all Mac OS X Finder windows, the Editing toolbar—the one that appears when you open a photo in its own window—can be customized to contain the particular editing tools you use the most.

With at least one photo open in its own window, start by choosing Window→ Customize Edit Toolbar. (Alternatively, you can Control-click a toolbar button and choose Customize Toolbar from the contextual menu.) The toolbar's customization panel fills the window (Figure 6-5); you now have a dozen more icons at your disposal, ready to be installed on the toolbar.

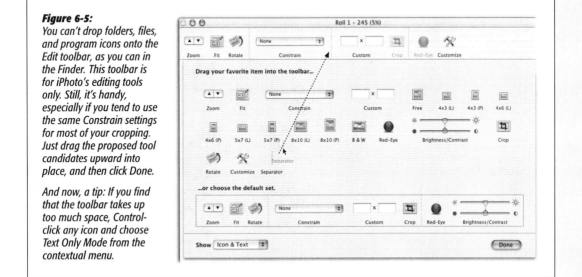

Figure 6-5:
You can't drop folders, files, and program icons onto the Edit toolbar, as you can in the Finder. This toolbar is for iPhoto's editing tools only. Still, it's handy, especially if you tend to use the same Constrain settings for most of your cropping. Just drag the proposed tool candidates upward into place, and then click Done.

And now, a tip: If you find that the toolbar takes up too much space, Control-click any icon and choose Text Only Mode from the contextual menu.

To put a new item on the toolbar, just drag it into position. To remove an existing tool, drag it anywhere off the toolbar. It vanishes Mac OS X–style—in a puff of smoke. Here are some of the changes you might consider making:

- There are buttons for each of the constrained cropping options described earlier. If there's one cropping size that you find yourself using frequently, put it in the toolbar.

- Get rid of the tools you never use, in order to keep the toolbar free from clutter. If you never crop to a custom size, for example, you can drag the Custom constraining fields out of the way. (You can always restore tools later.)

- Even if you don't add or remove any buttons, you can drag the ones that are already there into a new order, putting them exactly where you want them. (You can do this at any time, even when the customization panel isn't open, by ⌘-dragging the buttons on the toolbar.)

- Drop separator lines between the various tools to group them visually on the toolbar according to your preference.

No need to worry about adding too many items to this toolbar. If you keep piling on the icons, it sprouts a fly-out menu on the right side, listing every button, as shown in Figure 6-1.

When you're finished dragging extra buttons to the toolbar, click Done to close the Customize panel and activate your new icons.

Tip: You can restore the toolbar to its original condition by dragging the default set of tools at the bottom of the customization panel to the toolbar.

Beyond iPhoto

If you're serious about digital photographs, iPhoto's tools by themselves aren't going to cut it. You'll have to spring for a more full-featured image-editing program, such as Adobe Photoshop, Canvas 8, GraphicConverter, Corel Photo-Paint, or a similar program.

Photoshop is by far the most popular tool for the job, but at about $600, it's also one of the most expensive. Unless you intend to perform sophisticated image-editing and *compositing* (sandwiching together parts of different photos into one image), save yourself some money and buy Photoshop Elements, if a Mac OS X version is available as you read this. It's a trimmed-down version of Photoshop with all the basic image-editing stuff and just enough of the high-end features. It costs only about $100. (Your digital camera may even have come with Photoshop Elements right in the box.)

Before you go software shopping, though, check out your own hard drive. If you bought your Mac recently, you may already have the image-editing software you need. Apple now includes Lemke Software's GraphicConverter—a simple but powerful editing program with Photoshop-like tools—on some Mac models. You also might find a copy of Caffeine Software's PixelNhance. You can't paint, draw, mask, trim, copy, or paste images with PixelNhance, but you can fiddle with the color balance, sharpness, and other settings.

Opening Photos in Other Programs

To open a photo in a "real" editing program, first launch that program so that its icon appears in the Dock. Then simply drag a thumbnail from iPhoto's window directly onto the program icon. (Of course, you can also drag a picture from iPhoto's window onto the application's actual desktop icon, or an alias of it, even if it's not in the Dock.) In fact, you can even drag several thumbnails at once, to open all of them simultaneously.

If you've already been working in, say, Photoshop, you might be tempted to use its File→Open command to open an iPhoto photo directly. But the drag-and-drop method is far more efficient; if you use File→Open, you'll have to navigate through the oddly numbered folders of the labyrinthine iPhoto Library folder (page 90) to locate the picture you want.

Caution: When you edit photos in another program, you're essentially going behind iPhoto's back. Therefore, it won't be able to track the changes you make. As a consequence, you're sacrificing your ability to use the Revert to Original command to restore your photo to its original state in case of disaster. See "Reverting to the Original" later in this chapter for details.

Setting up a default editing program

The drag-and-drop approach is great if you *occasionally* want to open a photo in another program. But if you find yourself routinely editing your photos using another program, there's a much easier method: Just set up iPhoto to automatically open your photos in that program with a double-click. You set up this arrangement as follows.

1. **Choose iPhoto→Preferences.**

   The Preferences window opens.

2. **Under the "Double-click" preference settings, click the Other radio button.**

   A standard Open dialog box appears so you can navigate to your favorite photo-editing program.

3. **Choose the program you want to use for editing, then click Open.**

   When you're done, close the Preferences window.

Now, whenever you double-click a thumbnail, iPhoto will launch the designated editing program and use it to open your photo.

One big advantage in using this method is that it allows iPhoto to track your editing activity—yes, even when you use other programs. iPhoto can therefore update its thumbnail versions of your photos to reflect the changes. It can also preserve the original version of the photos you edit externally, so that you can later use the Revert to Original command if disaster should strike any time later, as explained later in this chapter.

Tip: Once you've slated an external program to open when you double-click a thumbnail in iPhoto, you can use this nifty trick. If *Option*-double-click a thumbnail, iPhoto reverses your preference. That is, if you've set iPhoto to open an iPhoto window when you double-click, Option-double-clicking opens the photo in GraphicConverter instead (if that's what you chose in step 3 above). And if you've set iPhoto to open GraphicConverter when you double-click a thumbnail, Option-double-clicking opens it into an iPhoto window instead.

Alternatively, you can click a thumbnail and then click the Edit mode button beneath it. That always opens the photo for editing right in iPhoto.

Fixing Digital Photos

Once you've moved beyond the world of iPhoto, there's plenty that you can do to improve the quality of digital photos. Programs like Photoshop let you make dozens

---

of different enhancements to your photos and apply a seemingly endless variety of wild special effects.

Still, you'll probably find yourself using only a handful of such features for most photo-fixing work. Here are some of the operations that are worth tackling.

Color correction

One of the most common failings of digital cameras (and many flatbed scanners, too) is that they don't capture color very accurately. Digital photos often have a slightly bluish or greenish tinge, producing dull colors, lower contrast, and sickly looking skin tones. Most image-editing programs let you bump up or lower each of the individual color channels in your photos, adding red values or decreasing green values, so that your photos have more balanced, lifelike color. Figure 6-6 shows how you can use PixelNhance to make corrections of this sort.

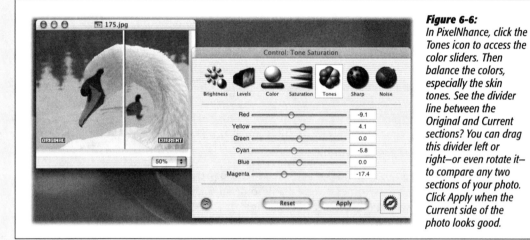

Figure 6-6:
In PixelNhance, click the Tones icon to access the color sliders. Then balance the colors, especially the skin tones. See the divider line between the Original and Current sections? You can drag this divider left or right—or even rotate it— to compare any two sections of your photo. Click Apply when the Current side of the photo looks good.

Sharpness

Another frequent complaint about digital cameras is that they don't produce the sharpest images. High-end programs like Photoshop and GraphicConverter can apply a sharpening filter that brings out edges and adds definition to a slightly blurry photo.

Figure 6-7 illustrates how you can use a Sharpen filter in an image-editing program (GraphicConverter, in this case) to give a photo the crisp focus it might have lacked straight from the camera or scanner.

Saturation

Another way to improve dull, washed-out colors is to increase the *saturation* in a photo—a standard operation in most image-editing programs. (Photoshop, Graphic-Converter, and PixelNhance all have Saturation controls.) You can increase the saturation to make colors look deeper and richer and less "gray." You can also improve photos that have harsh, garish colors by dialing down the saturation so that the colors end up looking a little less intense than they appeared in the original snapshot.

If you're using GraphicConverter, you can access the Saturation slider by choosing Picture→Brightness/Contrast.

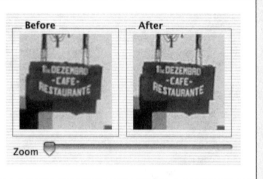

Figure 6-7:
Choose Effect→Sharpen Edges to open the sharpen window, then drag the slider to adjust the degree of sharpening, comparing the Before and After views to gauge the amount needed. Be careful to apply sharpening very conservatively; otherwise, you'll introduce artificially jagged edges into your pictures.

Reverting to the Original

iPhoto includes built-in protection against overzealous editing—a feature that can save you much grief. If you end up cropping a photo too much, or cranking up the brightness of a picture until it seems washed out, or accidentally turning someone's lips black with the Red-Eye tool, you can undo *all* your edits at once with the Revert to Original command. Revert to Original strips away every change you've made since the picture arrived from the camera. It leaves you with your original, unedited photo.

The secret behind the Revert to Original command lies in iPhoto's unique way of handling photo editing. Whenever you use any editing tools, iPhoto—without prompting and without informing you—instantly makes a *duplicate* of your original file. With an original version safely tucked away, iPhoto lets you go wild on the copy. You can remain secure in the knowledge that in a pinch, iPhoto can always restore an image to the state it was in when you first imported it.

Note: The unedited originals are stored in your Home→Pictures→iPhoto Library→Originals folder. (This folder doesn't exist until you start editing.)

To restore an original photo, undoing all cropping, rotation, brightness adjustments, and so on, select a thumbnail of an edited photo, or open the photo in Edit mode. Then choose File→Revert to Original. iPhoto swaps in the original version of the photo—and you're back where you started.

As noted earlier, iPhoto does its automatic backup trick whenever you edit your pictures (a) within iPhoto or (b) using a program that you've set up to open when you double-click a picture. It does *not* make a backup when you drag a thumbnail onto the icon of another program. In that event, the Revert to Original command will be dimmed out when you select the edited photo.

Bottom line: If you want the warmth and security of Revert to Original at your disposal, don't edit your pictures behind iPhoto's back. Follow the guidelines in the previous two paragraphs so that iPhoto is always aware of when and how you're editing your pictures.

FREQUENTLY ASKED QUESTION

In iPhoto, Less Is More

I just finished editing a batch of photos, cropping each picture to a much smaller size. But now my iPhoto Library is taking up more space on my hard drive! How can making the photos smaller increase the size of my photo collection? Shouldn't throwing away all those pixels have the opposite effect—shrinking things down?

Your cropped photos do, in fact, take up much less space than they did. Remember, though, that iPhoto doesn't let you monkey with your photos without first stashing away

a copy of each original photo, in case you ever want to use the Revert to Original command to restore a photo to its original condition.

So every time you crop a picture (or do any other editing), you're actually creating one new, full-size file on your hard drive, as iPhoto stores both the original *and* the edited versions of the photo. Therefore, the more photos you edit in iPhoto, the more hard drive space your photo collection will take up.

Part Three:
Meet Your Public

3

The iPhoto Slide Show

Photo's slide show feature offers one of the world's best ways to show off your digital photos. Slide shows are easy to set up, they're free, and they make your photos look fantastic. This chapter shows you not only how to put together an iPhoto slide show, but how to give presentations that make you and your photos look their absolute best.

About Slide Shows

When you run an iPhoto slide show, your Mac presents the pictures in full-screen mode—no windows, no menus, no borders, with your images filling every inch of the entire monitor. Each picture fades gently into the next, producing a smooth, cinematic effect. If you want, you can even add a musical soundtrack to accompany the presentation. The total effect is incredibly polished and professional looking— yet creating a slide show requires very little setup.

The One-Click Slide Show

If you haven't already tried iPhoto's slide show feature, give it a whirl right now. It requires only a single click.

With either a photo album or your entire Photo Library displayed in the iPhoto window, click the Play button under the Info pane (see Figure 7-1). A moment later, your Mac's screen fades to black, and then the show begins. Each photo is displayed full-screen for two seconds, and then softly fades out as the next one dissolves into view. The default musical soundtrack—J. S. Bach's *Minuet in G*—plays in the background.

As noted in Chapter 4, this is a great feature for reviewing photos you've just dumped into the Mac from the camera. In fact, that delicious moment when you first see the pictures at full-screen size—after having viewed them only on the camera's two-inch screen before that—is just what Apple's engineers had in mind when they designed the Play button.

When you've had enough, click the mouse or press any letter key to end the show and return to the iPhoto window. (Don't wait for the slide show to finish on its own; the default setting runs the show in a continuous loop, so it keeps going until you stop it.)

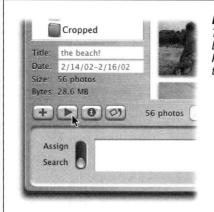

Figure 7-1:
The quickest way to kick off a slide show in iPhoto is to click the Play button in the main iPhoto window, shown by the cursor here. There's no keyboard shortcut, but you can hit any key except the arrow keys and the Space bar to stop a show once it's running.

Setting Up the Show

Of course, this canned slide show is just a starting point. To put together a presentation that will dazzle friends and family, you're invited to select the most impressive photos, choose the perfect background music, and even control how fast or slow the show moves along.

Choose Your Photos

When putting together a slide show, your first task is choosing the photos you want to include.

As a starting point, here's how iPhoto determines which photos *it* includes:

- If no photos are selected, iPhoto shows all the pictures currently in the photo viewing area, starting the show with the first photo in the album or Photo Library.

  Most people, most of the time, want to turn one album into a slide show. That's easy: just click the album before starting the slide show. As long as no individual pictures are selected, iPhoto will show all the pictures in the currently open photo album.

- If only one photo is *visible* (but not selected) in the photo viewing area, then the slide show consists of that one picture. The music still plays—you just end up with a one-picture show.

- If one photo is *selected,* iPhoto uses that picture as its starting point for the show, ignoring any that come before it. (Of course, if you've got the slide show set to loop continuously, iPhoto will eventually circle back to display the first photo in the window.)

- If you've selected more than one picture, iPhoto includes *only* those pictures in its slide show.

Not all pictures are good pictures

Choosing photos for your slide show involves more than just picking the photos you like the best. You also have to make sure you've selected pictures that are the right size.

Why is the size so important? Because iPhoto always displays slide show photos at full-screen dimensions—and on most of today's monitors, that means at least 1024 x 768 pixels. If your photos are smaller than that, iPhoto stretches them to fill the screen, often with disastrous results. If you include a tiny 320 x 240 pixel snapshot in a slide show, for example, the resulting slide-show image, blown up to more than ten times its normal size, turns into a chunky, jaggy-edged mess.

Note: Although iPhoto blows up images to fill the screen, it always does so proportionately, maintaining each photo's vertical-to-horizontal aspect ratio. As a result, some photos may appear with a black border around either the vertical or horizontal edges.

Figure 7-2:
Here's an example of what happens when a 240 x 180 pixel photo ends up in a slide show. Projected at full-screen dimensions, a portrait that looks great at its normal size becomes jaggy-edged and fuzzy—unflattering to both the subject and the photographer. If you plan to use your photos in a slide show, make sure your digital camera is set to capture pictures that are at least 1024 x 768 pixels.

Determining the size of your photos

If you're not sure that your photos are big enough to be slide show material, iPhoto provides two easy ways to check their size:

- Click a thumbnail in the photo viewing area, and then look at the Size field in the Info pane. You'll see something like "1600 x 1200." That's the height and width of the image, measured in pixels.

- Select a thumbnail and choose File→Show Info, or press ⌘-I to open the Show Info window. The width and height of the photo are the first two items listed in the Image section of the Photo pane.

Putting photos in the right order

iPhoto shows your pictures in the same order you see them in the photo viewing area. In other words, to rearrange your slide-show slides, drag the thumbnails around within their album (page 113). Remember that you can't drag pictures around in the Photo Library or the Last Import folder—only within a photo album.

Slide Show Preferences

With your photos selected, you're ready to configure iPhoto's slide show preferences (Figure 7-3). Go to iPhoto→Preferences, or press ⌘-Y, to explore your options.

Timing

If left to its own devices, iPhoto advances through your pictures at the rate of one photo every two seconds. If that seems too brisk or too slow, you can change the rate.

In the iPhoto→Preferences dialog box, use the "Play each slide for __ seconds" controls to specify a different interval, as shown in Figure 7-3.

UP TO SPEED

How Big Is My Monitor?

To know if your photos are large enough to be displayed distortion-free on your monitor, you have to know how many pixels it takes to fill your screen.

And to know that, you need to know your screen's *resolution*. Choose → System Preferences (or click the System Preferences icon on your Dock), and open the Displays panel. In the Resolutions list, you'll find all the resolutions that your monitor can handle, with the current resolution highlighted. If the selection says, for example, 1024 x 768, you know that photos must be at least 1024 pixels by 768 pixels to fill your screen without iPhoto having to stretch them to fit. (And once you're in the Displays panel, you may as well turn on "Show displays in menu bar." You'll get a handy menu of resolutions that, henceforth, you can consult with one click.)

The timing setting you choose also affects the speed of the cross-fade transition from photo to photo. Choosing a short playing time results in quick transitions, while a longer playing time produces long, slow crossfades as one photo dissolves into the next.

Note: You can't set different timings for different pictures. It's one-timing-fits-all.

Repeating a show

When iPhoto is done running through all your photos in a slide show, it ordinarily circles back and starts playing the whole sequence from the beginning again. If you want your photos to play just one time through, turn off the "Repeat slide show when finished" checkbox.

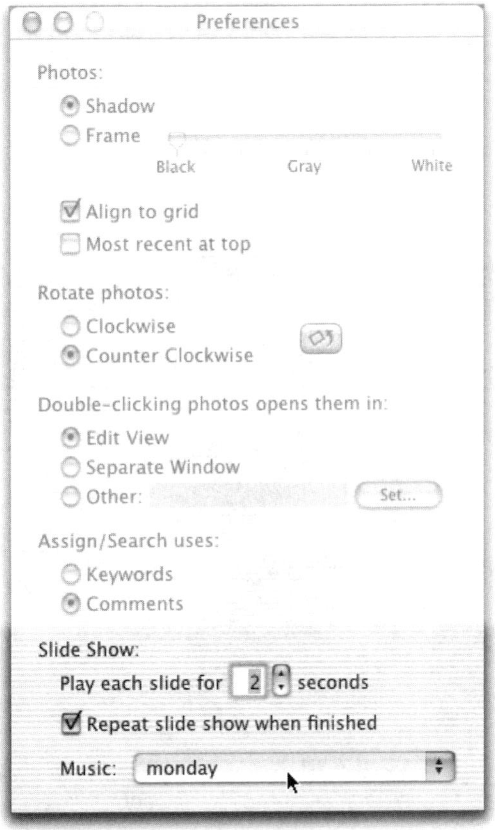

Figure 7-3:
The lower portion of the Preferences window is dedicated to iPhoto's slide show options. This is where you set slide show timing and pick the musical soundtrack that plays with each show. You can go as fast as one second per slide, or bump the number up to 60 seconds each for a very leisurely presentation. (You can type a number larger than 60 in the "Play each slide…" field, but iPhoto will ignore you. It refuses to spend any more than one minute on each shot, no matter how good a photographer you are.)

Adding Music

Perhaps more than any other single element, *music* transforms a slide show, turning your ordinary photos into a cinematic event. When you pair the right music with the right pictures, you do more than just show off your photos, you create a mood that can stir the emotions of your audience. So if you really want your friends and family to be transfixed by your photos, add a soundtrack.

iPhoto makes it remarkably easy to add music to your slide shows. To get you started, Apple sends iPhoto to you equipped with two classical music tracks by J. S. Bach: *Minuet in G* and *Jesu, Joy of Man's Desiring*.

To add one of these musical selections to a slide show, choose it from the Music pop-up menu at the bottom of the Preferences window. The music track you choose starts playing when the slide show begins and loops continuously for the duration of the slide show.

Tip: If you decide you don't want any music to play during a slide show, choose None from the Music pop-up menu.

About MP3 files

Not to knock Bach, but it's fortunate that you're not limited to his greatest hits. You can add any music you want to a slide show, using your own MP3 tracks.

WORKAROUND WORKSHOP

Small Photos, Big Show

You can't control the size of your pictures as they appear during a slide show; they always fill the screen. To ensure that the results look good, you need to make sure that all your photos are sized properly to fill the screen, as mentioned earlier in this chapter.

But what if you're *stuck* with photos that are simply not big enough? Suppose you're charged with putting together a slide show for the family reunion—and the only pictures you have of Uncle Rodney happen to be scanned photos that are only 640 x 480 pixels?

You can't hack Rodney out of the slide show, but at the same time, you know Aunt Lois won't take kindly to having her husband appear onscreen hideously distorted. ("Why does Rod look so jagged?" you can imagine her saying. "What did you do to him?") Here's one simple way to have smaller photos displayed perfectly in a slide show and keep everyone happy.

Using a program like Adobe Photoshop, GraphicConverter, or Photoshop Elements, create a new document that's exactly the right size for your screen. If your monitor's set to 1024 x 768 pixels, create a document of 1024 x 768 pixels. Fill the background of the blank document so that it's black, to match the black between slides. (Actually, you can use whatever background color you like.)

Now open the small photo that you want to include in your slide show. Paste a copy of it into the center of your blank document. Save the results and then import the image file into iPhoto.

You now have a new picture, perfectly sized for your slide show. Your small photo will appear onscreen at the proper size, with a black border around it. No, the photo won't fill the screen, but at least it will appear just as clear and distortion-free as the larger photos.

MP3 is short for *MPEG-1 Audio Layer-3*, a highly compressed file format that lets you store CD-quality music in remarkably small files. In recent years, MP3 has become the standard format for storing and playing digital music. Apple's iTunes software stores music in MP3 format, for example, as does the portable iPod music player and virtually all of the other Walkman-size digital music players.

There are at least two ways to get your hands on some MP3 files for use as slide show soundtracks:

- Convert tracks from your favorite CDs into MP3 files using iTunes, Apple's free digital music software. (If you don't have a copy of iTunes, you can download it from Apple's Web site.)

- Do a search on the Internet for *MP3*. You'll find literally thousands of Web sites offering downloads of free music. Just download the tracks you want. (You can use iTunes to play them and keep them organized.)

Note: In addition to MP3 files, iPhoto can also play music stored in two other common sound file formats: AIFF and WAV. These formats are considerably less popular than MP3, in part because they take up much more disk space (and require much more time to download). You can convert AIFF and WAV files into MP3s using iTunes.

Adding your own music track

To designate an MP3 track of your own as the standard iPhoto slide show music, choose Other from the Music pop-up menu in the Preferences window (shown in Figure 7-3). A standard Open dialog box appears (see Figure 7-4). Navigate to the

Figure 7-4:
Top: In the Preferences dialog box, choose Other from the Music pop-up menu.

Bottom: The Open dialog box lets you navigate to, for example, your iTunes music-library folder, the better to forage for good slide-show music. To find your iTunes collection of MP3 files, choose Documents from the From pop-up menu (top). Then click the iTunes folder, followed by the folder containing your iTunes music, the artist name folder, album folder, and so on, to find the MP3 file you want.

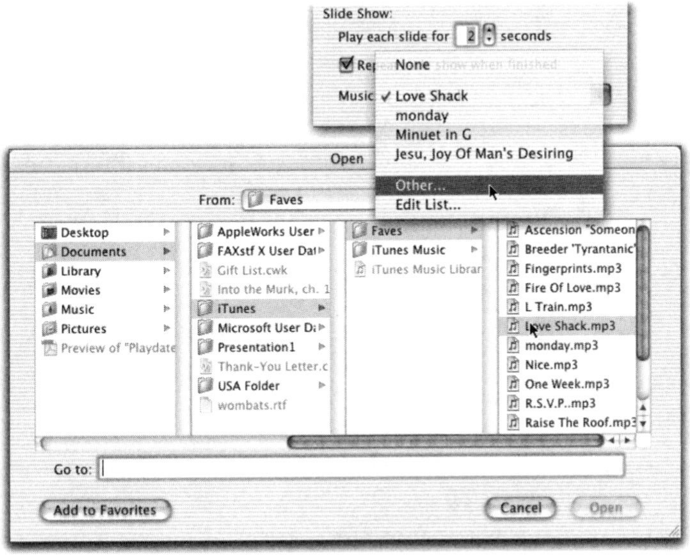

MP3 file you want and select it. The name of the track from then on appears in the Music menu.

Once you've added a music track, it remains in the Music pop-up menu permanently, so you can use it with additional slide shows in the future. (To remove these added tracks, use the Edit List command in the Music menu.)

Note: You can select only one music track per slide show; iPhoto will make it loop endlessly until you stop the show. If you want two different songs to play during one slide show, you'll have to use a sound-editing program to splice two sound files together to create one file containing both tunes. Amadeus II, available for download from *www.missingmanuals.com,* among other places, can fill the bill nicely.

Using music from iTunes

If, like most Mac OS X fans, you keep your MP3 files in iTunes, you've probably already got a good collection of MP3s on your Mac. Trouble is, from within iPhoto's Open dialog box, you might not know exactly where each of those MP3s are located on your hard drive. Here's some guidance:

- Most of your own files are in your personal iTunes library. To find it, open the From pop-up menu in the Open dialog box and choose Home. Now you see the contents of your Home folder. In successive panels, click Documents→iTunes→ iTunes Music, and then the name of the performing artist (or group), album, and song you want (see Figure 7-4).

- Some Macs come with a sampler of MP3 files already installed. To choose one of these songs, scroll all the way to the left in the Open dialog box. Now, in succes-

Figure 7-5:
To use a track in iTunes with a slide show, select the track in iTunes and choose File→Get Info to open the Song Information window. On the Info pane, you'll see the full path to the MP3 file that corresponds to the selected song. Once you know the name and location of the file you want, you can use the Music pop-up menu in iPhoto to select the MP3 file and add it as a soundtrack.

sive panels, click Macintosh HD→Library→Application Support→iTunes→
Sampler→Tunes Sampler, and then the song you want.

- If your copy of iTunes lists a song that you can't seem to find using either of the
two avenues listed above, launch iTunes. Use the Get Info command, as shown in
Figure 7-5, to figure out where the file is stored within the iTunes Music folder.

- You can also drag an entry from the iTunes window directly to the desktop or
into a folder, which makes a *copy* of the original MP3 file. You can drop this file
into a folder called something like "Soundtracks" and then point iPhoto to *that*
copy of the MP3.

If you decide you no longer want a particular track to appear in iPhoto's Music pop-
up menu, you can delete it. When you choose Edit List from the pop-up menu (shown
in Figure 7-4), a box listing all of the menu entries drops down from the top of the
Preferences window. Select the entries you no longer want and click the Delete button to remove them. Deleting these entries doesn't delete the music files themselves—
just the menu listing.

In any case, close the Preferences window when you're finished with your Music-
menu surgery.

Running the Show

Once you've picked your photos, set up your options, and selected a music track,
your show is ready to run. You can start it in one of two ways:

- **The short way.** Click the Play button (the triangular button beneath the album
list) in the main iPhoto window. The slide show begins instantly.

- **The long way.** Click the Share button in the main gallery area, and then click the
Slide Show button at the bottom of the screen.

Why would you use the second, more convoluted approach? Because this way,
you're offered the chance to change the slide show preferences before the show
begins. As shown in Figure 7-6, you get a miniature version of the Preferences

Figure 7-6:
*You can trigger the slide show in one of two
ways. If you just click the Play button, iPhoto
begins to "play" whatever is currently shown or
selected in the main gallery window—instantly. If
you click Share and then Slide Show, you get the
dialog box shown here, so that you can adjust
the music track and other options.*

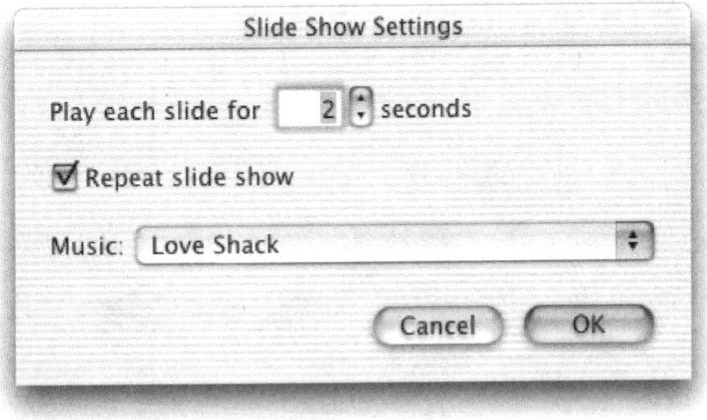

Slide Show Settings

Play each slide for [2] seconds

☑ Repeat slide show

Music: [Love Shack]

Cancel   OK

dialog box that you got to know so well in the preceding pages. Adjust the time-on-the-screen setting, turn "Repeat slide show" on or off, choose a music track from the Music pop-up menu, and then click OK to begin the show.

Control over the Show

iPhoto slide shows run themselves, advancing from photo to photo according to the timing you set in the Preference or Slide Show Settings dialog box. However, you can control a slide show after it starts running in the following, rarely discovered ways:

- **Pause it.** Press the Space bar at any point to pause a slide show. When you pause a show, the music keeps playing, but the photos stop advancing; a glowing Pause indicator briefly appears in the lower-right corner of the screen. When you're ready to move to the next slide and resume auto-advancing the pictures, press the Space bar again. A tiny Play indicator appears momentarily in the bottom right corner to confirm that iPhoto has understood your command.

- **Manual advance.** Press the right or left arrow keys to advance to the next or previous photo, overriding the preset timing. In fact, once you hit either arrow key, the slide show shifts into manual mode and stops automatically advancing the photos altogether.

POWER USERS' CLINIC

Screen Saver: The Other Slide Show

As good as iPhoto's slide show feature is, there's an even more impressive way to display your photos onscreen: turn an album into a Mac OS X *screen saver*.

In some ways, iPhoto's Slide Show feature and Mac OS X's screen saver module are very similar. Both completely fill the screen with your photos, and both cross-fade one image into the next for a very smooth, polished presentation. But the screen saver module adds another subtle effect—gently zooming in and out of each photo as it's displayed. When combined with the crossfades between shots, the result is a less static, more cinematic slide show.

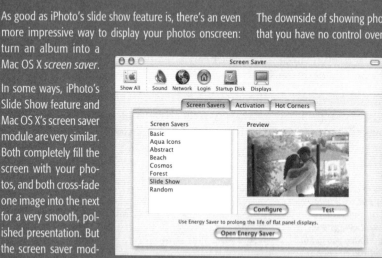

The downside of showing photos in screen saver mode is that you have no control over the speed (photos change every 8 to 10 seconds), you can't override the timing or advance photos manually, and there's no sound.

Still, photos look so good when displayed via the screen saver module, you might consider showing your photos this way and just playing the accompanying music on a CD player stuck under the desk.

See page 231 for instructions on setting up a photo album as a screen saver.

At this point, you can continue to use the arrow keys to move through all of the photos—or stay on one photo for the rest of your life, for all iPhoto cares. As with the pause command, the music track keeps on playing. (To stop the music, you have to end the slide show.)

In short, this is a terrific setup for a slide show that you're narrating in person.

- **Back to auto-advance.** To put a slide show back into auto-play mode after you've used one of the arrow keys, press the Space bar. The photos advance automatically once again.

- **Speed it up or slow it down.** Press the up or down arrow keys to speed up or slow down the slide show by one second per slide. You'll discover that iPhoto can't create a stroboscopic, three-frames-per-second effect; one picture per second is about its maximum speed. (Give the poor thing a break—it's got *a lot* of data to scoop off the hard drive and throw onto your screen.)

Note: The change you make here is temporary. The next time you run a slide show, you'll start again with the timing set in the Preferences window.

- **End it prematurely.** End a slide show by clicking the mouse button, or by pressing any keys other than the arrow keys and the Space bar. When a slide show ends, the screen fades to black, the musical track fades out gradually, and then you return to the iPhoto window.

Slide Show Tips

The following guidelines will help you build impressive slide shows that truly showcase your efforts as a digital photographer:

- Use images that are the right size. Photos that are too small will be ugly when blown up to full-screen size. Photos that are much too large will look fine, but iPhoto will take longer to display them and the cross-fade transitions might not look smooth. For the best possible results, make your photos roughly the same pixel size as your screen, as discussed on page 126.

- To whatever degree possible, stick with photos in landscape (horizontal) orientation. With portrait-oriented (vertical) photos, iPhoto has no choice but to display big black borders along the sides.

- For similar reasons, try to stick with photos with proportions of 4 to 3 (width to height), just as they came from the camera. Pictures that you've cropped to other proportions (4 x 6 or 5 x 7 for ordering prints, for example), won't fill the screen completely, either.

- Always preview images at full size before using them. You can't judge how sharp and bright an image is going to look based solely on the thumbnail.

- Keep the timing brief when setting the playing speed—maybe just a few seconds per photo. Better to have your friends wanting to see more of each photo than to have them bored, waiting for the show to advance to the next image. Remember, you can always pause a slide show if someone wants to take a long look at one picture.

- Give some thought to the order of your photos. A good slide show can tell a story. You might want to start with a photo that establishes a location—an overall shot of a park, for example—and then follow it with close-ups that reveal the details.

- If your viewers fall in love with what you've shown them, you have two options: (a) Save the slide show as a QuickTime movie that you can email to them or burn onto a CD for their at-home enjoyment (Chapter 11), or (b) Make them buy their own Macs.

FREQUENTLY ASKED QUESTION

Slide Show Smackdown: iPhoto vs. iMovie

I read in iMovie 2: The Missing Manual *that iMovie makes a great slide show program, too. It says there that I can import my photos, add music, and play it all back full-screen, just like you're saying here. Which program should I use?*

The short answer: iPhoto for convenience, iMovie for control.

In iMovie, you can indeed import photos. You can add them to the timeline at the bottom of the window in any order. What's more, you have individual control over their timing (1 second for the first slide, 3 seconds for the second, or whatever) and the crossfades between them (dissolve between slides 1 and 2, a left-to-right "wipe" between slides 2 and 3, and so on).

The music options are much greater here, too. Not only can you import music straight from a music CD (without having to visit iTunes as an intermediary), but you can actually record a narration into a microphone as the slide show plays. And, of course, you have a full range of title-

and credit-making features at your disposal, too.

When the show looks good, you can export it to a Quick-Time movie just as described in Chapter 11—or, for the absolute finest in picture quality, to Apple's iDVD software for burning onto a real DVD. (A Mac with a DVD burner, called an Apple SuperDrive, is required.)

But iPhoto has charms of its own. Creating a slide show is *much* less work in iPhoto, for one thing. If you want a slide show to loop endlessly—playing on a laptop at somebody's wedding, for example, or at a trade show—iPhoto is also a much better bet. (iMovie can't loop, and neither can a DVD, although you could export the iMovie movie to QuickTime Player for looping playback.)

Remember, too, that iPhoto is beautifully integrated with your various albums. Whereas building an iMovie project is a serious, sit-down-and-work proposition that results in *one* polished slide show, your iPhoto library has as many different slide shows as you have albums—all ready to go at any time.

CHAPTER 8

Making Prints

There's a lot to love about digital photos that remain digital. You can store hundreds of them on a single CD; you can send them anywhere on earth by email; and they won't wrinkle, curl, or yellow until your monitor does.

Sooner or later, though, most people want to get at least some of their photos on paper. You may want the printouts to paste into your existing scrapbooks, to put in a picture frame on the mantle, or to share with your Luddite friends who don't have computers.

Using iPhoto, you can create such prints using your own printer. Or, for prints that look, feel, and smell like the kind you get from a photo finishing store, you can transmit your digital files to Kodak Print Services, an online photo processing service. In return, you receive an envelope of professionally printed photos on Kodak paper that are indistinguishable from their traditional counterparts.

This chapter explains how to use each of iPhoto's printing options, including the features that let you print greeting cards, contact sheets, and other special items from your digital photo collection.

Making Great Prints

Using iPhoto to print your pictures is pretty easy. But making *great* prints—the kind that rival traditional film-based photos in their color and image quality—involves more than simply hitting the Print command.

One key factor, of course, is the printer itself. You need a good color inkjet printer that can produce photo-quality printouts. Fortunately, getting such a printer these days is pretty easy and inexpensive. Even some of the cheapo inkjet printers from Epson, Hewlett-Packard, and Canon can produce amazingly good color images—and they cost less than $100. (Of course, you make it up to the printer company on the back end: when you buy more ink cartridges. Depending on how many prints you make, what you spend on these expensive cartridges can easily double or triple the cost of the printer in a year.)

Tip: If you're really serious about producing photographically realistic printouts, consider buying a model that's specifically designed for photo printing, such as one of the printers in the Epson Stylus Photo series or the slightly more expensive Canon printers. What you're looking for is a printer that uses *six* different colors of ink instead of the usual "inkjet four." The extra colors do wonders for the printer's ability to reproduce a wide range of colors on paper.

Even with the best printer, however, you can end up with disappointing results if you fail to consider at least three other important factors when trying to coax the best possible printouts from your digital photos. These factors include the resolution of your images, the settings on your printer, and your choice of paper.

Resolution and Shape

Resolution is the number of individual pixels squeezed into each inch of your digital photo. The basic rule is simple: The higher your photo's resolution, or *dpi* (dots per inch), the sharper, clearer, and more detailed the printout will be. If the resolution is too low, you end up with a printout that looks blurry or speckled.

Low-resolution photos are responsible for more wasted printer ink and crumpled photo paper than any other printing snafu, so it pays to understand how to calculate a photo's dpi when you want to print it.

To calculate a photo's resolution, divide the horizontal or vertical size of the photo (measured in pixels) by the horizontal or vertical size of the print you want to make (usually measured in inches).

Suppose a photo measures 1524 x 1016 pixels. (How do you know? See Figure 8-1.) If you want a 4 x 6 printout, you'll be printing at a resolution of 254 dpi (1524 pixels divided by 6 inches = 254 dpi), which will look fantastic on paper. Photos printed on an inkjet printer look their best when printed at a resolution of 250 dpi or higher.

But if you try to print that same photo at 8 x 10, you'll get into trouble. By stretching those pixels across a larger print area, you're now printing at just 152 dpi—and you'll see a noticeable drop in image quality.

While it's important to print photos at a resolution of 250 to 300 dpi on an inkjet printer, there's really no benefit to printing at higher resolutions—600 dpi, 800 dpi, or more. That doesn't hurt anything, but you probably won't notice any difference in the printed photos—at least not on inkjet printers. Some inkjets can spray ink at finer resolutions—720 dpi, 1440 dpi, and so on—and using these highest settings produces very smooth, very fine printouts. But bumping the resolution of your *photos* higher than 300 dpi doesn't have any perceptible effect on their quality.

You also have to think about your pictures' *aspect ratio*—their proportions. Most digital cameras produce photos with 4-to-3 proportions, which don't fit neatly onto standard print paper (4 x 6 and so on). You can read more about this problem on pages 125 and 197.(Just to make sure you're completley confused, print paper is measured *height by width*, whereas digital photos are measured *width by height*).

If you're printing photos on letter-size paper, the printed images won't have standard Kodak dimensions. (They'll be, for example, 4 x 5.3); you may not particularly care. But if you're printing onto, say, precut 4 x 6 photo paper (which you choose in the File→Page Setup dialog box), you can avoid ugly white bands at the sides by first cropping your photos to standard print sizes (see page 125).

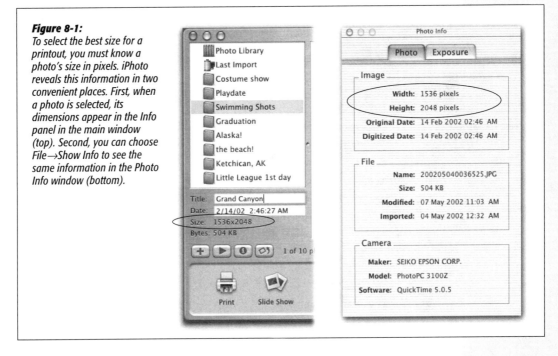

Figure 8-1:
To select the best size for a printout, you must know a photo's size in pixels. iPhoto reveals this information in two convenient places. First, when a photo is selected, its dimensions appear in the Info panel in the main window (top). Second, you can choose File→Show Info to see the same information in the Photo Info window (bottom).

Tweaking the Printer Settings

Just about every inkjet printer on earth comes with software that adjusts various print quality settings. Usually, you can find the controls for these settings right in the Print dialog box that appears when you choose File→Print. To reveal these printer-specific controls in iPhoto, you click the Advanced Options button in the Print dialog box, and then choose an additional command from the pop-up menu (Figure 8-2).

Before you print, verify that you've got these settings right. On most printers, for example, you can choose from several different quality levels when printing, like Draft, Normal, Best, or Photo. There might also be a menu that lets you select the kind of paper you're going to use—plain paper, inkjet paper, glossy photo paper, and so on.

Choose the wrong settings, and you'll be wasting a lot of paper. Even a top-of-the-line Epson photo printer churns out awful photo prints if you feed it plain paper when it's expecting high-quality glossy stock. You'll end up with a smudgy, soggy mess. So each time you print, make sure your printer is configured for the quality, resolution, and paper settings that you intend.

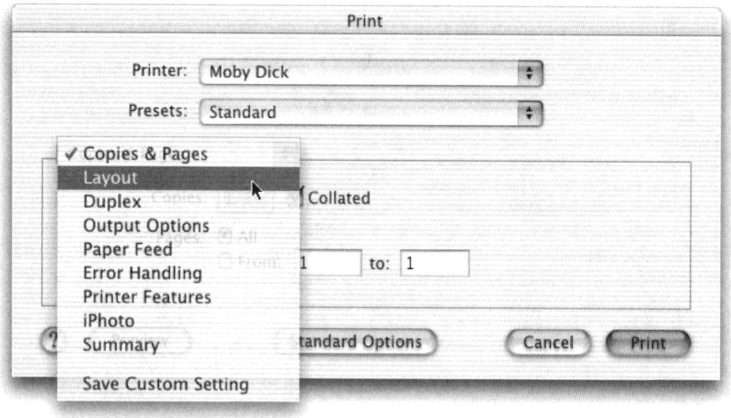

Figure 8-2:
Click Advanced Options in the standard iPhoto Print dialog box (shown in Figure 8-3) to open this important box. Here, the controls for paper type, print quality, and so on are hidden until you choose from a pop-up menu. The command you want might be called "Printer Features," "Quality & Media," or something else, depending on your printer.

Paper Matters

When it comes to inkjet printing, paper is critical. Regular typing paper—the stuff you'd feed through a laser printer or copier—may be cheap, but it's too thin and absorbent to handle the ink that gets sprayed on when you print a full-color digital photo. If you try to print large photos on plain paper, you'll end up with flat colors, slightly fuzzy images, and paper that's rippled and buckling from all the ink. For really good prints, you need really good paper.

Most printers accommodate at least four different grades of paper. Among them:

- Plain paper (the kind used in most photocopiers)

- High resolution paper (a slightly heavier inkjet paper—not glossy, but with a silky-smooth white finish on one side)

- Glossy photo paper (a stiff, glossy paper resembling the paper that developed photos are printed on)

- Glossy *film* (a more expensive option made of polyethylene rather than paper), feels even more like traditional photographic paper.

These better photo papers cost much more than plain paper, of course. Glossy photo paper, for example, might run $18 for a box of 20 sheets, which means you'll be spending about 90 cents per 8 x 10 (or letter-size) print—not including ink. (You can find good deals on printer paper at, for example, Staples.com and Buy.com.)

Still, by using good photo paper, you'll get much sharper printouts, more vivid colors, and results that look and feel like real photographic prints. Besides, at sizes over 4 x 6 or so, making your own printouts is still less expensive than getting prints from the drugstore, even when you factor in printer cartridges and photo paper.

> **Tip:** To save money and avoid wasting your high-quality photo paper, use plain inkjet paper for test prints. When you're sure you've got the composition, color balance, and resolution of your photo just right, load up your expensive glossy photo paper for your final printouts.

Printing from iPhoto

When you choose File→Print (⌘-P) in iPhoto, you don't see the standard Mac OS X Print dialog box—the one that asks you how many copies you want to print, which pages you want included, and so on. (As shown in Figure 8-2, you must click Advanced Options to see these controls.)

Instead, you're presented with iPhoto's own private version of the Print command, with four photo-specific printing options at your disposal: Standard Prints, Full Page, Greeting Cards, and Contact Sheet.

Each of these four printing styles is discussed in detail on the following pages.

POWER USERS' CLINIC

Advanced Printing Options

As mentioned earlier, the "advanced" printing options that appear when you click the Advanced Options button in the Print dialog box aren't really advanced. They're the standard, everyday options that you find in the Print dialog box when printing from any other Mac OS X program, as shown in Figure 8-2.

You can safely ignore many of these options, which vary depending on which printer you're using. For example, unless you're using a fancy printer equipped with multiple paper trays and double-sided printing capabilities, there's no need to concern yourself with the Duplex and Paper Feed options. The Error Handling panel, which appears if you're using a PostScript printer, controls arcane details about how your printer reports PostScript errors; you'll be happier if you don't even think about it. And the Summary panel is just a window showing your current printer settings, with nothing to turn on or off.

Some of these other printing options are more useful:

- **Copies & Pages.** You don't have to use this panel to choose the number of copies you want printed; you do that using the standard iPhoto print options. However, this panel does allow you to set a specific *range* of pages for printing, which can be helpful. You can print just the first page or two of a 26-page contact sheet, for example, to test your print settings.

- **Output Options.** This panel offers another way to save your print job as a PDF file, exactly like the one described on page 163.

- **Printer Features.** This panel is important, since it's where you can make adjustments that are specific to *your* particular printer. Depending on the make and model of your printer, this might be where you set print resolution, quality, and speed settings.

Standard-Sized Prints

Use this method to print out photos that conform to standard photo sizes, like 5 x 7 or 8 x 10. This is especially useful if you intend to mount your printed photos in store-bought picture frames, which are designed to hold photos in these standard sizes.

Tip: Once again, printing photos at standard sizes works best if your digital photos are trimmed so that they fit perfectly into one of the three pre-set proportions—4 x 6, 5 x 7, or 8 x 10. Use iPhoto's Constrained Cropping tool, explained on page 125, to trim your photos to precisely these sizes.

---

1. **Select the thumbnail(s) of the photo(s) you want to print.**

   Alternatively, you can open the photo in Edit mode before you print it; the Print command is accessible in all of iPhoto's five modes. You can also select more than one photo—a good idea if you want to get the most out of your expensive inkjet paper. Just highlight the ones you want, using the techniques described on page 97.

2. **Choose File→Print, or press ⌘-P.**

   The iPhoto Print dialog box appears.

3. **From the Style pop-up menu, choose Standard Prints.**

   This is the default setting, but if you've been printing using other styles, you may have to switch it back.

4. **Using the Size buttons, choose the size of prints you want.**

   You have three standard photo sizes to choose from—4 x 6, 5 x 7, and 8 x 10. Remember, though, that choosing a larger size stretches the pixels of your photo across a larger area, reducing the photo's resolution and potentially degrading its print quality. For best results, don't choose 8 x 10 unless the picture you're print-

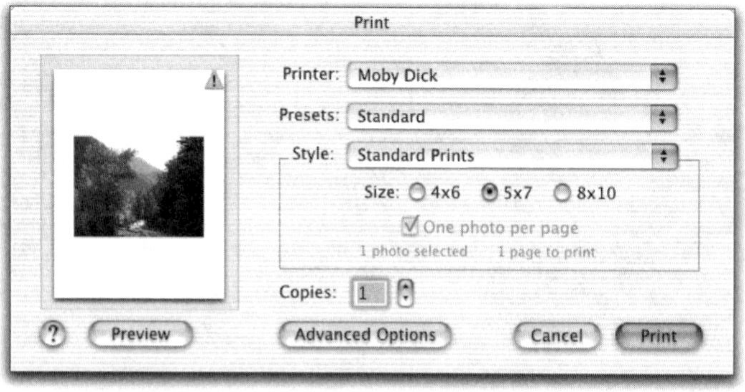

Figure 8-3:
The Preview panel on the left side of the Print Dialog box does more than show you how your photo is going to look on the printed page. See that warning icon on the top right corner of the preview image? That's iPhoto's way of warning you that you've chosen a print size that's too large, given the resolution of your digital photo. If you ignore the warning, your printout will likely have jagged edges or fuzzy detail.

ing is at least 1800 x 2200 pixels. (A yellow triangle warns you if the resolution is too low; see Figure 8-3.)

The Preview panel displays how your photo will be positioned on the paper, as shown in Figure 8-3.

5. **Select the number of photos you want printed on each page.**

When the "One photo per page" checkbox is turned off, iPhoto fits as many photos as it can on each page, based on the paper size (which you select using the File→Page Setup command) and the photo size that you've chosen. Conversely, when the checkbox is turned on, you get one photo at the center of each page.

When printing to letter-size paper, iPhoto can fit two 4 x 6 or 5 x 7 pictures on each page.

6. **Choose the number of copies you want to make.**

You can either type the number into the Copies field or click the arrows to increase or decrease the number.

7. **Click the Print button (or press Enter).**

Your printer scurries into action, printing your photos as you've requested.

Greeting Cards

When you choose Greeting Card from the Style pop-up menu of the Print dialog box, iPhoto automatically rotates and positions your photo (Figure 8-4). You could conceivably print out cards on standard letter-size paper and then fold it into halves or quarters, but this option is actually designed for printing on special inkjet greeting-card paper. This kind of glossy paper stock, made by Epson and others, comes prescored and perforated for tidy edge-to-edge printing and crisp folding.

Here's how you print out a greeting card:

Figure 8-4:
iPhoto's Greeting Card printing doesn't create any actual greeting card content—no titles, holiday-themed icons, fancy borders, or pithy verses. All you get is a printout of your photo on an otherwise blank sheet of paper, ready to be folded into a greeting card–shaped configuration. Coming up with an actual greeting and writing it on the card is entirely up to you.

1. **Select or open the photo(s) you want to print.**

   Only one photo goes on each card. If you've selected more than one picture, you'll see only the first one illustrated in the preview.

2. **Choose File→Print, or press ⌘-P.**

   The Print dialog box appears.

3. **From the Style menu, choose Greeting Card. Pick a greeting card style using the radio buttons.**

   You have two choices: Single-fold, which prints your photo onto a half sheet of paper; or Double-fold, which fits your photo into a quarter-page printing area. The Preview panel on the left side of the Print dialog box illustrates how each of these options will appear in the final printout.

4. **In the Copies field, enter the number of copies you want to make.**

   If you selected multiple photos in step 1, iPhoto will print multiple greeting cards, one per photo. The number you enter here is different, in that it tells iPhoto how many *duplicates* of each one to print.

5. **Click the Print button (or press Enter).**

   Print, fold, sign, and mail.

Printing Full Page Photos

iPhoto's Full Page printing option reduces or enlarges each photo so that it completely fills a single page.

Figure 8-5:
Use the Margins slider to change the width of the margins around your photo. You can add margins of up to one inch. You can also specify zero margins, although that doesn't mean you'll get edge-to-edge printing. You will, however, get the smallest margins your particular printer can muster.

FREQUENTLY ASKED QUESTION

Changing Page Sizes

iPhoto's Print command lets me choose the size of the photos I want to print, but not the size of the paper I'm printing them on. Can't I pick a different paper size?

Yes, but remember that you change this kind of setting in the Page Setup dialog box, not the Print dialog box. Choose File→Page Setup, and then select the paper size you want using the Paper Size pop-up menu.

To make Full Page prints, select the photos you want to print, press ⌘-P, and then choose Full Page from the Style pop-up menu in the Print dialog box (Figure 8-5).

With Full Page printing, it takes ten pages to print ten photos, of course—but when you make Standard Prints or Contact Sheets, iPhoto can fit more than one photo on each page.

Tip: iPhoto's Print dialog box tells you how many photos you've selected and how many pages it will take to print them all. However, this information is easy to miss because it appears in dim, grayed-out text near the center of the dialog box (in Figure 8-5, directly under the Margins slider).

Contact Sheets

The Contact Sheet option prints out a *grid* of photos, tiling as many as 112 different pictures onto a single page—eight columns, fourteen rows.

Photographers use contact sheets as quick and useful references when organizing or looking for photos—a poor man's iPhoto, if you think about it. But this printing option is also handy in some other practical ways.

POWER USERS' CLINIC

Professional Print Output

As Chapter 8 makes clear, iPhoto has plenty of printing options: greeting cards, contact sheets, and multiple standard prints side by side on a single sheet of paper. But without help, iPhoto can't print specialized *combination* templates like the portrait galleries delivered by professional photographers.

Fortunately, a $20 companion program called Portraits & Prints nicely fills in iPhoto's printing weaknesses. (You can download it either from *www.missingmanuals.com* or from Econ Technologies at *www.econtechnologies.com/site/Pages/pnp_overview.html.*)

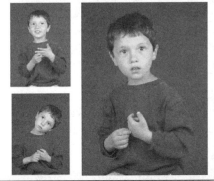

Once again, the idea is that you'll drag selected photos directly out of the iPhoto window and into the Portraits & Prints window. There, you can boost or reduce color intensity, sharpen, crop, rotate, add brightness, and remove red eye. But all that is just an appetizer for Portraits & Prints' main dish: a delicious variety of printing templates, like the one shown here.

The program comes with six different "portrait sets" that let you arrange different pictures at different sizes on the same sheet of paper. You can even save your layouts as *catalogs*, so that you can reuse them, or reprint them at a later date. If you designate Portraits & Prints as your preferred external photo editing program (page 135), any changes you make while in Portraits & Prints will be reflected in iPhoto's thumbnails.

If you do much photo printing at all, you'll probably find Portraits & Prints well worth its price—which is about half that of a color ink cartridge.

- By printing several pictures side by side on the same page, you can easily make quality comparisons among them without using two sheets of paper.

- Use contact sheet printing to make test prints, saving ink and paper. Sometimes a 2 x 3 print is all you need to determine whether a picture is too dark or whether its colors are wildly off when rendered by an inkjet printer. Don't make those full-page prints until you're sure you've adjusted your photo to print correctly.

- If you're willing to settle for printed photos that are smaller that 4 x 6, you can save yourself a lot of paper by printing four, six, or eight photos on each sheet of paper. Cut them apart with a paper cutter, scissors, or an X-Acto knife.

- Contact sheet printing is the easiest way to print multiple copies of a *single* picture if you want to produce lots of wallet-sized (or smaller) copies.

Contact Sheet printing options

To make Contact Sheet prints, choose Contact Sheet from the Style pop-up menu in the Print dialog box. Your printing options vary, depending on how many photos you selected in the Print command. To wit:

- If no photos are selected, the Contact Sheet option will print *all* the photos in the current album (or the Photo Library, if that's what's selected). Use the Across slider to change the size of the grid, and therefore the number of photos that will appear on each printed page. iPhoto will print as many pages as needed to include all the photos in your current view.

- If several photos are selected, iPhoto will print a contact sheet containing only the selected photos.

Tip: The Save Paper checkbox appears only when you're printing more than one photo. It reduces the amount of white space that iPhoto puts between each photo, squishing the pictures closer together on the page. With more photos squeezed onto each page, you end up using less paper to print your contact sheet pages.

- When only *one* photo is selected, iPhoto clones that one photo across the whole grid, printing one sheet of duplicate images at whatever size you specify using the slider control, as shown in Figure 8-6.

Using the Preview Button

A mini preview of your printout-to-be is always visible at the left side of the Print dialog box. But this postage stamp preview is far too small to show much detail. Worse, it shows you only the *first page* of a multipage job.

For a better preview, click the Preview button. iPhoto processes the print job, just as if you had hit the Print button—a "Print" progress bar appears at this point, indicating that the job is "on its way" to the printer. Instead of transmitting the job to your printer hardware, however, iPhoto creates a temporary PDF (Acrobat) file. This file opens in Preview, the free graphics-viewing program that comes with Mac OS X.

Tip: *Depending on the size of your print job, building a preview can take awhile. iPhoto has to process all the image data involved, just as if it were really printing.*

You end up with a full-size, full-resolution electronic version of your print job. Using the commands in Preview's Display menu, you can zoom in or out to view details, scroll across pages, and move from page to page (to preview every page of a contact sheet, for example). You're seeing exactly how iPhoto is going to render your job when it is actually printed, using the print options you selected.

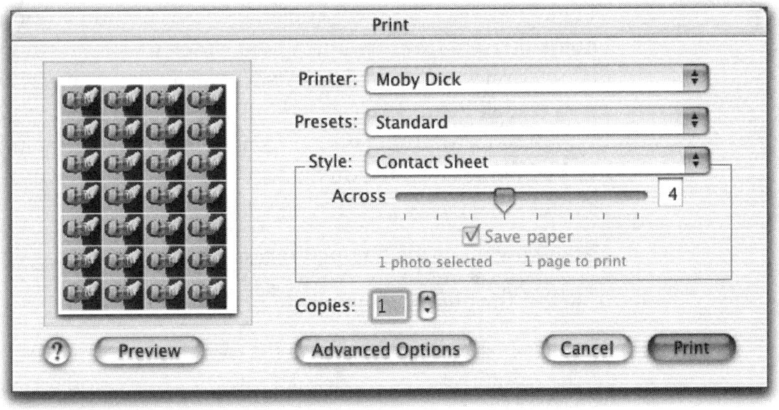

Figure 8-6:
Need a sheet of wallet-sized photos to send to relatives? The easiest way is to use the Contact Sheet printing option. The trick is to select just one photo before choosing the Print command. Then drag the grid slider so that you have three or four rows of duplicate photos.

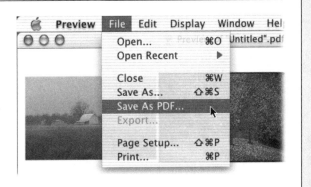

If you like what you see in the PDF preview, you have the following two choices:

- If you want to *keep* the preview—in order to distribute an electronic version of a contact sheet, for example—you can save it, using one of the options shown in Figure 8-7. The result is a PDF file, which anyone with a Mac, Windows PC, or Unix machine can open using the free Acrobat Reader program that comes on every computer.

Figure 8-7:
The documents generated by the Preview command are intended to be temporary files; if you close one, it will disappear without even asking if you want to save it. But you can save a preview document permanently by choosing File→Save As or File→Save As PDF. Note this important difference between the two commands: Save As preserves only the first page of the preview as a TIFF file, while the Save As PDF command captures all the preview pages as a stand-alone PDF file.

• Close the Preview window, return to iPhoto, and choose File→Print again (the Print dialog box will have closed itself automatically). Now, confident that you're going to get the results you expect, click the Print button and send the job to your printer.

Ordering Prints Online

Even if you don't have a high-quality color printer, traditional prints of your digital photos are only a few clicks away—if you have an Internet connection and you're willing to spend a little money, that is.

Thanks to a deal between Apple and Kodak, you can order prints of your digital photos directly from within iPhoto. After you select the size and quantity of the pictures you want printed, one click is all it takes to have iPhoto transmit your photos to Kodak Print Services and bill your credit card for the order. The rates range from 49 cents for a single 4 x 6 print to about $20 for a jumbo 20 x 30 poster. Your finished photos, printed on high-quality glossy photographic paper, are sent to you within two days.

Here's how the print-buying process works:

1. **Select the photos you want to print.**

   Click an album in the album list to order prints of everything in it, or select only the specific photos you want. Only the photos you select will appear in the Order Prints window.

2. **Put iPhoto into Share mode by clicking the Share button below the main iPhoto window. Then click the Order Prints icon on the bottom panel.**

   Now the Mac must go online to check in with the Kodak processing center. (If the Mac can't make an Internet connection at all, the Order Prints window shown in Figure 8-8 won't open.)

3. **Click "Enable 1-Click Ordering." Surrender your identity and credit card info.**

   You can't even *play* with the Order Prints window without first enabling and configuring Apple's 1-Click Ordering system. This involves first filling in your

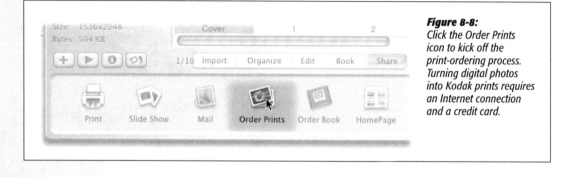

Figure 8-8:
Click the Order Prints icon to kick off the print-ordering process. Turning digital photos into Kodak prints requires an Internet connection and a credit card.

Apple ID (your email address) and matching password. Once you've got an Apple ID, fill in your contact information, credit card details, shipping address, and so on. (This is a one-time task designed to save you time when you place subsequent orders.)

In fact, you must do all of this even if you have no intention of buying anything yet. (Of course, you won't be charged unless you actually order prints.)

For details on the process, see page 210. When the 1-Click Summary screen finally appears, click Done to return to the Order Prints window.

4. **Select the sizes and quantities you want.**

If you want 4 x 6 or 5 x 7 prints of every photo you've selected, just use the text boxes at the top of the dialog box to specify how many copies you want of each.

For more control over sizes and quantities of individual photos, fill in the numbers individually for each photo, scrolling down through the dialog box as necessary. The total cost of your order is updated as you make selections.

Tip: If you want *mostly* prints of one size—5x 7's, for example—type the quantity into the "5x7 prints, quantity" box at the top of the window, so that iPhoto fills in that number for every photo. Now you're free to *change* the quantity for the few photos that you *don't* want to order at 5 x 7.

Figure 8-9:
The Order Prints window lets you order six different types of prints from your photos—from a set of four wallet-sized prints to mammoth 20 x 30 posters. Use the scroll bar on the right to scroll through all the photos you've selected to specify how many copies of each photo you want to order. If you need to change your shipping, contact, or credit card information, click the Edit 1-Click Settings button to modify your Apple ID profile.

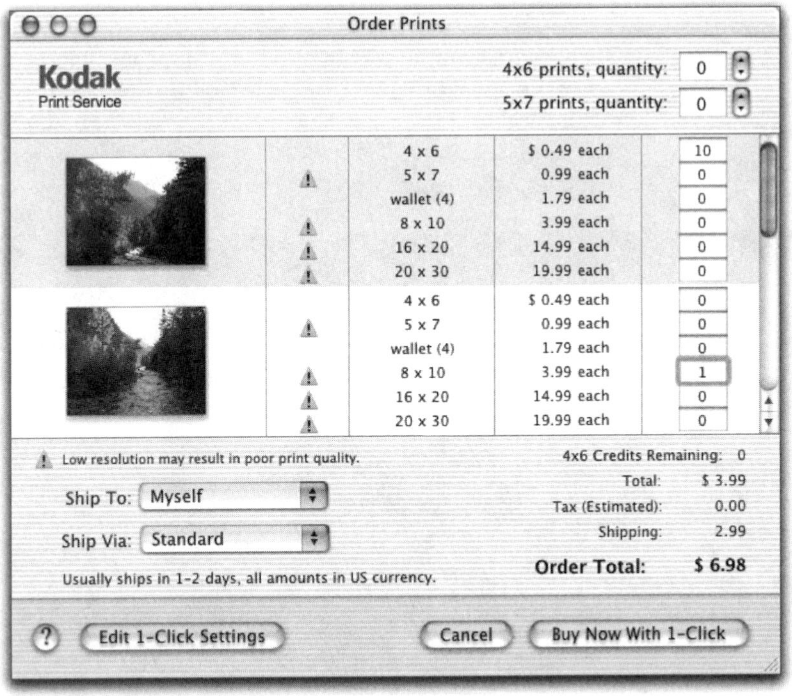

As you order, pay heed to the alert icons (little yellow triangles) that may appear on certain lines of the order form (visible, in spades, in Figure 8-9). These are iPhoto's standard warnings declaring that certain photos don't have a high enough resolution to be printed at some of the sizes offered. A 1600 x 1200 pixel photo makes a great 5 x 7, but a terrible 16 x 20 enlargement. *Never* order prints in a size that's been flagged with a low-resolution alert (unless you're the kind of person who thrives on disappointment).

Tip: You'll see the same warning icon when you print your own photos and order photo books (Chapter 10). As always, you have few attractive choices: Order a smaller print, don't order a print at all, or order the print and accept the lower quality that results.

---

5. **Click the "Buy Now With 1-Click" button to order the prints.**

   "Buy Now" means just that. You don't receive an "Are you sure?" message, allowing you to back out of your purchase. Your photos are transferred, your credit card is billed, and you go sit by the mailbox.

   A dialog box appears, showing the reference number for your order and a message saying that you'll be receiving a confirmation by email.

As you may have discovered, ordering from iPhoto is not the most economical way to get prints. A batch of 24 standard 4 x 6 snapshots costs about $12, plus shipping, which is considerably more than you'd pay for processing a role of film at the local drugstore.

On the other hand, you get to print only the prints that you actually want, instead of developing a roll of 36 prints only to find that two of them are any good. This feature is ideal for creating enlargements that would be impossible to create on the typical inkjet printer. And it's a handy way to send top-notch photo prints directly to friends and relatives who don't have computers.

UP TO SPEED

How Low Is Too Low?

When you order photos online, the Order Prints form automatically warns you when a selected photo has a resolution that's too low to result in a good-quality print. But just what does Kodak consider too low? Here's the list of Kodak's official minimum resolution recommendations.

To order this size picture:	Your photo should be at least:
Wallet-sized	640 x 480 pixels
4 x 5	768 x 512 pixels
5 x 7	1152 x 768 pixels
8 x 10	1536 x 1024 pixels

These are *minimum* requirements, not suggested settings. Your photos will look better in print, in fact, if you *exceed* these resolution settings.

For example, a 1536 x 1024 pixel photo printed at 8 x 10 inches meets Kodak's minimum recommendation, but has an effective resolution of 153 x 128 dpi—a relatively low resolution for high-quality printing. A photo measuring 2200 x 1760 pixels, printed at the same size, would have a resolution of 220 dpi—and look much better on paper, with sharper detail and subtler variations in color.

CHAPTER 9

Photos Online

Holding a beautifully rendered glossy color print created from your own digital image is a glorious feeling. But unless you have an uncle in the inkjet-cartridge business, you could go broke printing your own photos. Ordering high-quality prints with iPhoto is terrific fun, too, but it's slow and expensive.

For the discerning digital photographer who craves both instant gratification and economy, the solution is to put your photos *online*—either by emailing them to others, or by posting them on the Web.

Fortunately, transferring your pictures from iPhoto to the Web doesn't require that you buy a Web server, register a domain (dot-com) name, or even design HTML pages. With minimal setup, iPhoto can connect directly to Apple's own iTools Web site and publish your photos automatically. And emailing photos is even easier.

Note: In the summer of 2002, Apple changed both the name and the price for its Web-hosting services. As you read the following chapters, please mentally substitute ".Mac" for "iTools," and "$100 per year" for "free."

Emailing Photos

Emailing from iPhoto takes just a few clicks and doesn't require you to sign up for anything—assuming that you already have an email account. It's perfect for quickly sending off a single photo—or even a handful of photos—to friends, family, and co-workers. (If you have a whole *batch* of photos to share, on the other hand, consider using the Web publishing feature described later in this chapter.)

The most important thing to know about emailing photos is this: *full-size photos are usually too big to email.*

Suppose, for example, that you want to send three photos along to some friends—terrific shots that you captured with your 3-megapixel camera.

First, a little math: A typical 3-megapixel shot might consume a megabyte of disk space. So sending along three shots would constitute a 3-megabyte package.

Why is that bad? Let us count the ways:

- It will take you 12 minutes to send (using a standard dial-up modem).

- It will take your recipients 12 minutes to download. During that time, the recipients must sit there, not even knowing what they're downloading. And when you're done hogging their time and account fees, they might not consider what you sent worth the wait.

- Even if they do open the pictures you sent, the average high-resolution shot is much too big for the screen. It does you no good to email someone a 3-megapixel photo (2048 x 1536 pixels) when his monitor's maximum resolution is only 1024 x 768. If you're lucky, his graphics software will intelligently shrink the image to fit his screen (otherwise, he'll see only a quarter of the photo)—but you'll still have to contend with his irritation at having waited 12 minutes for so much superfluous resolution.

- The typical Internet account has a limited mailbox size. If the mail collection exceeds 5 MB or so, that mailbox is automatically shut down until it's emptied. Your massive 3-megabyte photo package might be what pushes your hapless recipient's mailbox over its limit. She might miss out on important messages that get bounced as a result.

For years, this business of emailing photos has baffled beginners and enraged experts—and for many people who haven't yet discovered iPhoto, the confusion continues.

It's all different when you use iPhoto. Instead of unquestioningly attaching a multi-megabyte graphic to an email message and sending off the whole bloated thing, its first instinct is to offer you the opportunity to send a scaled-down, reasonably sized version of your photo instead (see Figure 9-1). If you take advantage of this feature, your modem-using friends will savor the thrill of seeing your digital shots without enduring the agony of a half-hour email download.

The Mail Photo Command

iPhoto doesn't have any emailing features of its own. All it can do is get your pictures ready and hand them off to Apple's Mail program, the email program that came with your copy of Mac OS X. Here's how the process works:

1. Select the thumbnails of the photo(s) you want to email.

   You can use any of the picture-selecting techniques described on page 97. (If you fail to select a thumbnail, you'll get an error message asking you to select a photo and try again.)

2. **In the main iPhoto window, click the Share button.**

   iPhoto enters Share mode, with its expanse of nine buttons at the bottom of the window.

3. **On the panel at the bottom of the iPhoto window, click the Mail icon.**

   The dialog box shown in Figure 9-1 appears.

Figure 9-1:
The Mail Photo dialog box not only lets you choose the size of photo attachments, it also keeps track of how many photos you've selected and estimates how large your attachments are going to be, based on your selection.

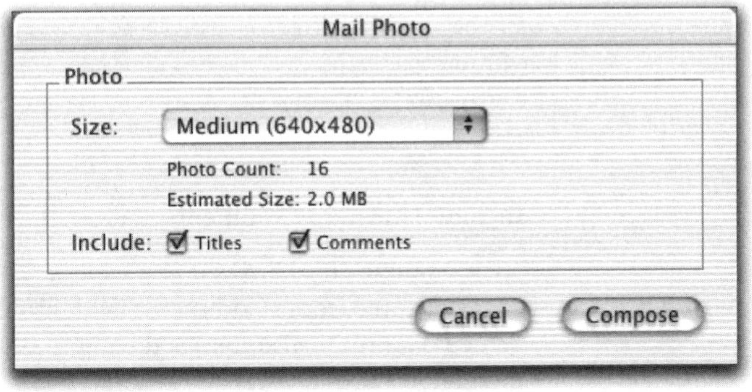

Mail Photo

Photo

Size: Medium (640x480)

Photo Count: 16
Estimated Size: 2.0 MB

Include: ☑ Titles ☑ Comments

Cancel   Compose

4. **Choose a size for your photo(s).**

   This is the moment. As noted above, iPhoto offers to send a scaled-down version of the photo. The Size pop-up menu in the Mail Photo dialog box, shown in Figure 9-1, offers four choices.

   Choose **Small (240x320)** to keep your email attachments super-small—and if you don't expect the recipient of your email to print the photo. (A photo this size can't produce a quality print any larger than a postage stamp.) On the other hand, your photos will consume less than 100 K apiece, making downloads quick and easy for those with dial-up connections.

Note: Don't be weirded out by the fact that iPhoto, for the first and only time, displays these dimensions backwards (height by width). How it should read, of course, is "Small (320x240)."

   Choosing **Medium (640x480)** yields a file that will fill a nice chunk of your recipient's screen, with plenty of detail. It's even enough data to produce a slightly larger print—about 2 x 3 inches. Even so, the file size (and download time) remains reasonable; this setting can trim a 2 MB, 4-megapixel image down to an attachment of less than 150 K.

   The **Large (1280x960)** setting downsizes even your large photos to about 450 K, preserving enough pixels to make good 4 x 5 prints and completely fill the typical recipient's screen. Don't send more than one photo this way to the same person at the same time, however (unless she has a high-speed connection like a cable modem or DSL).

Despite all of these cautions, there may be times when a photo is worth sending at **Full Size.** Maybe both you and the recipient have high-speed Internet connections, or maybe you're submitting a photo for printing or publication.

In any case, this option attaches an exact copy of your original photo, at its original dimensions. If your original is in a file format other than JPEG (a Photoshop file, for example), this setting still converts the photo *to* JPEG, which can reduce its file size.

Note: iPhoto retains each picture's proportions when resizing it. But if a picture doesn't have 4:3 proportions (maybe you cropped it, or maybe it came from a camera that isn't set to create 4:3 photos), it may wind up *smaller* than the indicated dimensions. In other words, think of the choices in the Size pop-up menu as meaning, "this size or smaller."

---

5. **Include Titles and Comments, if desired.**

   Turn on these checkboxes if you want iPhoto to copy the title of the photo and any text stored in the Comments field into the body of the email. When Titles is turned on, iPhoto also inserts the photo's title into the Subject line of the email message.

Note: If multiple photos are selected when you generate an email message, the Titles option produces a generic Subject line: "5 great iPhotos" (or whatever the number is). You can edit this proposed text, of course, before actually sending your email.

---

6. **Click Compose.**

   At this point, iPhoto processes your photos—converting them to JPEG format and, if you requested it, resizing them. It then launches the Mail program, creates

---

FREQUENTLY ASKED QUESTION

Using iPhoto with Entourage, Eudora, MailSmith...

Hey, I don't use Apple Mail as my email program! But iPhoto doesn't give me a choice— it's Mail or nothing. How can I get iPhoto to send my photos via Entourage?

You're absolutely right. Even if you have a different email program selected in the Internet panel of your Mac OS X System Preferences, iPhoto stubbornly refuses to launch anything but Mail when you click Compose.

There's a great workaround, though, thanks to the pro-

gramming efforts of Simon Jacquier. Using his free utility, iPhoto Mailer Patcher, you can make iPhoto work obediently with Microsoft Entourage, Eudora, Mailsmith, PowerMail, or QuickMail Pro. As shown here, it replaces the actual Mail button on iPhoto's bottom-edge panel with the icon of your preferred email program.

Sound good? You can download iPhoto Mailer Patcher from *http://homepage.mac.com/jacksim/software.*

a new email message, and attaches your photos to the message. (Behind the scenes, iPhoto uses AppleScript to accomplish these tasks.)

7. **In the To box, type your recipient's email address, and then click Send.**

Your photos are on their merry way.

Tip: iPhoto always converts photos into JPEG format when emailing them. If you want preserve a file's original format when emailing a Photoshop file or a PDF, *don't* use the Mail Photo feature. Instead, create a new message in the Mail program manually, then drag the thumbnails from iPhoto directly into the message window to attach them. (If you want them scaled down, you'll have to edit them in another program, as described on page 135.)

Publishing Photos on the Web

Putting your photos on the Web is the ultimate way to share them with the world. If the idea of enabling the vast throngs of the Internet-using public to browse, view, download, save, and print *your* photos sounds appealing, read on; it's amazingly easy to get your photos from iPhoto to the Internet.

Before you can post photos online using iPhoto's built-in Web tools, you'll need a free *iTools* account. iTools is Apple's online suite of Internet services, which includes

---

UP TO SPEED

Getting a Free iTools Account

iTools, Apple's free online service, provides everything you need to put a collection of your photos online. Mac OS X makes it easier than ever to sign up for an iTools account. If you don't already have an account, here's how to get one.

Choose →System Preferences, or click the System Preferences icon on your Dock. When you click the Internet icon, the iTools tab is staring you in the face. Click Sign Up.

Now you go online, where your Web browser opens up to the iTools sign-up screen. Fill in your name and address, make up an account name and password, and, if you like, turn off the checkbox that invites you to receive junk mail.

You're also asked to make up a question and answer (such as, "First grade teacher's name?" and "Flanders"). If you ever forget your password, the iTools software will help you— provided you can answer this question correctly. Click Continue.

An account summary screen appears (print it or save it). On the next screen, the system offers to email your friends to let them know about your new address (which is *whatever-name-you-chose@mac.com*).

The final step is to return to the Internet pane of System Preferences. On the iTools tab, fill in the account name and password you just composed. You're now iTools-ready!

---

email accounts, secure file-backup, Web-site hosting, and a bunch of other freebies. If you don't already have an iTools account, see the "Getting a Free iTools Account" box on the previous page. You'll have one in less than five minutes.

Three Roads to Webdom

iPhoto actually provides three different Web publishing routes (two of which require iTools), offering varying degrees of sophistication and complexity.

- **The easiest, most hands-off approach:** Use the HomePage feature within iPhoto. With only a couple of mouse clicks, this feature lets you construct Web pages, transfer them to the Internet, and make them available to the public. (An iTools account is required.)

What's especially nice about the resulting Web page is that it presents a tidy collection of thumbnail images—a gallery that downloads relatively quickly into your audience's browsers. Then, when they click one of the thumbnails, a new window opens up to display the picture at full size (see Figure 9-2).

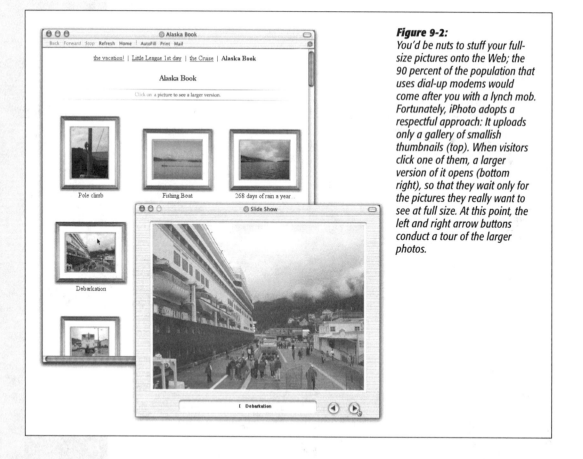

Figure 9-2:
You'd be nuts to stuff your full-size pictures onto the Web; the 90 percent of the population that uses dial-up modems would come after you with a lynch mob. Fortunately, iPhoto adopts a respectful approach: It uploads only a gallery of smallish thumbnails (top). When visitors click one of them, a larger version of it opens (bottom right), so that they wait only for the pictures they really want to see at full size. At this point, the left and right arrow buttons conduct a tour of the larger photos.

- **More effort, more design and layout options:** Copy photos from iPhoto to the Pictures folder of your iDisk (a free, 20 MB "virtual hard drive" based on the Internet). Then use the HomePage features at Apple's Web site (instead of the layout tools in iPhoto) to set up your pages.

- **For the experienced Web-page designer:** If you already have a Web site, you can use iPhoto's Export command to generate Web pages (HTML documents) that already contain your photos. You can upload these files, with the accompanying graphics, to your Web site, whether that's an iTools account or any other Web-hosting service. (Most Internet accounts, including those provided by America Online, Earthlink, and other service providers, come with free space for Web pages uploaded this way.)

This is the most labor-intensive route, but it offers much more flexibility if you know how to work with HTML to create more sophisticated pages.

All three of these methods are detailed in the following pages.

Method 1: Use HomePage in iPhoto

Web publishing doesn't get any easier than with iPhoto's built-in HomePage feature. Your photos end up on a handsome-looking Web page in just a few quick steps—and you don't have to know the first thing about HTML.

1. **In iPhoto, select the photos you want to put on the Web—or click the album that contains them.**

   Make sure you've got iPhoto in Share mode. If you don't, click the Share button on the row of mode buttons just under the main photo-viewing pane.

Note: The HomePage feature in iPhoto can't handle more than 48 photos per Web page. If you want to "publish" more than that, you'll have to create a series of separate pages to stay within the limit.

---

2. **Click the HomePage button.**

   After it connects to the Internet, iPhoto opens its Publish HomePage window, which offers a visual menu of predesigned frame styles for your photos (see Figure 9-3).

Note: If you don't have an iTools account when you click this button, iPhoto alerts you to this fact and opens the Internet panel of System Preferences so that you can sign yourself up for an account. Follow the steps in the "Getting a Free iTools Account" box on page 171 to create an account.

Another note: If nothing happens when you click the HomePage button, it's because your Mac can't establish an Internet connection.

---

3. **Click a frame style.**

   The Publish HomePage window immediately displays a mock-up of how your finished Web page is going to look (Figure 9-3), displaying the thumbnails in

---

whatever order they appear in iPhoto. You can choose from five different frame and text styles by clicking on the photo thumbnails along the bottom of the window.

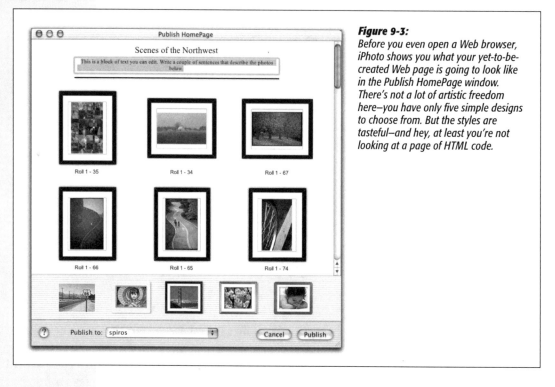

Figure 9-3:
Before you even open a Web browser, iPhoto shows you what your yet-to-be-created Web page is going to look like in the Publish HomePage window. There's not a lot of artistic freedom here—you have only five simple designs to choose from. But the styles are tasteful—and hey, at least you're not looking at a page of HTML code.

4. **Edit the page title, subtitle, and individual photo titles.**

   Just click on a text block to edit it. You can use iPhoto's spelling checker, if you need the help (page 205).

   If you don't bother changing the photo names, iPhoto will simply use whatever titles the photos have in the program itself. (On the other hand, be careful: Any changes you make to the photo titles here are reflected in iPhoto.)

Tip: There's a 40-character limit on the captions you can create using iPhoto's HomePage feature. You can, however, expand these into longer captions—up to 80 characters—if you later edit the Web pages you create here using the page-editing tools in the HomePage section of the iTools Web site.

---

5. **Click the Publish button.**

   This is the big moment: iPhoto connects to the iTools Web site, scales down your photos to a reasonable size, and then transfers them to the server (shown in Figure 9-4, top).

When the process is complete, as indicated by the alert dialog box shown in Figure 9-4 (bottom), you can go to the page and see your results.

Note: If you include larger photos in your Web page, iPhoto automatically scales them down to 800 x 600 pixel JPEG files, so they can be more easily loaded and displayed within a Web browser. If you want your Web pages to include *exact* copies of your original photos—regardless of size or file format—you must copy them to your iDisk yourself and then use the online HomePage tools to create your Web pages, as described later in this chapter.

In any case, beware: Your iDisk holds only 20 MB of data—a limit that's easy to hit once you're addicted to self-publishing. (If you're *really* addicted, Apple is happy to raise the ceiling to 100 MB or even a gigabyte—for an annual fee.)

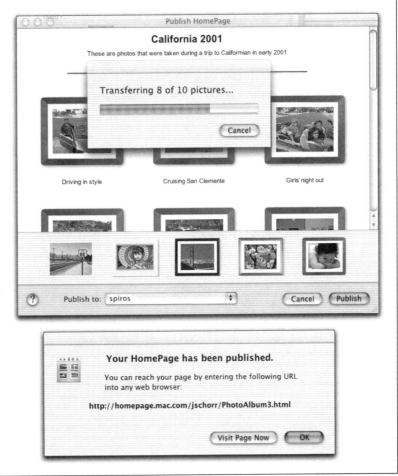

Figure 9-4:
Top: When you've got titles and captions looking the way you want, clicking Publish uploads the photos to your iTools account. Depending on the size and number of the photos you've selected, and the speed of your Internet connection, this can take some time.

Bottom: Once iPhoto is done transferring photos to your iTools account, you see this confirmation message, indicating that your new Web page has been born. You can see your finished page on the Web immediately by clicking Visit Page Now, but pay heed to the URL listed above the buttons; that's the Web address you need to give out if you want others to come visit the page. (This address is "live," meaning you can either click it to visit the page or drag across it to copy it.)

What you get when you're done

When you see what you've created with iPhoto, you'll be impressed: It's a sharp-looking, stylishly titled Web page with thumbnails neatly arranged in a three-column grid. Clicking one of these thumbnails opens an enlarged version of the picture, complete with Previous and Next buttons (Figure 9-2). You can return to your main index page at any time, or use the buttons in the slide show window to navigate through the larger versions of your pictures.

Tip: The URLs for your iTools-hosted Web sites (such as *http://hompage.mac.com/yackell/ PhotoAlbum2.html*) are case-sensitive—a point not to be forgotten when you share the site's address with friends. If you type one of these addresses into a Web browser without the correct capitalization, you'll get only a "missing page" message.

Editing the text of the Web page

To touch up the picture names or page title, visit *http://itools.mac.com,* click the HomePage icon, click the name of the page you want to edit (in the list depicted in Figure 9-5), and then click the Edit button beneath it. You wind up on a Web-based page-editing window like the one shown in Figure 9-3, where you're free to change the text in any of the title or caption boxes.

Editing the pictures on a Web page

Remember that your photo gallery Web page depicts *all* of the photos in a specific folder in your iDisk's Pictures folder. Adding, rearranging, or deleting photos from your Web page is therefore something of a hassle.

On the other hand, why bother? Publishing Web pages like this is easy, relatively quick, and absolutely free; in many cases, the simplest way to make changes to a page is simply to re-publish it from within iPhoto.

Of course, then you'll want to delete the original Web page. To do that, visit *http:// itools.mac.com.* Click the HomePage icon; proceed as shown in Figure 9-5.

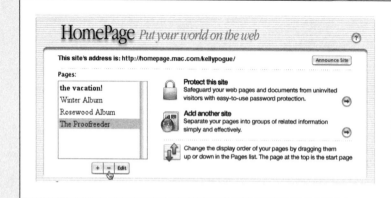

Figure 9-5:
Deleting a Web page is easy once you've signed onto the iTools HomePage Web site. Click the name of the page you want to delete, and then click the minus-sign (–) button, as shown here by the tiny pointing-hand cursor at bottom. "Are you sure?" you're asked; click Yes.

Note: Deleting a Web page doesn't delete the photos that were on it; they remain in your iDisk's Pictures folder. If iTools ever reports that your iDisk is out of room, you may want to burrow into that Pictures folder (specifically, into its Photo Album Pictures folder) for some housecleaning. See the box at the bottom of this page for more about this folder's contents.

Method 2: Use iTools

The incredible simplicity of iPhoto's HomePage feature comes at a price: The design options available are strictly limited. You're stuck with a three-column grid, one thumbnail size, a white background, and five picture-frame styles for all of your Web pages.

If you'd like a lot more flexibility—different colors, more font choices, and so on—consider bypassing the HomePage feature in iPhoto completely. Instead, use the much more powerful version of HomePage that lives on the iTools Web site. Composing your page online with HomePage takes a bit more effort than using iPhoto's built-in Web-site-making features, but it's still a breeze.

To get started with HomePage, you must copy the photos you want to publish from iPhoto to the Pictures folder of your iDisk—in fact, into a *new folder* in the Pictures folder, one folder per Web page. (If your iDisk isn't already onscreen, just choose Go→iDisk in the Finder, so that its icon appears on your desktop.) You can drag thumbnails directly out of iPhoto and into the Pictures folder on the iDisk.

Once your photos are in the iDisk's Pictures folder, you're ready to create your Web pages. Go to *www.itools.com*, sign in, click the HomePage icon, then click one of the "Create a page" tabs on the HomePage screen to view the styles of pages you can create.

The first tab, Photo Album, is probably the one you'll want to use for photos. Some of the formatting options available are shown in Figure 9-6.

FREQUENTLY ASKED QUESTION

Where Did All the Photos Go?

When iPhoto transfers my photos to the iTools Web site, where do they go?

Everything gets stored on your iDisk, the free 20 MB virtual disk that comes with your iTools account. (Your iDisk looks and behaves like a miniature hard drive, but it's really just a privately reserved chunk of space on one of Apple's secure servers.)

The HTML pages generated by HomePage automatically go in the Sites folder on your iDisk. (In fact, if you know how to use a Web-page creation program like Dreamweaver, you can make changes to your Web pages by editing these documents.)

The photos get dumped into Pictures→Photo Album Pictures on the iDisk, where you'll find each separately exported group of Web-page pictures housed in its own time-stamped folder.

To set up an online photo album, click the miniature image of the design you want. HomePage next asks which photos folder in your Picture folder you want to place on your new Web page, as shown in Figure 9-7. Select a folder of pictures, and then click Choose. After a few moments, your new photo album page appears, with photos already inserted in the appropriate spots.

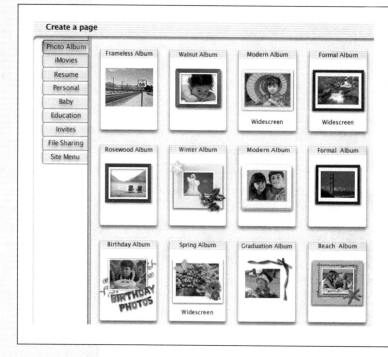

Figure 9-6:
Your Web-publishing options multiply considerably once you hit HomePage. In addition to the photo album themes shown here, you can also create résumés, personal newsletters, baby announcements, and party invitations. You can find these other options by clicking the "Create a page" tabs along the left side of the screen in the main HomePage screen.

(The template thumbnails that say "Widescreen" at the bottom represent Web pages shaped for happiness on extra-wide screens like Apple's Cinema Display and PowerBook G4.)

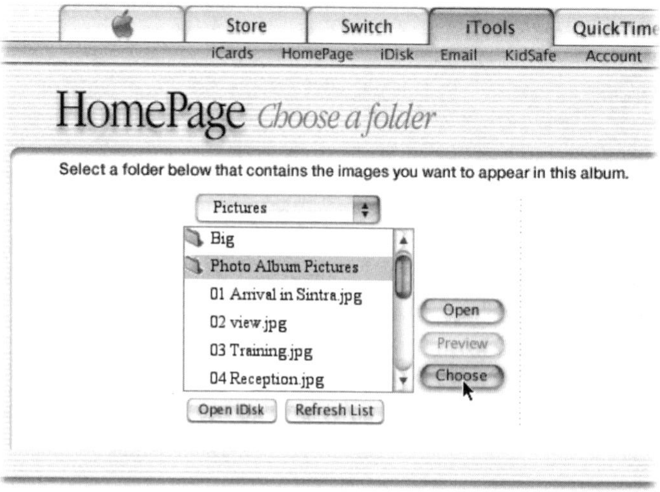

Figure 9-7:
Tell HomePage which photos to use. Two important things to remember here: First, the pictures you choose must be in the Pictures folder of your iDisk at this point, or HomePage won't see them. Second, you can only choose a folder, not individual files. To include a specific set of photos on one page, put them into a folder of their own inside your Pictures folder before you start building the Web page with HomePage.

To finish the project, click Edit at the top of the page to change the chunks of dummy text on the page. (Try to avoid misspellings and typos, unless you want an audience of 300 million to consider you educationally challenged.)

Finally, click Preview to see how the Web page will look. When everything is just the way you want it, click the Publish button. The page goes live, as indicated by the confirmation dialog box shown at the bottom of Figure 9-4.

Tip: You can create as many Web pages as your iDisk will hold, by the way. When you return to the main HomePage screen, a list of your existing Web pages appears, complete with New Page (+), Edit Page, and Delete Page (−) buttons.

Corporations and professional Web designers may sniff at the simplicity of the result—but it takes *them* a lot longer than ten minutes, and more than $0, to do their thing.

Method 3: Export Web Pages

If you already have your own Web site, you don't need iTools or HomePage to create an online photo album. Instead, you can use iPhoto's Export command to generate HTML pages that you can upload to any Web server. You're still saving a lot of time and effort—and you still get that handy, thumbnail gallery page shown in Figure 9-2.

POWER USERS' CLINIC

Adding Password Protection

When you publish your photos using HomePage, the pages you create become accessible to the entire Web-browsing world. Specifically, anyone with a Web browser and an Internet connection can view, and even download, your pictures.

If you don't feel comfortable sharing your photos quite so freely, you can add a password to your HomePage-generated sites, thereby controlling access to your photos. All right, you may not particularly care who sees your dog photos—indeed, you may be trolling for a dog-photo agent. But if you'd rather eliminate the possibility that your boss might see your bachelor party shots, or that your husband might see shots of your old boyfriend, password-

protect the page, and then distribute the password only to those who need to know.

To password-protect your site, access the screen shown in Figure 9-5. Select the name of your site from the Site list at the left side of the page, and then click the "Protect this site" button. On the "Edit your site" screen, turn on the Password On checkbox, insert the password of your choice, and then click Apply Changes.

After you've turned on password protection, anyone who comes to one of your iTools-hosted Web pages will be prompted to enter the password (as shown here) before gaining access to your photos.

The Web pages you export directly from iPhoto don't include any fancy designs or themed graphics. In fact, they're kind of stark; just take a look at Figure 9-10.

But they offer more flexibility than the pages made with HomePage. For example, you can select the background color (or image) that appears on each page, specify the dimensions of thumbnails and images, and choose exactly how many thumbnails you want included on each page.

This is the best method to use if you plan to post the Web pages you create to a Web site of your own—especially if you plan to tinker with the resulting HTML pages yourself.

Preparing the export

Here are the basic Web exporting steps:

1. **In iPhoto, select the photos you want to include on the Web pages.**

   Unlike the HomePage feature, the Export command puts no limit on the number of photos you can export to Web pages in one burst. Select as many photos as you want; iPhoto will generate as many pages as needed to accommodate all of the pictures into your specified grid.

Tip: If you don't select any photos, iPhoto assumes that you want to export all of the photos in the current album (or even the Photo Library or Last Import category).

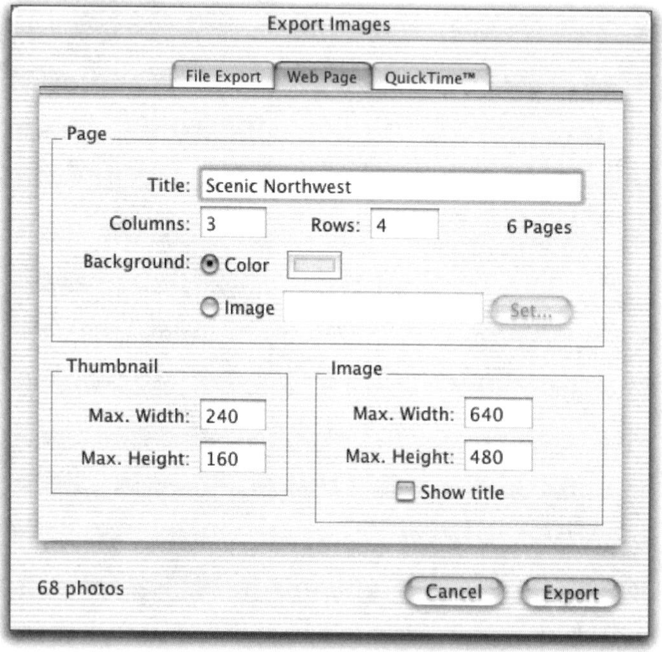

Figure 9-8:
As you change the size of the thumbnail grid or the size of the thumbnails, the number of pages generated to handle the images changes. The page count, based on your current settings, appears just to the right of the Rows field. The total count of the photos you're about to export appears in the lower-left corner of the window.

2. **Choose File→Export, or press ⌘-E.**

   If you have iPhoto in Share mode, you can also click the Export button on the far right side of the Share pane. In any case, the Export Images dialog box now appears before you.

3. **Click the Web Page tab.**

   You see the dialog box shown in Figure 9-8.

4. **Set the Page attributes, including the title, grid size, and background.**

   The title you set here will appear in the title bar of each exported Web page and as a header in the page itself.

Tip: For maximum compatibility with the world's computers and operating system, use all lowercase letters and no spaces.

Use the Columns and Rows boxes to describe your "index" gallery page, insofar as how many thumbnails you want to appear across and down. (The little "1 page" indicator lets you know how many pages this particular index requires.)

If you'd like a background page color other than white, click the rectangular swatch next to the word Color, and follow the instructions in Figure 9-9.

You can even choose a background *picture* instead of a solid background color by clicking the Image button and then the Set button to select the graphics file on your hard drive. Be considerate of your audience, however. A background graphic

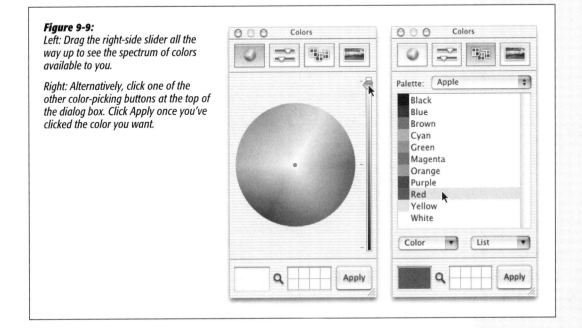

Figure 9-9:
Left: Drag the right-side slider all the way up to see the spectrum of colors available to you.

Right: Alternatively, click one of the other color-picking buttons at the top of the dialog box. Click Apply once you've clicked the color you want.

will make your pages take longer to load, and a noisy background pattern can be very distracting.

5. **Specify how big you want the thumbnail images, as well as the expanded images that appear when you click them.**

   The sizes iPhoto proposes are fine *if* all of your photos are horizontal (that is, in *landscape* orientation). If some are wide and some are tall, however, you're better off specifying *square* dimensions for both the thumbnails and the enlarged photos—240 x 240 for the thumbnails and 640 x 640 for the biggies, for example.

6. **Turn on "Show title," if desired.**

   Even though it may sound like your Web pages will sprout show titles ("Phantom of the Opera," "Oklahoma!," "Mame"), this option actually draws upon the *photo* titles you've assigned in iPhoto. They'll appear centered under each thumbnail, as well as under the larger version of each picture when it opens into its own window.

7. **Click Export.**

   The Save dialog box appears.

8. **Choose (or, by clicking New Folder, create) a folder to hold the export files and then click OK.**

   The export process gets under way.

Examining the results

When iPhoto is done with the export, here's what you'll find in the folder you specified (see Figure 9-10):

- **index.html.** This is the main HTML page, containing the first thumbnails in the series that you exported. It's the home page, the index page, and the starting point for the exported pages.

Figure 9-10:
This is what a Web site looks like before it's on the Internet. All the pieces are here, filed exactly where the home page (index.html) can find them.

- **Page1.html, Page2.html,**... You'll see these only if you exported enough photos to require more than one page of thumbnails—that is, if iPhoto required *multiple* "home" pages.

- **Thumbnails.** This folder holds the actual thumbnail graphics that appear on each of the index pages.

- **Pages.** This folder contains the HTML documents (named Image1.html, Image2.html, Image3.html, and so on) that open when you click the thumbnails on the index pages.

- **Images.** This folder houses the larger JPEG versions of your photos. Yes, these are the *graphics* that appear on the Image HTML pages.

Once you've created these pages, it's up to you to figure out how to *post* them—hanging them on the Internet where the world can see them. To do that, you must upload all of the exported files to a Web server, using an *FTP* program like the Mac OS X versions of Fetch or Interarchy (both available from *www.versiontracker.com*).

Only then do they look like real Web pages, as shown in Figure 9-11.

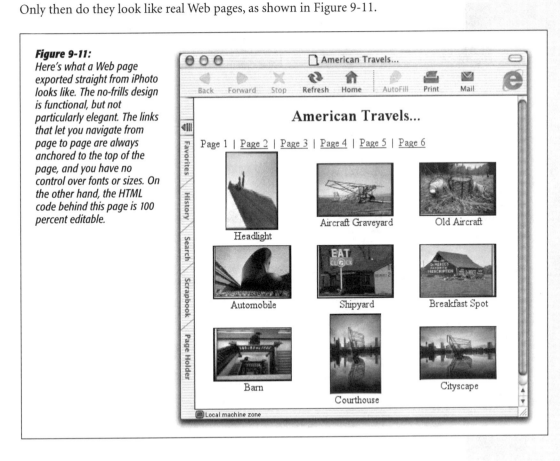

Figure 9-11:
Here's what a Web page exported straight from iPhoto looks like. The no-frills design is functional, but not particularly elegant. The links that let you navigate from page to page are always anchored to the top of the page, and you have no control over fonts or sizes. On the other hand, the HTML code behind this page is 100 percent editable.

Enhancing iPhoto's HTML

If you know how to work with HTML code, you don't have to accept the unremarkable Web pages that iPhoto exports. You're free to tear into them with a full-blown Web-authoring program like Adobe GoLive, Macromedia Dreamweaver, or the free Netscape Composer (*www.netscape.com*) to add your own formatting, headers, footers, and other graphics (Figure 9-12). (Heck, even Microsoft Word lets you open and edit HTML Web pages—plenty of power for changing iPhoto's layout, reformatting the text, or adding your own page elements.)

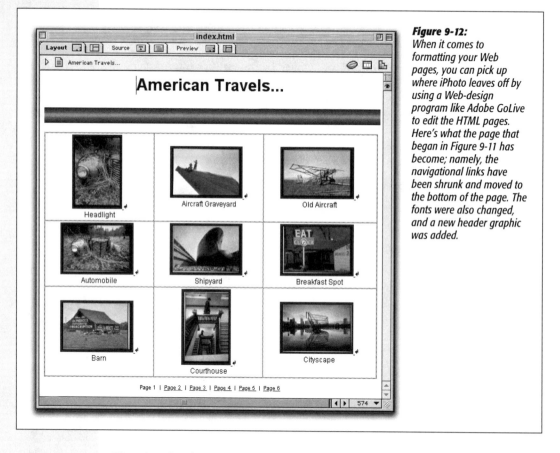

Figure 9-12:
When it comes to formatting your Web pages, you can pick up where iPhoto leaves off by using a Web-design program like Adobe GoLive to edit the HTML pages. Here's what the page that began in Figure 9-11 has become; namely, the navigational links have been shrunk and moved to the bottom of the page. The fonts were also changed, and a new header graphic was added.

If you're a hard-core HTML coder, you can also open the files in a text editor like BBEdit or even TextEdit to tweak the code directly. With a few quick changes, you can make your iPhoto-generated Web pages look more sophisticated and less generic. Some of the changes you might want to consider making include:

• Change font faces and sizes.

• Change the alignment of titles.

• Add a footer with your contact information and email address.

- Add *metadata* tags (keywords) in the *page header*, so that search engines can locate and categorize your pages.

- Insert links to your other Web sites, or other relevant sites on the Web.

If you're *not* an HTML coder—or even if you are—you can perform many of these adjustments extremely easily using the free BetterHTMLExport plug-in for iPhoto, described next.

Better HTML

iPhoto's Export command produces simple, serviceable Web-page versions of your photo albums. Most people assume that if they want anything fancier, they need either HTML programming chops or a dedicated Web design program.

Burning Pro Caliber Photo CDs

iPhoto's ability to export complete Web sites into a folder is the first step in creating a terrific, self-contained photo gallery *on a CD*. This, by the way, is exactly the way many professional photographers distribute their own catalogs. Their clients insert the CD into their own computers, double-click the "Double-click Me" icon, and then view the main "gallery" page of thumbnails in their Web browsers—even though these Web pages and graphics are actually right there on the CD. There's nothing to stop you from stealing this technique for use with your own photo gallery.

After exporting a Web page as described on these pages, insert a blank CD into your Mac's CD burner, give it a descriptive name, and then drag the three folders and index.html file (Figure 9-10) onto the CD's icon.

If you think your audience might need a little hint as to how to get started, you have three options. You might create a simple Read Me text file that says nothing more than, "To get started, double-click the document called *index.html.*"

If that seems a bit inelegant, you can also add an empty folder to the CD window—a folder named, "Double-click index.html icon to start. " (You can even paste a more attractive icon onto that folder icon. You might swipe the iPhoto icon for this purpose, for example. To do that, highlight the iPhoto program icon, choose File→Show Info, click the iPhoto icon in the corner of the dialog box, choose Edit→Copy, click your empty folder on the CD, click *its* icon in the Show Info window, and then choose Edit→Paste.)

The third option for giving your viewers a clue is to display the CD window in Icon view. Then, by choosing View→Show View Options, you summon the dialog box containing a Picture option. Click Picture, and then click the Select button next to it. Now you can choose a graphics file that you carefully designed to be the same size and shape as the CD window itself—a graphic image that not only forms a lovely backdrop for the CD window, but contains typographically attractive instructions for getting started with it, as shown here.

Finally, burn the CD (choose File→Burn Disc). The result is a portable gallery that plays in the Web browser of any Windows PC or Macintosh.

Web pages: they're not just for the Internet anymore.

Actually, though, you can add a number of elegant features to your photo site using a quick piece of free add-on software that requires no hand coding—or special editing software—at all.

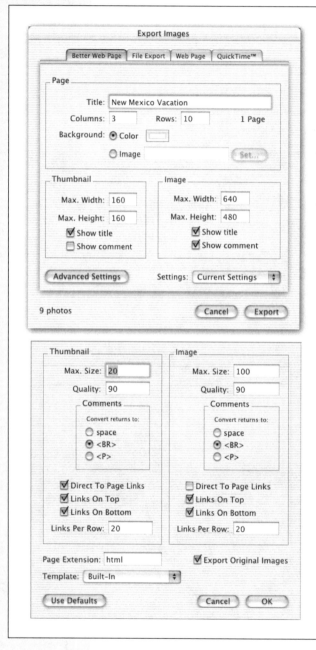

Figure 9-13:
Top: BetterHTMLExport works by adding a new tab to the standard Export Images dialog box: a tab called Better Web Page. Already, you have a few more features than you did before, including a Show Comment option for thumbnails. But this plug-in's real magic lies behind the Advanced Settings button.

Bottom: Here's the hidden screen behind that Advanced Settings button. Its gems include the "Links On Bottom" and "Links On Top" checkboxes, which add a row of links to the top of every page of your Web catalog, as shown in Figure 9-14.

It's the fittingly named BetterHTMLExport, a free iPhoto plug-in by Simeon Leifer that extends the features of iPhoto's own HTML Exporter. (See page 262 for more about plug-ins.)

You can download a free copy of BetterHTMLExport from *www.droolingcat.com*. (As for that Web address—well, apparently all of the good names were taken.)

Here are some of the great things you can do with BetterHTMLExport:

• Add comments (not just titles) on index and image pages.

• Insert "Previous" and "Next" links on each individual image page, so you can jump from picture to picture without returning to the index (thumbnail) page.

• Control the JPEG quality/compression setting that iPhoto uses to create copies of your photos.

• Create links to your *original* images instead of just JPEG versions of them.

• Choose where on the page you want to include navigation hyperlinks.

See Figure 9-13 for a quick tour of this valuable add-on, and Figure 9-14 for an example of what it can do.

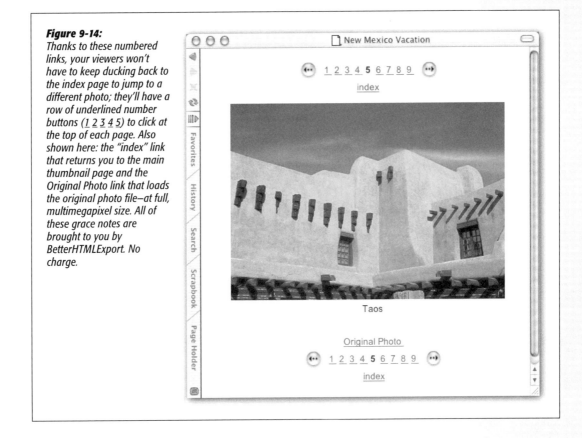

Figure 9-14:
Thanks to these numbered links, your viewers won't have to keep ducking back to the index page to jump to a different photo; they'll have a row of underlined number buttons (1 2 3 4 5) to click at the top of each page. Also shown here: the "index" link that returns you to the main thumbnail page and the Original Photo link that loads the original photo file—at full, multimegapixel size. All of these grace notes are brought to you by BetterHTMLExport. No charge.

Publishing a Photo Book

At first, gift-giving is fun. During those first 20, 30, or 40 birthday, anniversary, Christmas, thank-you, welcome-to-the-neighborhood, good-luck-in-your-new-location, sorry-about-the-car, or I-think-you're-the-cutest-one-in-the-whole-tenth-grade-class events, you might actually *enjoy* picking out a present, buying it, wrapping it, and delivering it.

After a certain point, however, gift-giving becomes exhausting. What the heck do you get your dad after you've already given him birthday and holiday presents for 15 or 35 years?

If you have iPhoto, you've got an ironclad, perennial answer. The program's Book feature lets you design and order (via the Internet) a gorgeous, linen-covered, 9-by-11-inch hardbound book, printed at a real bindery and shipped back to you in a slipcover. Your photos are printed right on the glossy, acid-free, single-sided pages, complete with captions, if you like.

A ten-page book costs $30 (extra pages are $3 each). That's about the least you could hope to pay for a handsome, emotionally powerful gift *guaranteed* never to wind up in an attic, garage sale, or Goodwill shop. In short, it's a home run gift every time.

But the iPhoto book is not *only* a gift. You should also consider ordering them for yourself—one each for your vacation, wedding, child, or whatever. These books are amazing keepsakes to leave out on your coffee table—the same idea as most families' photo albums, but infinitely classier and longer lasting (and not much more expensive).

Phase 1: Pick the Pix

The hardest part of the whole book-creation process is winnowing down your photos to the ones you want to include. Many a shutterbug eagerly sits down to create his very first photo book—and winds up with one that's 49 pages long (that is, $147).

As a general rule, each page of your photo book can hold a maximum of four pictures. (iPhoto also offers canned book designs called Catalog and Yearbook, which hold up to 32 tiny pictures per page in a grid. At that size, however, your pictures don't exactly sing; instead, the whole thing more closely resembles, well, a catalog or yearbook.)

Even the four-per-page limit doesn't necessarily mean you'll get 40 photos into a ten-page book, however. The more pictures you add to a page, the smaller they have to be, and therefore the less impact they have. The best-looking books generally have varying numbers of pictures per page—one, four, three, two, whatever. In short, the number of pictures you'll fit in a ten-page book may be far lower than 40—25, say.

The first step is to create an album (page 109). In Organize mode, fill it with the pictures you really want in the book. This can be an excruciating experience, especially if you and a collaborator are trying to work together. ("You can't get rid of that one! It's adorable!" "But honey, we've already got 139 pictures in here!" "I don't care. I love that one.")

As you work, constantly keep in mind the photo *sequence*. Drag them around in the album to determine a preliminary order. You'll have plenty of opportunity to fine-tune each page of the book (and rearrange the pictures on it) later in the process. When you're still in Organize mode, the only critical task is to place the two most sensational or important photos first and last (for the cover and the last page of the book).

Caution: Don't include black-and-white photos. They may look great when you order *prints* (page 164), but they look mottled when published in a photo book—a casualty of the printing technology used by the bindery.

Phase 2: Choose a Theme

Once you've corralled the book's pictures into an album of their own, click the album, and then click the Book button below the main picture area (Figure 10-1). (If you forget to click the album before clicking Book, iPhoto will scold you.)

Tip: If you've been working in some other album, you can save a click by Option-clicking the album that you want to become a book. Option-clicking a different album in the list always switches into the mode you're *not* currently in: Organize or Book.

Now you see something like Figure 10-1: a large preview page above, and a scrolling bank of thumbnails below, representing the book's pages. iPhoto has just turned into a page-layout program.

Tip: Light blue lines surround each photo and text box. These *guides,* as they're called, won't appear in the printed book. They're there just for your convenience, to help you visualize how the finished layout will look. Still, if they bother you, turn off the Show Guides checkbox in the lower-left corner of the window.

Before you dive in, take a moment to get your bearings. Note that the thumbnails are numbered—an early-warning system that shows you how many pages long your book will be (read: how expensive). If you're like most people, your initial layout will be much too long. Not to worry; you'll fix that in a moment.

In book-design mode, you can't add photos to your album, take any photos out, or even rearrange them. You can perform tasks like these as you work on your book—but you must click the Organize button to do so.

What you can do, however, is design your book pages, and that process begins when you choose a *theme* for the book—a canned design, in other words. Use the Theme pop-up menu at the lower-left corner of the iPhoto screen for this purpose (shown in Figure 10-1). Before you begin fiddling with individual pages, try each of the themes in turn, studying the thumbnails and page previews to get a feeling for the effect.

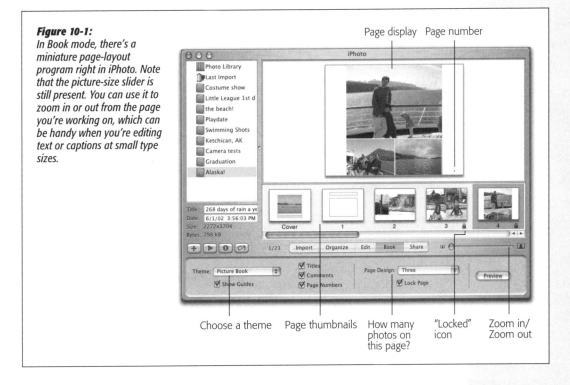

Figure 10-1:
In Book mode, there's a miniature page-layout program right in iPhoto. Note that the picture-size slider is still present. You can use it to zoom in or out from the page you're working on, which can be handy when you're editing text or captions at small type sizes.

Page display   Page number

Choose a theme   Page thumbnails   How many photos on this page?   "Locked" icon   Zoom in/ Zoom out

Caution: Choose carefully. You can switch to a different theme for this album later, but you'll lose *all the custom text and photo groupings* you've performed so far.

You won't lose your captions, because those are the Comments stored with every photo in your collection. "Custom text" refers to the text you type into Introduction pages (page 196) and onto every page of the Story Book design (page 194). (If you have, in fact, typed any custom text, iPhoto warns you about this loss when you try to switch layout themes.)

If you want to experiment with a different theme once you've spent some time with one, *duplicate the album first.* (With the album highlighted in the list, choose File→Duplicate.) Now you can change the theme on the duplicate without destroying the work you've done on the original.

Your choices are:

- **Catalog.** This design looks exactly like a mail order catalog: a picture on the left, and a name and description on the right—all eight times per page (or one, or four). It's neatly aligned and some-what conservative. For ex-ample, there's a page design called Introduction, where you can pour a lot of text, such as your shipping poli-cies, a letter from the founder, what this season's catalog offers, and so on.

  It's also good for more than just designing catalogs, however. It would be an ideal "face book" (with mini biographies) for, say, a dating agency or personnel direc-tor. It's also a candidate for a regular photo album, in the event you're the kind of person who wants it to look square and gridlike, like a *real* photo album book from Office Max.

- **Classic.** It's easy to deduce the philosophy behind this conservative, clean design: maximum photos, mini-mum text. Photos are as large as possible on the page (up to four per page), and each offers only enough room for a title and a very short caption.

- **Picture Book.** This design's philosophy is even starker: maximum photos, period. There's no text, and only minimum margins. Thus, on one-photo-per-page pages, the photo stretches gloriously from one edge of the page to the other—a *full bleed*, as publishers might say.

This dramatic design can be emotionally compelling in the extreme. The absence of text and minimization of white space seems to make the photos speak—if not shout—for themselves.

As you build your first book, you may be compelled to choose a theme that offers space for captions. But if your text is no more illuminating than, "Timmy doing a belly-flop" or "Dad falls asleep at the bar," consider the Picture Book theme instead. This is, after all, a *photo* album, and so it may be worth giving the photos all the space they deserve. You don't need to eat into their space by restating the obvious.

Tip: Keeping in mind that the book is published *horizontally,* in landscape mode, will help you maximize page coverage. For example, on pages with only one photo, a horizontal shot looks best. It will fill the page, edge to edge. On pages with two photos, two side-by-side vertical (portrait-mode) shots look best. They'll appear side by side, filling the page top to bottom.

- **Portfolio.** Modeled after a photographer's portfolio, this design has elements of both Catalog and Picture Book. Like Catalog, it provides text boxes that accommodate a title and description for each photo. But as with Picture Book, the photos are otherwise displayed at maximum size, with very little white space between them.

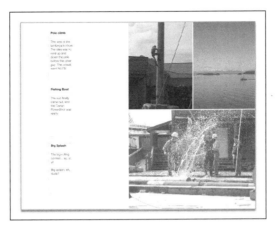

The whole effect is a tad industrial-looking, so you probably wouldn't want to use it as a "memory book" for some trip or event. It's useful in situations where Catalog would be right, except that it's more interesting to look at, thanks to the varied photo sizes.

• **Story Book.** Here's a wackier, more energetic layout in which *no* photos are square with the page. Everything falls at a tilt, as though tossed onto a coffee table helter-skelter. If there's more than one photo per page, they may even *overlap*.

The layout isn't complete chaos, however, thanks to the text boxes for captions, which are always parallel to the page edges and therefore anchor the design. Overall, this theme sings a little more than the others; use it when fun, craziness, or light-heartedness is your desired effect.

• **Year Book.** This theme lets you fit up to 32 photos on each page—just as in a high school yearbook. Of course, if you choose greater quantities, the photos themselves get smaller—but iPhoto always leaves you enough room for a title ("Chris Jones") and a little description ("Swim team '02; voted Most Likely to Enter the Priesthood").

Tip: Make an effort to choose a quantity of photos that neatly fills the final page, or at least a row of it. Otherwise, the final page can look a bit half-finished.

Try choosing each of these themes in turn from the Themes pop-up menu. The thumbnails of your pages should give you immediate feedback about the suitability of each design for your book project.

Phase 3: Design the Pages

Once you've selected an album and a theme, the most time-consuming phase begins: designing the individual pages.

It's important to understand that iPhoto thinks of the pictures in your book as a *continuous stream* that flows from left to right, in precisely the same order as they appear in the album you've selected. You can drag your page thumbnails around with the mouse to rearrange them—but behind the scenes, you're simultaneously rearranging the photos in the album. Similarly, if you drag photos around in the Organize window for your album, you'll wind up rearranging the pages of your book. Figure 10-2 should drive this point home.

Tip: You'll soon discover that designing a book is a much happier experience if you work on your pages strictly from *left to right*. Doing so reduces the likelihood that your photos will sproing out of order unexpectedly, as described on page 199.

To begin work on a page, click its thumbnail. Now you have three decisions to make: how many photos should appear on this page, what text should appear, and what the text should look like.

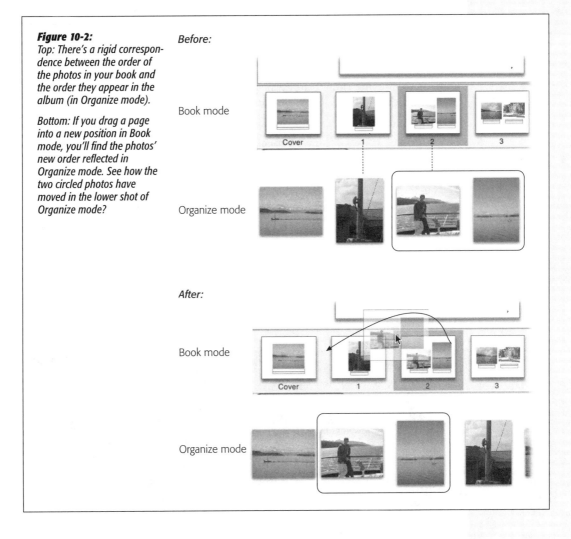

Figure 10-2:
Top: There's a rigid correspondence between the order of the photos in your book and the order they appear in the album (in Organize mode).

Bottom: If you drag a page into a new position in Book mode, you'll find the photos' new order reflected in Organize mode. See how the two circled photos have moved in the lower shot of Organize mode?

Before:

Book mode

Organize mode

After:

Book mode

Organize mode

Tip: Even in Book mode, you can still rotate photos, rename them, change their dates, or delete them, just as you would thumbnails in Organize mode (see Chapter 5).

The Cover

Start with the Cover page—the first thumbnail in the row. When it's selected, the cover photo appears in the main picture area. This is the picture that will be pasted (and centered) on the linen cover of the actual book. (The cloth cover of your book will be one of several handsome dark colors, *not* white as it appears here.)

You can't do much with the cover except to change the title or subtitle; see "Editing titles and captions," below. You'll choose the cover color in a later step.

Tip: The picture you see here is the *first picture* in the album. If it's not the photo you want on the cover, click the Organize button and drag a different photo to the beginning of your album.

Pictures per Page

Click the thumbnail for page 2. If you did some preliminary arranging work in your album, your photos should already be in roughly the right *order* for the book pages—but not necessarily the right *groupings*.

You control how many pictures appear on a page—and, to an extent, their layout—by choosing a number from the Page Design pop-up menu. Your choices are:

- **Cover.** The first thumbnail in your book *must* have the Cover design.

  On the other hand, subsequent pages can *also* have the Cover layout. You can use this quirk to your advantage. For example, in a book that documents your trip to three countries, you can have a "cover" layout that introduces each country's batch of photos.

- **Introduction.** In most themes, this special page design has no photos at all. It's just a big set of text boxes that you can type (or paste) into. Here's where you can let the audience know about the trip, the company, or the family; tell the story behind the book; praise the book's lucky recipient; scare off intellectual-property thieves with scary-sounding copyright notices; and so on.

FREQUENTLY ASKED QUESTION

Cover = Page in the Album

I want to use my cover photo as one of the pages in the book, just like they do in real coffee-table photo books. How do I do it?

In Organize mode, click the photo and then choose File→Duplicate (⌘-D).

Now you have two copies of the photo. Drag one to the front of the line in the album (to use as the cover). Drag the other into the mass of other photos, so that you can now use it in one of the interior page layouts.

- **One, Two, Three, Four….** Use these commands to specify how many photos appear on the selected page. iPhoto automatically arranges them according to its own internal sense of symmetry.

First-time iPhoto book designers frequently complain that they have no control over the placement of the photos *within* the page. You can't drag the bottom picture up to the top, for example.

It's true that you can't rearrange pictures by dragging them—but that doesn't mean you can't rearrange them at all. Remember that the photos' order on the book pages is a mirror of their order in the *album*. Just click Organize, drag the

---

FREQUENTLY ASKED QUESTION

Case of the Hideous Layout

Oh my gosh, you can't believe how ragged my book pages look. They don't look anything like the tidy illustrations in this chapter, or the examples on the Apple Web site. What's going on?

iPhoto's design templates operate on the simple premise that all of your photos have a *4:3 aspect ratio.* That is, the long and short sides of the photo are in four-to-three proportions (four inches to three inches, for example).

In most cases, that's what you've already got, since those are the standard proportions of standard digital photos. If all your pictures are in 4:3 (or 3:4) proportions, they will fit neatly and beautifully into the page-layout slots iPhoto provides for them.

A few cameras produce photos in the more traditional 3:2 film dimensions (1800 x 1200 pixels, for example), and some cameras let you choose. That feature will make you very happy when it comes time to order Kodak prints of your pictures (Chapter 8)—but will cause you nothing but headaches when you want to lay out a photo book. They won't align with the canned iPhoto designs, and full-bleed (edge-to-edge) pictures won't go edge to edge. They'll leave unsightly strips of white along certain edges.

Another possibility: You may have made the mistake of *cropping* your photos in iPhoto. When you arbitrarily chop out excess portions of your pictures, you lose the tidy 4:3 aspect ratio they were born with. You wind up with one picture that's 4:2.5, another that's 5:3, and so on. These photos won't line up when placed into a book layout, either.

The simple way to avoid these problems is to crop your non-4:3 photos using the Constrain pop-up menu (page 125). Choose "4 x 3 (Book, DVD)" from this menu to crop safely. Now, even though you're chopping away edges of your photo, you're maintaining the ideal book proportions.

If you've already done unconstrained cropping—if you're reading this advice too late, and you've got uneven layouts in your book—you have only one recourse. Click Organize, click the pictures you cropped, and choose File→Revert to Original. Thanks to iPhoto's secret backup system (page 137), you now have the photos as they were when they first arrived from the camera. You can now re-crop them, this time using the Constrain menu to keep the dimensions pure.

---

photos into a new sequence, and then click the Book button again. You'll see the change reflected immediately.

Otherwise, you are indeed at the mercy of iPhoto's design templates. In the Story Book theme, for example, you can't dictate which photos overlap their neighbors or how they overlap. In the Picture Book theme, you can't control which photos are half-size and which are quarter-size. And so on.

- **End.** The Page Design pop-up menu for the Story Book theme offers a bonus page design called End. Use it for the last page of the book.

The End page is designed to hold three pictures, and you'd be well advised to fiddle with your album until the last page does, in fact, have three photos on it. Otherwise, you'll wind up with a strange, half-filled look on the End page. For example, if there's only one photo on it, that picture will sit halfway off the left margin, as though sailing off to the left ("later dude!"), and the rest of the page will be blank.

Each time you change the number of photos on a page, something happens that you may find disconcerting: Pictures on the *following* pages slide onto earlier or later pages. Figure 10-3 illustrates this phenomenon.

This syndrome can drive you wiggy if it winds up disrupting a page that you've already tweaked to perfection—a problem you'll almost certainly encounter if you don't work on your pages from left to right.

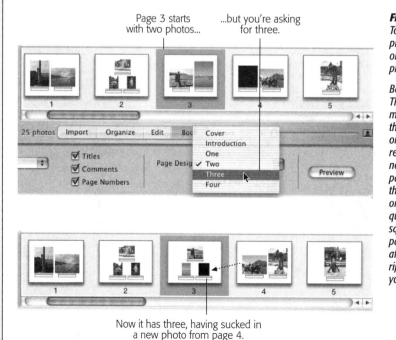

Page 3 starts with two photos...   ...but you're asking for three.

Now it has three, having sucked in a new photo from page 4.

Figure 10-3:
Top: Suppose iPhoto proposes putting two photos on page 3. (Note the all-black photo on page 4.)

Bottom: When you choose Three from the Page Design menu, you're telling iPhoto that you want three photos on page 3. The program responds by sucking in the next photo (on the next page) to fill its quota. Yes, there are now three pictures on page 3, as you re-quested—but the all-black square photo has now left page 4, causing all photos after it to slide leftward, rippling all the way through your book.

The solution is simple. Once a page has the right photos on it (and the right *number* of photos), lock it by turning on the Lock Page checkbox at the lower edge of the window. (A tiny padlock icon appears on the page's thumbnail, as shown in Figure 10-1.)

From now on, even if you change the number of shots on an earlier page, the page you locked will remain undisturbed.

Even this trick, though, requires some caution. Keep in mind the following gotchas:

- Once you've locked a page, the Page Design pop-up menu no longer functions for that page. You have to unlock a page before you can change the number of pictures on it.

- If you do unlock a page, watch out…you're taking the muzzle off of a spring-loaded design. Because iPhoto is maintaining a picture group that, in its head, is out of sequence (relative to Organize mode), unlocking a page may cause its pictures to explode into other locations. As a result, you'll witness a ripple effect that's likely to scramble *all* unlocked pages in your book.

- If you use the Theme pop-up menu to change themes, all bets are off. Changing themes blasts *all* layout work into oblivion, locked or not.

FREQUENTLY ASKED QUESTION

The Save Command

Yo…where's the Save command?

There isn't one. iPhoto automatically saves your work as you go.

If you want to make a safety copy along the way—a fallback version—highlight the *album* from which the book is de-rived and choose File→Duplicate. This process takes virtually no extra memory or disk space, but it's good insurance. If you change the layout or theme of a book, iPhoto vaporizes all the text you've entered (and, often, a lot of the layout work). If that happens, you'll be glad you had a backup.

Page Sequence

As you work, continue to consider the overall effect of your layout. You already know that you can rearrange the photos (by clicking the Organize button and then dragging them), but you can also rearrange entire *pages*. Just drag the thumbnails left or right in their track. (If you return to Organize mode, you'll see that the photos have shifted there, too, to reflect their new order in the book; see Figure 10-2.)

Sometimes chronological order is the natural sequence, especially for books that will be mementos of special events like trips, parties, and weddings. But there's nothing to stop you from cheating a bit—rearranging certain scenes—for greater impact and variety.

As you drag your pictures into order, consider these effects:

• Intersperse group shots with solo portraits, scenery with people shots, vertical ones with horizontals.

• On multiple-photo pages, exploit the direction your subjects face. On a three-picture page, for example, you could arrange the people in the photos so that they're all looking roughly toward the center of the page, for a feeling of inclusion (Figure 10-4). You might put a father looking upward to a shot of his son diving on a photo higher on the page, or a brother and sister back-to-back facing outward, signifying competition.

• Group similar shots together on a page.

Figure 10-4:
Variety is good—but thematic unity is good, too. Here, two photos taken at the same event, moments apart, feel good together. They tell a little scene and add a little action to your book.

Page Limits

The book can have anywhere from 10 to 50 pages. If you create fewer pages, you'll be warned during the book-ordering process that you're about to pay for a ten-page book with blank pages at the end. If you create more than 50 pages, you won't be allowed to place the order at all.

There's nothing to stop you from creating multiple books, however. ("Our Trip to New Jersey, Vol. XI," anyone?)

Hiding Page Numbers

Each built-in theme includes page numbers stamped on the lower-right corner of each page. You never have to worry about a page number winding up superimposed on one of your pictures, though. A picture *always* takes priority, covering up the page number.

Even so, you may feel that page numbers intrude on the mood your book creates. If so, just eliminate them by turning off the Page Numbers checkbox at the lower-left corner of the window.

Tip: As you work, you may discover photos here and there that need a little editing—cropping, brightening, and so on (Chapter 6). No problem: Just double-click a picture right in the book-page display window to open it into either Edit mode or an external photo-editing program, as described on page 135. Click the Book button again when you're finished.

Phase 4: Edit the Titles and Captions

In every theme, iPhoto offers you text boxes that you can fill with titles, explanations, and captions. Most layouts have space for this kind of text on every page. Only the Picture Book design is text-free (except for the cover and introduction page).

In any case, taking the time to perfect this text is extremely important. A misspelling or typo you make here may haunt you (and amuse the book's recipient) forever.

In general, iPhoto offers the following four kinds of text boxes:

- **The book title.** This box appears on the book's cover and (if you've added one) Introduction page. When you first create a book, iPhoto proposes the *album's* name as the book name, but you're welcome to change it.

  A second text box, all set with slightly smaller-type formatting, appears below the title. Use it for a subtitle: the date, "A Trip Down Memory Lane," "Happy Birthday Aunt Enid," "A Little Something for the Insurance Company," or whatever.

- **The introduction.** Applying the Introduction page design to a page gives you a huge text block that you can fill with any introductory text you think the book needs.

Tip: An Introduction page doesn't need to be the first page of the book (after the cover). You can turn *any* page into an all-text Introduction page. Such pages make great section dividers.

They're especially useful in Picture Book designs that otherwise have no text at all. Whatever you type or paste into the Introduction page can set the scene and explain the following (uncaptioned) pages of pictures.

- **Photo titles.** In most layouts, iPhoto displays the name of each photo. If you haven't already named each picture as described on page 103, you'll get only the internal iPhoto name of each picture—"Roll 132-101," for example. You can edit this name either in the text box on your page preview, or in the Title text box at the left side of the iPhoto window (Figure 10-5).

- **Comments.** The larger text box that appears for each photo (in some layouts) is for a caption. It automatically displays any comments you've typed into the Comments box for a photo at the left side of the iPhoto screen (see page 105). Or, to be precise, it displays the first chunk of that text (Figure 10-5).

Note, by the way, that some of the layouts don't show nearly as much text as the "real" Title or Comments box does. In these cases, iPhoto has no choice but to chop off the excess, showing only the first sentence or two. A yellow, triangular exclamation point appears next to any text box that has overflow of this kind—your cue to edit down the text to fit the text box on the layout (Figure 10-5).

Note: On the other hand, iPhoto 1.1.1 may give you "false positives," showing a yellow triangle (and text visually wrapping on the screen) when, in fact, the text will look just fine when it's printed. (This problem is especially apparent with small text and a reduced-size display of the page.) To find out what you'll *really* get, make a final proofreading pass using one of the techniques described on page 207.

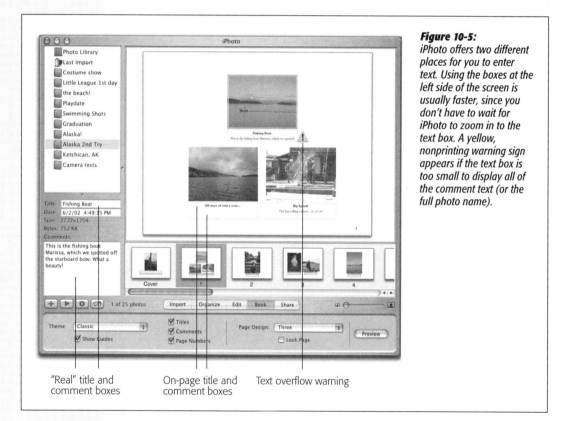

Figure 10-5:
iPhoto offers two different places for you to enter text. Using the boxes at the left side of the screen is usually faster, since you don't have to wait for iPhoto to zoom in to the text box. A yellow, nonprinting warning sign appears if the text box is too small to display all of the comment text (or the full photo name).

"Real" title and comment boxes

On-page title and comment boxes

Text overflow warning

Editing Text

You're welcome to edit the photo titles or comments in either place: right here in the layout, or back in the Info box for the individual photos (page 101). In general, the editing process is straightforward. Just proceed like this:

• Click inside a text box to activate the insertion-point cursor, so you can begin typing. iPhoto zooms in on the page and scrolls it, if necessary, so that the type is large enough to see and edit. When you click outside of a text box—on another part of the page, for example—the page shrinks again to fit the window.

• You can select text and then use the Edit menu's Cut, Copy, and Paste commands to transfer text from box to box.

• You can also move selected text *within* a text box by dragging it and dropping it. The trick is to *hold down* the mouse button for a moment before dragging. Add the Option key to make a *copy* of the selected text instead of moving it.

• Double-click a word, or triple-click a paragraph, to neatly highlight it.

• Press Control-right arrow or Control-left arrow to make the insertion point jump to the beginning or end of a text box.

• To make typographically proper quotation marks ("curly like this" instead of "this"), press Option-[and Shift-Option-[, respectively. And to make a true long dash—like this, instead of two hyphens—press Shift-Option-hyphen.

But here's the biggest tip of all: *Edit your text in Preview mode.* (Click the Preview button at the lower-right corner of the window; see Figure 10-9.) In Preview mode, each page appears in its own window, which you can make as large as you like. iPhoto therefore doesn't have to zoom and unzoom as you click each text box, which makes the editing go faster. And because you can see the whole page (instead of only the portion that fits within the photo viewing area), you have a better sense of your text block's look and proportions relative to the picture.

Tip: Click the green Zoom button at the left end of the title bar to make the page fill your screen. The result: An even more expansive canvas in which to work.

Hiding Text

As noted earlier, the Picture Book theme is especially dramatic because it *lacks* text. The pictures spill across the pages, strong and big.

Bear in mind, though, that you can turn off the text for *any* of the layout themes. Just turn off the corresponding checkbox (Titles or Comments) in the lower-left corner of the iPhoto window. (You can also leave *individual* boxes empty, of course.)

Note: You can't *add* titles or comment boxes to a theme that doesn't have them, however. The pages in the Picture Book theme don't have any text on them, and no amount of turning the Titles and Comments checkboxes on or off can change that.

Formatting Text

To a certain extent, you can change the fonts, sizes, and styles of type in your book. To begin, choose Edit→Font→Show Fonts (or press ⌘-T). As shown in Figure 10-6, Mac OS X's standard Font panel appears.

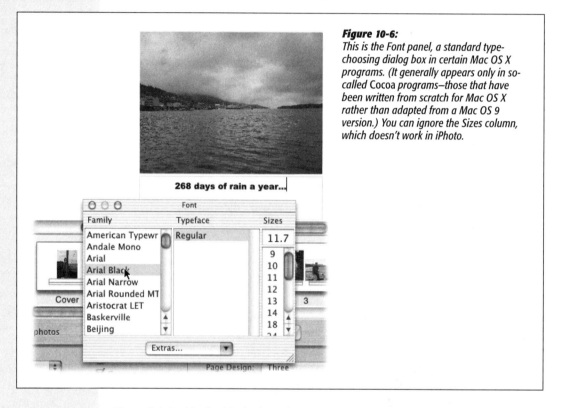

Figure 10-6:
This is the Font panel, a standard type-choosing dialog box in certain Mac OS X programs. (It generally appears only in so-called Cocoa *programs—those that have been written from scratch for Mac OS X rather than adapted from a Mac OS 9 version.) You can ignore the Sizes column, which doesn't work in iPhoto.*

Now click inside the kind of text box you want to change, and then click any font, style, or type size you like. All right, "any" may be stretching it. The truth is:

- You can't change the *size* of the type—only the font and style.

- In general, whatever changes you make apply to *every* title or comment box in the entire book. There's no way to make one caption look different from other captions, or to format only part of a sentence (so that you can italicize a single word, for example).

- There are two exceptions to the previous point. If you select some words and then Control-click them, a contextual menu appears. Choosing Italic or Bold from its Font submenu affects all text in all boxes—but choosing *Underline* affects only the selected words. (It looks pretty crude, but that's a different conversation.)

  The Font submenu even offers a Show Colors command. It opens a color palette; using it, you can apply different colors, too, to individual text selections. Yes, the bright, multicolored result might look a little bit like it was designed by Barney the Dinosaur, but the Color option is worth keeping in mind when you're preparing books about, for example, someone's fourth birthday party.

Check Your Spelling

Ordinarily, you might scoff at the overkill—what difference does a typo make in a photo-organizing program, for goodness' sake? But your tune will change the very day you get your $30 (or $150) hardbound photo book in the mail, proudly titled, "Our Trip to the Grand Canon."

As in a word processor, you can ask iPhoto to check your spelling several ways:

- **Check a single word or selection.** Highlight a word, or several, and then choose Edit→Spelling→Check Spelling (⌘-;). If the word is misspelled in iPhoto's opinion, a red, dashed line appears under the word. Proceed as shown in Figure 10-7.

- **Check a whole text block.** Click inside a title or comment box and then choose Edit→Spelling→Spelling (Shift-⌘-;). The standard Mac OS X Spelling dialog box appears, also shown and described in Figure 10-7.

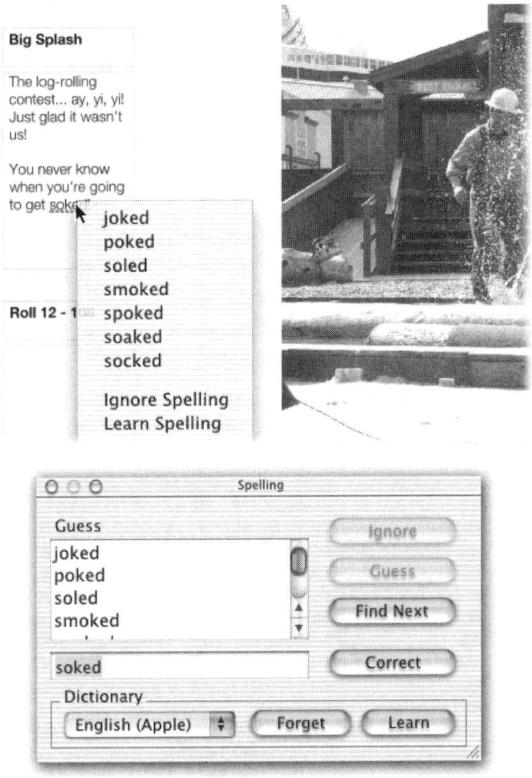

Figure 10-7:
Top: Control-click any word that's underlined with dashed, red line. If the resulting contextual menu contains the correct spelling, choose it. Otherwise, choose Ignore or Add (to teach Mac OS X that wor for future spell checks).

Bottom: If you prefer a more word-processorish spelling check, you can summon this box.

The first "misspelled" word already appears. If the correct version appears in the list, double-click it (c single-click it and then click Correct). If not, type th correct word into the box below the list and then click Correct.

On the other hand, if the word in your caption is fir as it is, click either Ignore ("Stop underlining this, iPhoto. It's a word I want spelled this way; let's go on") or Add ("This is a name or word that not only is correctly spelled, but I may use again. Add it to your dictionary so you'll never flag it again"). Alas, iPhoto forgets everything you've told it to Ignore as soon as you click into a different text box.

- **Check as you type.** The trouble with the spelling commands described above is that they operate on only a single, tiny text block at a time. To check your entire photo book, you must click inside each title or caption and invoke the spelling command again. There's no way to have iPhoto sweep through your entire book at once.

Your eyes might widen in excitement, therefore, when you spot the Edit→Spelling→Check Spelling As You Type command. You'd expect it to make iPhoto flag words it doesn't recognize *as you type them.*

Sure enough, when this option is turned on, whenever you type a word not in iPhoto's dictionary, iPhoto adds a colorful dashed underline. (Technically, it underlines any word not in the *Mac OS X* dictionary, since you're actually using the

---

The Heartbreak of the Yellow Exclamation Point

As you work on your book design, you may encounter the dreaded yellow-triangle-exclamation point like the one shown here. It appears everywhere you want to be: on the corresponding page thumbnail, on the page display, on the page preview (which appears when you click Preview), and so on.

If you actually try to order the book without eliminating the yellow triangles, you even get a warning in the form of a dialog box. "Low Quality Warning: One or more photos in your book may print at too low a quality based on the design you have chosen. Do you want to continue?"

All of this boils down to one heartbreaking problem: At least one of your photos doesn't have enough resolution (enough pixels) to reproduce well in the finished book. If you ignore the warning and continue with the ordering process, you're likely to be disappointed by the blotchy, grainy result in the finished book.

You may remember from Chapter 1 that the resolution of your digital camera is relatively irrelevant if you'll only be showing your pictures onscreen. It's when you try to *print* them that you need all the megapixels you can get—like now.

The easiest solution is to shrink the photo on its page. And the easiest way to do *that* is to increase the *number* of pictures on that page. (Some layouts put both large and small photos on the same page. In that case, you may have to click Organize and drag photos around so that your low-res, problem-child picture lands in one of the smaller slots.)

Decreasing a picture's size also squeezes its pixels closer together, improving the dots-per-inch shortage that iPhoto is warning you about.

If even that dramatic step doesn't eliminate the yellow warning emblems, try to remember if you ever cropped this photo. If so, your last chance is to click Organize, double-click the photo, and then choose File→Revert To Original. Doing so will undo any *cropping* you did to the photo, which may have thrown away a lot of pixels that you suddenly find yourself needing. (If Revert To Original is dimmed, then you never performed any cropping, and this last resort is worthless.)

Finally, if nothing has worked so far, your only options are to eliminate the photo from your book or to order the book anyway.

---

standard Mac OS X spelling checker—the same one that watches over you in
Mac OS X's Mail program, for example.)

To correct a misspelling that iPhoto has found in this way, Control-click it. A
contextual menu appears. Proceed as shown in Figure 10-7.

There's only one problem: This option turns itself *off* every time you click into a
new text box. Using the mouse (there's no keyboard shortcut), you have to turn it
on again for every title and caption. The regular Check Spelling command looks
positively effortless by comparison.

Listen to Your Book

Unfortunately, even a spelling checker won't find missing words, inadvertently re-
peated words, or awkward writing. For those situations, what you really want is for
iPhoto to *read your captions aloud* to you.

No problem: Just highlight some text by dragging through it, and then Control-
click the highlighted area. As shown in Figure 10-8, a contextual menu appears,
containing the Speech command.

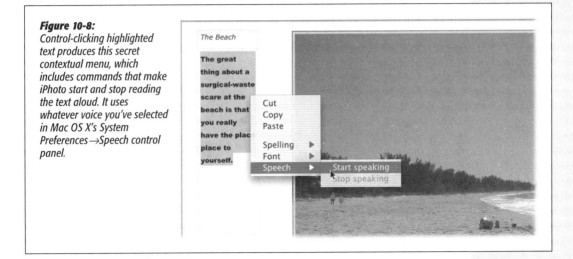

Figure 10-8:
*Control-clicking highlighted
text produces this secret
contextual menu, which
includes commands that make
iPhoto start and stop reading
the text aloud. It uses
whatever voice you've selected
in Mac OS X's System
Preferences→Speech control
panel.*

Phase 5: Preview the Masterpiece

Ordering a professionally bound book is, needless to say, quite a commitment. Before blowing $30 or more on a one-shot deal, you'd be wise to proofread and inspect
it from every possible angle.

Preview It Onscreen

One easy way to inspect your book is to click the Preview button in the lower-right
corner of the screen. iPhoto fills your screen with an electronic version of the selected page for your inspection, as shown in Figure 10-9.

Print It

As any proofreader can tell you, though, looking over a book on paper is a sure way to discover errors that somehow elude detection onscreen. That's why it's a good idea to print out your own, low-tech edition of this book at home before beaming it away to Apple's bindery.

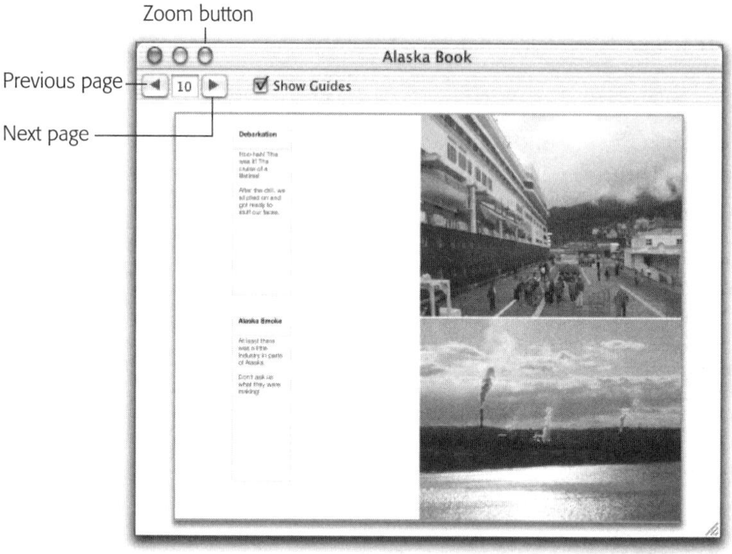

Zoom button

Previous page

Next page

Alaska Book

10 ☑ Show Guides

Figure 10-9:
In Preview mode, you can flip through your book one page at a time by clicking the arrows at the top. (You can also jump to a certain page by typing a number into the box and then pressing the Return key.) For best results, click the Zoom button to make the window as large as possible on your screen. You can turn off the light blue box boundaries, if you like, by turning off "Show Guides."

While you're in Book mode, choose File→Print. After the standard Mac OS X Print dialog box appears, fire up your printer and click Print when ready. The result may not be linen-bound and printed on acid-free paper, but it's a tantalizing preview of the real thing—and a great way to give the book one final look.

Turn It into a PDF File

Sooner or later, almost everyone with a personal computer encounters PDF (Portable Document Format) files. Many a software manual, Read Me file, and downloadable "white paper" comes in this format, for many of the following reasons:

- **Other people see your layout.** When you distribute PDF files to other people, they see precisely the same fonts, colors, page design, and other elements that you did in your original document. They get to see all of this even if they don't *have* the fonts or the software you used to create the document. (Now contrast this with the alternative: sending somebody, for example, a Microsoft Word document. In this scenario, if your correspondents don't have precisely the same fonts as you, then they'll see a screwy layout. And if they don't have Microsoft Word, they'll see nothing at all.)

- **It's universal.** PDF files are very common in the Macintosh, Windows, and even Unix/Linux worlds. When you create a PDF file, you can distribute it (by email, for example) without ever worrying about what kind of computers your correspondents are using. All the recipient needs is a copy of the free Adobe Acrobat Reader program, which now comes on every computer.

- **It has very high resolution.** PDF files print at the maximum quality of any printer. A single PDF file prints great both on cheapo inkjets and on high-quality image-setting gear at professional print shops. (You're looking at a PDF file right now, in fact, which was later printed at a publishing plant.)

- **You can search it.** Although you may be tempted to think of a PDF file as something like a captured graphic of the original document, it has several key differences. Behind the scenes, its text is still text. You can search it using a Find command.

If you suspect other people might want to have a look at your photo book before it goes to be printed—or if they'd just like to have a copy of their own—a PDF file makes a convenient, emailable package.

Here's how to create a PDF file:

1. **With your book design on the screen in front of you, choose File→Print.**

   The print dialog box appears.

2. **Click the Preview button.**

   After a minute of processing, the book appears in Mac OS X's Preview program— rotated 90 degrees, unfortunately. You can flip through its pages by clicking the < and > buttons at the lower-left corner of the window.

3. **Choose File→Save As PDF.**

   The Save sheet appears.

4. **Type a name for the file, choose a folder location for it, and click Save.**

   Your PDF file is ready to distribute. (Fortunately, the recipients will be able to correct the rotation within Adobe Acrobat, using its View→Rotate Counterclockwise command.)

Phase 6: Send the Book to the Bindery

When you think your book is ready for birth, click the Share button. In the row of icons at the bottom of the screen, click Order Book.

After several minutes of converting your screen design into an Internet-transmittable file, iPhoto offers you a screen like the one shown in Figure 10-10. (If your book is *shorter* than ten pages, iPhoto first warns you that you're about to pay for a bunch of blank pages. Ten pages is the *minimum* for a book.)

Note: If you receive a Low Quality Warning at this stage, see the box on page 206.

At this stage, your tasks are largely administrative.

- **Choose a cover color.** Use the Cover Color pop-up menu to choose Black, Burgundy (red), Light Gray, or Navy (blue). The books in the illustration, including the handy magnified swatch, change color to show you what you're getting. (If you're ordering more than one book, they must all have the same color.)

- **Inspect the charges.** If you've gone beyond ten pages, you'll see that you're about to be charged $3 per additional page.

- **Indicate the quantity.** You can order additional copies of the same book. Indeed, after you've spent so much time on a gift book for someone else, you may well be tempted to order yourself a copy.

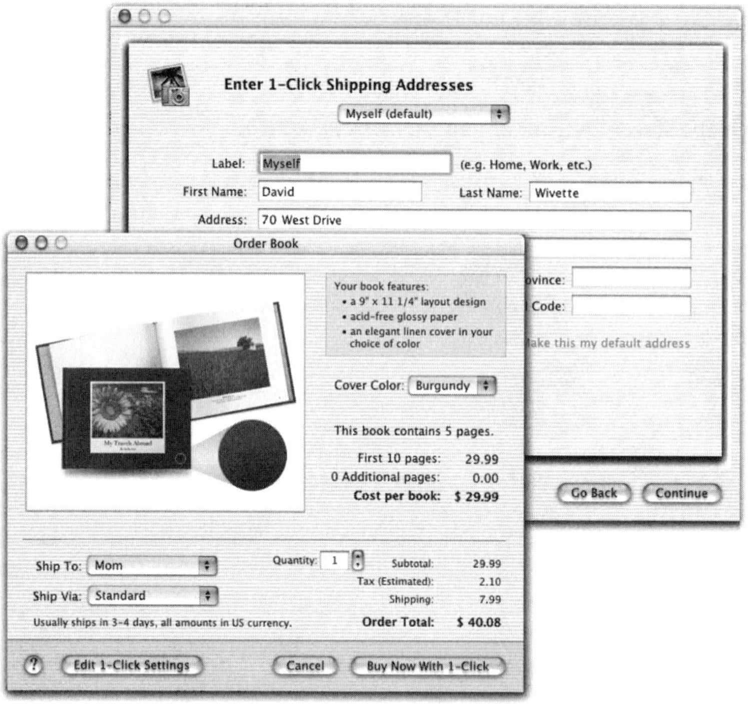

Figure 10-10:
Bottom left: Choose a color, a quantity, and a recipient.

Top right: You won't be allowed to choose a quantity or recipient, though, until you've first signed up for an Apple ID and turned on 1-Click Ordering, which you'll enjoy using over and over again to order books and stuff from the Apple online store.

Later, if you want to troubleshoot or change your Apple ID settings, visit www.myinfo.apple.com.

Your Apple ID

You can't change the quantity, however, or indeed make any additional progress until you've signed up for Apple's 1-Click Ordering system. And to do *that* you need an Apple ID. And to do *that* you must proceed like this:

1. **Click "Enable 1-Click Ordering."**

   Now you see a dialog box that invites you to type in your Apple ID and password, if you have them. If so, fill them in by all means. An Apple ID is your email address. It's the same ID you use to customize the look of Apple's help Web site (if you've ever done that) or to buy something from the Apple store.

2. **Click Create Apple ID.**

   The Create an Apple ID screen appears.

3. **Fill in your email address, a password (twice), a question (which you'll be asked if you forget your password) and its answer, and your date of birth.**

   Unless you enjoy receiving junk email, turn off "I would like to receive Apple news, software updates, special offers, and information…from other companies." Note, too, that Apple ships books only to people in the U.S. and Canada.

4. **Click Continue; on the Terms of Use screen, click Accept.**

   Now you're asked for your billing information (top right in Figure 10-10). This is how you'll pay for the book, and all books to come.

WORKAROUND WORKSHOP

Secrets of the Apple Book Publishing Empire

It's no secret that when you order prints of your photos via the Internet, Kodak makes the prints. But neither temptation nor torture will persuade Apple to reveal who makes the gorgeous iPhoto photo books.

It didn't take long for Mac fans on the Internet, however, to discover some astonishing similarities between the iPhoto books and the books created by a firm called MyPublisher.com. The pricing, timing, and books themselves are all identical. (When asked if it's Apple's publishing partner, MyPublisher.com says, "We don't discuss our partner relationships," which probably means "Yes.")

The truth is, iPhoto-generated books are more elegantly designed than the ones you build yourself at MyPublisher.com. And it's certainly easier to upload books

directly from iPhoto, rather than uploading photo files one at a time using your Web browser.

Still, you should know that building your books directly at MyPublisher.com offers greater design freedom than iPhoto does. You have greater choices of cover colors and materials (even leather), you can add a glossy dust jacket, you can add borders around the pages, you have your choice of lightly patterned backgrounds, and you have much more flexibility over the placement of photos and text.

In fact, it's easy to get carried away with these options and produce something absolutely ghastly, which is probably why Apple chose to limit your options so you simply can't go wrong.

---

5. **Fill in your billing information, and then click Continue.**

   iPhoto lets you set up a number of addresses for people you may want books shipped to. The next screen proposes that you add *yourself* to this list.

6. **Click Continue.**

   You wind up right where you started: at the Order Book screen. This time, however, the controls at the bottom are "live" and operational.

7. **From the Ship To pop-up menu, choose the lucky recipient of this book.**

   If it's you, choose Myself. If not, choose Add New Address from this pop-up menu. Fill in your Apple ID and password to prove that you're you (you certainly wouldn't want some hacker adding addresses to your list!). Click Sign In, and then, on the next screen, fill in the new address. When that's done, click Apply (if you intend to add yet *another* address) or Save (if that's it for now).

POWER USERS' CLINIC

Complete Design Freedom for Geeks

iPhoto may come with only six basic book designs. But for the creatively and technically inclined, that's only the beginning. You're free to design new layouts of your own—or modify Apple's—if you know the secret.

All of the book designs are stored in a secret location as *.nib files,* which you can edit using Apple's free Developer Tools suite. The hardest part of the whole process may just be getting a copy of these programs. Here's what you do:

Method 1: If you bought Mac OS X, you'll find this program on the CD called Developer Tools that came with your Mac OS X CD.

Method 2: You can get the Developer Tools from Apple's Web site. That, however, entails becoming a member of Apple's developer's club; an "Online" membership is free. Sign up at *http://connect.apple.com.*

Once you're on board, return to *http://connect.apple.com* and sign in. Click the Download Software link, then the Mac OS X link. You at last arrive at the Mac OS X software download page. Download the most recent version of the "Mac OS X Developer Tools" disk image.

Either way: Open the Packages folder of your Developer Tools disk or disk image, and then double-click the DevTools.pkg icon to install Apple's suite of programming tools. When the installation is complete, you'll find a new Developer folder on your hard drive.

Now you're ready to view and edit Apple's book-layout files. To view them, Control-click the iPhoto program icon in your Applications folder. From the contextual menu, choose Show Package Contents. (Mac OS X programs may *look* like single, self-contained icons, but most are in fact cleverly disguised folders. Control-clicking is the key to opening them up.)

In the iPhoto window, open the Contents→Resources folder. Here you find hundreds of tiny graphics, each of which constitutes one small piece of iPhoto's interface. You could, if you had very little else to do, open these graphics in a program like Photoshop and edit them, taking care not to change their dimensions. In that way, you could modify the look of the buttons at the bottom of the Share screen, for example. *(Continued)*

But enough ogling the scenery! Find and open the English.lproj→Books folder. Here are six folders with familiar names: Catalog, Classic, Picture Book, and so on, as shown on the previous page. They correspond to the canned book themes within iPhoto.

Duplicate the folder of the book design that comes closest to your dream design. Name the new folder whatever you like—let's call it *Ansel & Gretel*—and then open it. Deciphering the names of these files isn't especially difficult:*Page-Storybook00Cover.nib* is the cover, *Page-Storybook1.nib* is the 1-photo-per-page layout, and so on. (The letters P and L in the various file names—like *Portfolio4PPLL.nib*—refer to various combinations of *portrait* and *landscape* photos on each page.) Double-click the layout document that you want to edit first.

The page opens into a program called Interface Builder, which is one of your Developer Tools. It works much like a standard Mac drawing program. You can drag the text and photo boxes around, make them bigger or smaller, indent them (as shown here at top), change their fonts using the Format menu, and so on. In the Story-book layouts, you can use the Layout→Send to Back (and Bring to Front) commands to control how the photos overlap each other. You have multiple Undo's at your disposal. (Unless you're an XML geek who knows what you're doing, limit your editing to moving text or photo boxes around, resizing them, and overlapping them.)

When you're finished tinkering, quit Interface Builder and save your changes. In the next step, you have to make iPhoto sit up and notice its newly enhanced layouts.

First, open the Developer→ Applications folder and launch the program called PropertyListEditor. Choose File→Open, and navigate to the Applications→ iPhoto→Contents→Resources→ English.lproj→ Books folder. (Yes, PropertyListEditor treats the iPhoto application icon as a folder.) Open the Ansel & Gretel folder, and then open the *book.xml* file inside.

When the book.xml window opens, click the flippy triangle next to the word Root. Scan the list (illustrated at left) until you see the row called Name. Double-click in the Value column and change the old layout name (such as Catalog or Picture Book) to the name you want, such as Ansel & Gretel (shown here). Choose File→Save, and quit PropertyListEditor.

Finally, open your Home→Library→ Caches folder and throw away the iPhoto Cache folder.

When you next start up iPhoto, you'll see your new book layout listed in the Book mode's Theme pop-up menu (left)—and the changes you made to its page designs.

All of this, of course, is at your own risk. If a book you order based on your design doesn't look right, and you call Apple to complain, you're not likely to get a sympathetic ear.

If you wind up at the 1-Click Account Summary screen, click Done.

8. **From the Ship Via pop-up menu, indicate how you want the finished book shipped.**

"Standard" shipping takes about a week and costs $8. "Express" means overnight or second-day shipping (depending on when you place the order) and costs $13. An additional book sent to the same address costs another $1 for Standard shipping, or $2 for Express.

9. **Indicate how many copies of this book you want, using the Quantity control.**

You'll see the Order Total updated.

10. **Click "Buy Now With 1-Click."**

You've already stored your credit card information, so there's nothing to do now but wait for your Mac to upload the book itself. After a few minutes, you'll see a confirmation message.

11. **Go about your life for a week, holding your breath until the book arrives.**

You'll certainly be impressed by the linen-covered cover and the heavy, glossy pages. The photos themselves are printed on Indigo digital presses (fancy digital four-color offset machines), but aren't what you'd call Kodak quality—or even photo-inkjet-on-glossy-paper quality.

But the book itself is classy, it's handsome…and it smells good!

CHAPTER 11

From iPhoto to QuickTime

As Chapter 7 makes clear, once you select your images and choose the music to go with them, iPhoto orchestrates the production and presents it live on your Mac's screen as a slide show.

Which is great, as long as everyone in your social circle lives within six feet of your screen.

The day will come when you want friends and family who live a little farther away to be able to see your slide shows. Sure, you could pack up your Mac and fly across the country, but then you'd have to deal with lousy airline food and cramped seating. Wouldn't it be easier to simply send the slide show as a file that people can play on their own computers?

That's the beauty of QuickTime, a portable multimedia container built into every Mac. Even if the recipient uses a Windows PC (every family has its black sheep), your photos will meet their public; QuickTime movies play equally well on Gateways and Dells as they do on iMacs and PowerBooks.

The trick is to convert your well-composed iPhoto slide show into a stand-alone QuickTime movie: a file on your hard drive that you can email to other people, post on your Web page for downloading, burn on a CD, and so on.

Exporting a Slide Show to QuickTime

Fortunately, iPhoto makes creating the movie as simple as creating the original show itself. You just have to know which buttons to click.

Step 1: Perfect the Slide Show

Before you pack up your slide show for release to the public, review it to make sure it plays the way you want it to. You'll probably find it easiest to create a new album just for your QuickTime slide show (Chapter 5), so that you can fool around with the sequence and photo selection without messing up the album designed for such purposes as photo books and *onscreen* slide shows.

Thinking like a focus group

As you review your presentation, place the pictures into the proper sequence, remembering that you won't be there to verbally "set up" the slide show and comment as it plays. Look at it with fresh eyes and ask yourself, "If I knew nothing about this subject, would this show make sense?"

During this exercise, you might decide that your presentation could use a few more descriptive images to better tell the story. If that's the case, go back through your master photo library and look for pictures of landmarks and signs that are easily recognizable. Put one or two at the beginning of the show to set the stage. For example, if your slide show is about a vacation in Washington, D.C., then you might want to open with a picture of the Capitol, White House, or Lincoln Memorial.

Tip: If you don't have any suitable opening shots in your library, or even if you do, another option is to begin your show with a few words of text, like opening credits. To do so, create a JPEG graphic containing the text in a program like AppleWorks, Photoshop, or GraphicConverter. (Make sure this graphic matches the pixel dimensions of your slide show, as described in the following section.) Then drag and drop the file into iPhoto; drag it into your slide-show album; and place it first in the sequence. You've got yourself an opening title screen.

Which photos make the cut

If you're used to the slide show feature described in Chapter 7, the method for specifying which photos are exported to your QuickTime movie might throw you.

- If *one* thumbnail is selected, that's all you'll get in the finished QuickTime movie—the world's shortest slide show. (This is the part that might throw you: An iPhoto slide show would begin with that one selected photo and then move on from there, showing you all the rest of the photos in the album.)

- If *several* thumbnails are selected, only they make it into the QuickTime slide show movie.

- If *no* thumbnails are selected, the entire album's worth of photos wind up in the show.

When you're ready to convert your presentation to a QuickTime movie, click the Share button to summon iPhoto's bottom row of icons. Click the Export option in the lower-right corner.

The Export Images dialog box appears, as shown in Figure 11-1. Click the Quick-Time tab, where you have some important decisions to make.

Step 2: Choose the Movie Dimensions

Specifying the width and height for your movie affects not only how big it is on the screen during playback, but also its file size, which may become an issue if you plan to email the movie to other people.

Figure 11-1:
The Export dialog box with the QuickTime tab selected. This is the airlock, the womb, the last time you'll be able to affect your movie before it's born.

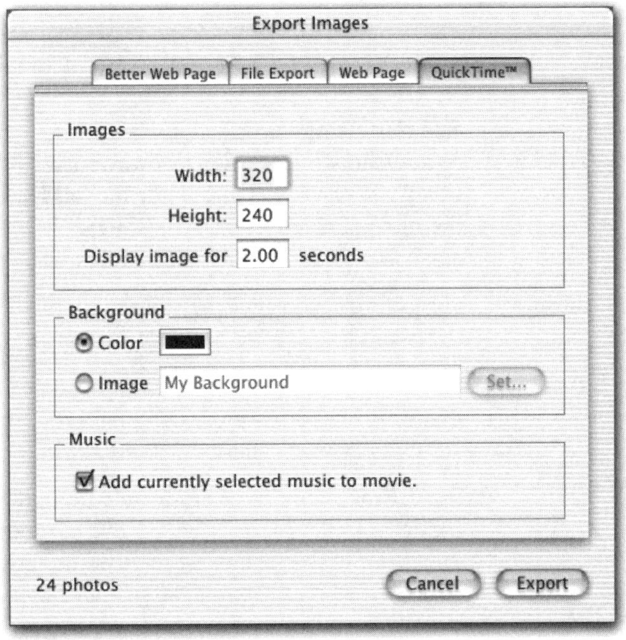

iPhoto generally proposes 640 x 480 pixels. That's a great size: big enough for people to see some detail in the photo, but not so big that the resulting movie won't play from, say, a CD. (CDs are much slower than hard drives.)

You're free to change these dimensions, however. If the movie will be played back from a hard drive, you may want to crank up the dimensions all the way to the size of the screen itself: 800 x 600 is a safe bet if you're not sure. You can go larger (1024 x 768, for example), but only if you're certain that your audience's screen is that big.

Proportion considerations

All of these suggestions assume, by the way, that your photos' dimensions are in a 4:3 ratio, the way they come from most cameras (see page 125). That way, they'll fit nicely into the standard QuickTime playback window.

But there's nothing to stop you from typing other numbers into the Width and Height boxes. If most of the shots are vertical, for example, you'll want to reverse the proposed dimensions so that they're 480 x 640, resulting in a taller, thinner playback window.

In any case, it would be hard to imagine why you'd want to choose dimensions other than those in a 4:3 ratio unless:

• You've cropped the photos for use in ordering prints (page 155).

• Your camera doesn't produce 4:3 images. (Some produce photos with a 3-to-2 width-to-height ratio instead, in which case you'd want your movie dimensions to match.)

• You're going for a bizarre, distorted look in your finished film.

Size considerations

As you choose dimensions, however, bear in mind that they also determine the *file size* of the resulting QuickTime movie. That's not such an issue if you plan to play the movie from a CD, DVD, or hard drive. But if you plan to send the movie by email or post it on a Web page, watch out.

For example, consider the slide-show movie shown in Figure 11-2. It contains 24 slides and has an MP3 music soundtrack.

At 640 x 480 pixels, this movie would take up 3 MB on your hard drive—and at least that much in your recipients' email Inboxes. Scaling it down to a quarter that size (320 x 240) would shave off about a third of that, resulting in a 2.1 MB file.

But 2.1 megabytes is a very big file to send as an email attachment to anyone who connects to the Internet with a dial-up modem. You could, of course, reduce the dimensions even further. At some point, though, you'd reach a point of diminishing returns; the pictures would be so microscopic, the project wouldn't be worth doing.

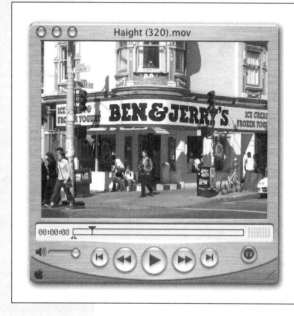

Figure 11-2:
This sample QuickTime movie has dimensions of 320 x 240 pixels. This is not what you'd call an Imax movie; it will play in a fairly small window on your audience's screens.

In that case, you might want to start whittling down the music rather than the photos (see the box below).

Managing Music

In the Music section of your QuickTime export dialog box, you have the option of including the soundtrack you originally selected for your movie (page 146) by turning on the box labeled, "Add currently selected music to movie." (If you want a different soundtrack, click Cancel, choose File→Preferences, and choose a different song as directed on page 147. Then start over with step 1 on page 216.)

To save file size, you could turn off this box. That 320 x 240 movie would shrink to a mere 440 K—less than one-fourth the size of the presentation with the original soundtrack—but, of course, you'd wind up with a silent movie.

Fortunately, there is a middle road. It involves some work in iTunes and a slight reduction in sound quality, but reducing the file size of the music track can result in a substantial file shrinkage. See the box below for details.

Step 3: Seconds per Photo

How many seconds do you want each picture to remain on the screen before the next one appears? You specify this number using the "Display image for ___ seconds" box in the QuickTime Export dialog box.

When you first open the dialog box, iPhoto proposes whatever frame rate you used in your original slide show. You're free to change it to other timings.

POWER USERS' CLINIC

Musical Liposuction

If you're struggling with the size of a QuickTime–movie slide show that's too big for emailing, consider shrinking the size of the music track. By cutting its *bit rate* (a measure of its sound quality) from 192 to 128 Kbps, the file size for a hypothetical 320 x 240–pixel movie would shrink from 2.1 MB to 1.5 MB—and your ears would hardly be able to tell the difference.

This kind of surgery requires iTunes, the music management software that comes with every Mac (you can also download it from the Apple Web site).

Once in iTunes, choose File→Preferences; in the dialog box, click the Importing tab. Choose MP3 Encoder from the Import Using pop-up menu, if it's not already selected, and choose "Good Quality (128 kbps)" from the Configuration pop-up menu.

Now choose Advanced→Convert to MP3. Navigate to the song on the original music CD (insert it if necessary), or from within your existing iTunes library on your hard disk. (It's in your Home→Documents→iTunes folder.)

iTunes imports the song at the new, lower *sample rate* (quality setting). The song's name appears in your iTunes library list. (If this song had already been imported into iTunes, you might want to rename the new version. Highlight it and then choose File→Get Info to rename it.)

Now return to iPhoto. Choose File→Preferences. From the Music pop-up menu, choose Other. Navigate to and open your new, resampled song.

When you export the slide show to QuickTime, you'll find that it's much more svelte—but sounds practically identical to the puffier version.

In fact, what's especially nice about exporting your show to QuickTime is that you're allowed to use faster frame rates than the "1 second per image" maximum in iPhoto slide shows. That's worth keeping in mind when you want to create (a) a time-lapse effect of photos flying by, or (b) a slide show that looks hallucinogenic.

Step 4: Background Colors

The color or image you choose in the Background section of the dialog box will appear as the first and last frames of the export. It will also fill in the margins of the frame when a vertically oriented or oddly proportioned picture appears.

Solid colors

To specify a solid color, click the color swatch next to the Color button. The color picker described in the figure on page 181 appears.

Generally speaking, white or black makes the best background.

POWER USERS' CLINIC

When Photos and Backgrounds Match

If you're getting seriously hooked on this iPhoto thing, here's a trick that will make you the envy of your nerd friends: Use the Color background option to create an illusion that your photos are appearing and disappearing on a constant background.

For example, consider this photo of a Moon Jelly jellyfish swimming in an aquarium tank. It was photographed so there were no distracting elements in the background—just the subject in blue water.

If you create a background the same color as the water, the movie will begin by showing your solid color—and then moon jelly will just *blink* into existence, without an apparent frame change or background shift. It looks really cool.

What's the trick to creating a backdrop that matches the water? First,

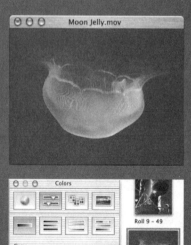

in the Export dialog box, choose the Color option. Click the rectangular swatch. When the Color Picker dialog box appears, click the magnifying-glass icon at the bottom of the box.

Now your cursor is, in fact, a functional magnifying glass that you can move to any part of the screen. The trick here is to position it over the actual iPhoto photo whose background color you want to clone, as shown here. Click the mouse button to capture that color, and then click Apply in the color picker box. You'll notice that the rectangle next to the color radio button has now changed to the color of the background you cloned.

When you export the movie, this custom color will fill in the first and last frames—and your jellyfish (or whatever the first photo is) will seem to pop into existence on top of it.

Background graphics

If you click the Image button and then the Set button next to it, you can navigate your hard drive in search of a *graphics* file to use as the slide show background. This is where handiness with a graphics program like AppleWorks, Photoshop, or Graphic-Converter comes in handy; by designing a picture there (in dimensions that match your movie) and exporting it as a JPEG file, you have complete freedom to control the kind of "movie screen" your QuickTime slide show will have (Figure 11-3).

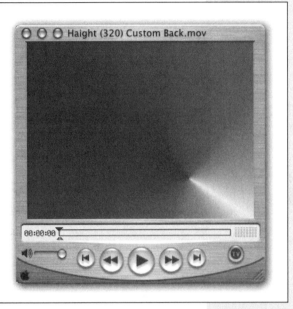

Figure 11-3:
*Here's a custom background created in AppleWorks
and saved in JPEG format. This is the underlying
"placemat" that will show through from behind
photos in the QuickTime slide show that don't quite
fill the frame.*

Step 5: Export the Movie

Having specified the dimensions, frame rate, music, and background for your movie, there's nothing left but to click the Export button in the dialog box. You'll be asked to specify a name and folder location for the movie (leave the proposed suffix *.mov* on the end of the name), and then click Save. After a moment of computing, iPhoto returns you to its main screen.

Press ⌘-H to hide iPhoto; then navigate to the folder you specified and double-click the movie to play it in QuickTime Player (a program that comes with every Mac). When it opens, click the Play triangle, or press the Space bar, to enjoy your newly packaged slide show (Figure 11-4).

Whenever playback is stopped, you can even "walk" through the slides manually by pressing the right-arrow key twice (for the next photo) or the left-arrow key once (for the previous one).

Tip: Even Windows PC users can enjoy your QuickTime movies—if they visit *www.apple.com/quicktime /download* to download the free QuickTime Player program for Windows.

Fun with QuickTime

The free version of QuickTime Player is, well, just a player. If you're willing to pay $30, however, you can turn it into QuickTime Player Pro, which offers a few special features relevant to iPhoto movie fans:

Figure 11-4:
Once you're in QuickTime Player, you can control the playback of the slide show in a number of ways. If you don't feel like clicking and dragging onscreen controls, the arrow keys adjust the volume (up and down) or step through the photos one at a time (right or left).

- **Play movies in full screen mode**. QuickTime Player Pro can play slide shows in full-screen mode—no menu bar, Dock, window edges, or other distracting elements—turning your laptop screen into a portable theater (among other advantages).

- **Edit your flicks**. QuickTime Player Pro lets you trim off excess footage or add an additional soundtrack, or even a text track for subtitles (captions).

- **Adjust video and audio**. Only the Pro version lets you fine-tune your video and audio controls—Brightness, Treble, Bass, and so on—and then save those settings with your movie.

- **No more nagware**. Upgrading eliminates the persistent "Upgrade Now" dialog box that appears when you open the regular Player program.

If you don't care much about customizing your movies after you export them from iPhoto, then apply that $30 to another memory card for your digital camera.

But if you decide that the upgrade is worthwhile, visit *www.apple.com* and click the QuickTime tab. There you'll find the links that let you upgrade your free QuickTime player to the Pro version. In exchange for $30, you'll be given a registration number that "unlocks" QuickTime's advanced features. (To input the serial number

in QuickTime Player, choose QuickTime Player→Preferences→Registration, and
then click Edit Registration.)

Then you'll be ready for the following tricks.

Play Movies at Full Screen

If you've upgraded to QuickTime Player Pro, here's how to create a full-screen, cinematic experience.

First, use a black background when you export your movie from iPhoto. That way,
there will be no frame marks or distracting colors to detract from your images. Furthermore, the black bars on the sides of vertically oriented photos will blend in
seamlessly with the rest of the darkened monitor, so that nobody is even aware that
the photo has been rotated. Those black bars will also fill in the gap between the
standard monitor shape and the nonstandard ones preferred by Apple these days
(such as the screens on the extra-wide Cinema Display or PowerBook G4 Titanium).

Second, export your movie in as large a size as will fit on your screen. Most often,
that means dimensions of 800 x 600 or 1024 x 768—whatever matches your monitor's
current setting. (To find out, choose →System Preferences and click the Display
icon.) Your images will occupy more of your Mac's display area, imparting greater
impact.

Once you've exported your movie, presenting it in "theater mode" depends on which
version of QuickTime you're using.

- **QuickTime 5.** Once you've opened the slideshow movie file, choose Movie→
  Present Movie. Fill in the dialog box as shown in Figure 11-5.

Tip: In the Present Movie dialog box, you have a choice of presentation mode (but only when working
with *slide-show* movies–not regular QuickTime movies).

Click Normal for automatic playback of the whole show, with music. Click Slide Show if you want to
advance the photos manually, by pressing the right and left arrow keys. (Here again, you press the right
arrow key *twice* for the next photo, the left arrow key *once* for the previous one. Double-clicking the
mouse also advances to the next photo.) You don't get music this way, however.

Figure 11-5:
*From the Movie Size pop-up menu, choose Normal. (Yes,
you could choose Full Screen—but that would stretch
your photos to fill the screen, often resulting in
distortion.) Click Play, sit back, and enjoy.*

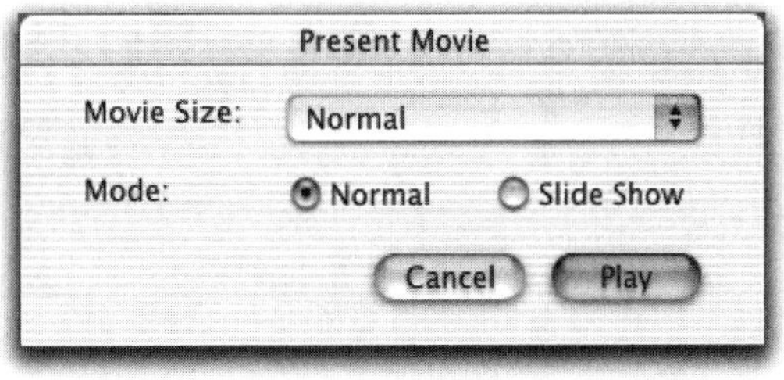

Present Movie	
Movie Size:	Normal
Mode:	● Normal ○ Slide Show
	Cancel Play

- **QuickTime 6.** Choose Movie→Full Screen. Then proceed exactly as described on the previous page.

To end a self-playing show, click the mouse; to end one in Slide Show mode, press ⌘-period.

Once you've created a slide-show movie, keep in mind that nothing's etched in stone—at least not if you have QuickTime Player Pro. Suppose you don't care for the empty frames of background color (or background picture) that iPhoto adds automatically at the beginning and end of your movie. Or what if, thanks to an unforeseen downsizing, a graduation, or a romantic breakup, you want to delete a photo or two from an existing movie? Using QuickTime Player Pro, you can snip unwanted photos or frames right out.

Selecting footage

Before you can cut, copy, or paste footage, QuickTime Player needs to provide a way for you to specify *what* footage you want to manipulate. Its solution: the two tiny black triangles that sprout out of the left end of the horizontal scroll bar, as shown in Figure 11-6. These are the "in" and "out" points; by dragging these triangles, you can enclose the scene you want to cut or copy.

Click in this bar
to place starting handle.

Shift-click in the bar
to place the ending handle.

Figure 11-6:
To select a particular scene, drag the tiny black triangles apart until they enclose the material you want, or use the clicking/Shift-clicking trick shown here. As you drag or click, QuickTime Player updates the movie picture to show you where you are. The material you select is represented by a gray strip of the scroll bar.

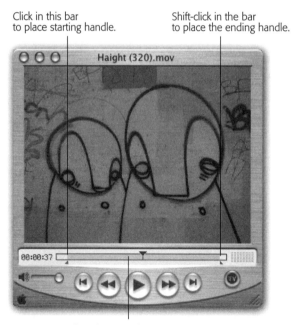

Everything between them is selected.

Tip: You can gain more precise control over the selection procedure shown in Figure 11-6 by clicking one of the black triangles and then pressing the right or left arrow key. Doing so expands or contracts the selected chunk of footage by one frame at a time.

You may also prefer to select a piece of footage by Shift-clicking the Play button. As long as you hold down the Shift key, you continue to select footage. When you release the Shift key, you stop the playback; the selected passage then appears in gray on the scroll bar.

Once you've highlighted a passage of footage, you can proceed as follows:

- Jump to the beginning or end of the selected footage by pressing Option-right arrow or -left arrow key.

- Deselect the footage by dragging the two triangles together again.

- Play only the selected passage by choosing Movie→Play Selection Only. (The other Movie menu commands, such as Loop, apply only to the selection at this point.)

- Drag the movie picture out of the Player window and onto the desktop, where it becomes a *movie clipping* that you can double-click to view.

- Cut, copy, or clear the highlighted material using the commands in the Edit menu.

Tip: Here's a great way to add opening credits or other titles to your slide shows. If you paste some copied text directly into QuickTime Player Pro, you get a two-second title at the current frame, professionally displayed as white type against a black background. QuickTime Player automatically uses the font, size, and style of the text that was in the text clipping. You can paste a graphic image, too; once again, you get a two-second "slide" of that still image.

If you find it easier, you can also drag a text or picture *clipping file* directly from the desktop into the QuickTime Player window; once again, you get a two-second insert. To make the text or picture appear longer than two seconds, drag or paste it several times in a row.

In either case, you need to specify the fonts, sizes, and styles for your low-budget titling feature by formatting the text the way you want it *before* you copy it from your word processor.

Exporting Edited Movies

After you've finished working on a sound or movie, you can send it back out into the world by choosing File→Save As. At this point, you can specify a new name for your edited masterpiece. You must also choose one of these two options:

- **Save normally.** The term "normally" is a red herring—in fact, you'll almost never want to use this option, because it produces a very tiny file that contains no footage at all. Think of it as an alias of the movie you edited. A file that you edited and saved "normally" works only as long as the original, *unedited* movie remains on your hard drive. If you try to email the newly saved file, your unhappy recipient won't see anything at all.

• **Make movie self-contained.** This option produces a new QuickTime movie—the one you've just finished editing. Although it consumes more disk space, it has none of the drawbacks of a "save normally" file.

Advanced Audio and Video Controls

One of the difficulties of creating multimedia productions is that there's no standard calibration for all the various computers that might play them. For example, a slide show that your friend creates on his Dell computer might look very washed-out on your Mac.

Should you inherit movies with poor audio and video, QuickTime Player Pro gives you some nifty audio and video controls to compensate.

To summon these controls, open a movie in QuickTime and choose Movie→Show Sound Controls (or Movie→Show Video Controls). See Figure 11-7.

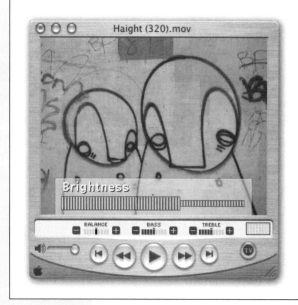

Figure 11-7:
You can adjust the brightness, balance, bass, or treble using these generally hidden controls. The trick is to click the control you want (in the light gray strip near the bottom) and then, once the "graph" has appeared on the movie frame, click anywhere along its length to adjust the strength of the selected quality (bass, brightness, whatever).

Burning a QuickTime Movie CD

If your QuickTime slide show lasts more than a minute or two, it's probably too big to send to people by email, unless they have cable modems or DSL boxes. In that and other situations, the ideal distribution method for your masterpiece may be a CD that you burn yourself. Assuming your Mac has a CD burner—and most models do these days—here's how the process goes:

1. **Prepare your QuickTime movie.**

   Since file size isn't an issue, you can make your slide show dimensions 640 x 480, 800 x 600, or any other size that will fit on the computer screen. There's no need to throttle down the music quality (page 219), either.

   Tip: To make things easy for the audience (even if it's only you), you can turn on the Auto Play feature, which will make the movie play immediately after being double-clicked. (Savings: One click on the triangular Play button.)

   To turn on Auto Play, start by opening the movie in QuickTime Player Pro. Choose Movie→Get Movie Properties. In the Properties dialog box, choose Auto Play from the drop-down box on the right, and then turn on the Auto Play Enabled checkbox. Save the movie as usual.

   ---

2. **Put a blank CD in your burner.**

   A few seconds after you insert the CD-R (recordable) or CD-RW (rewriteable) disc, you'll be asked to name the disc and choose the format (Figure 11-8). Leave the Format pop-up menu set to Standard.

Figure 11-8:
Top: After you insert a blank CD-R or CD-RW, you'll need to name it and select the "Standard" format.

Bottom: You have one last chance to change your mind before you burn the CD. If everything's a go, then click Burn.

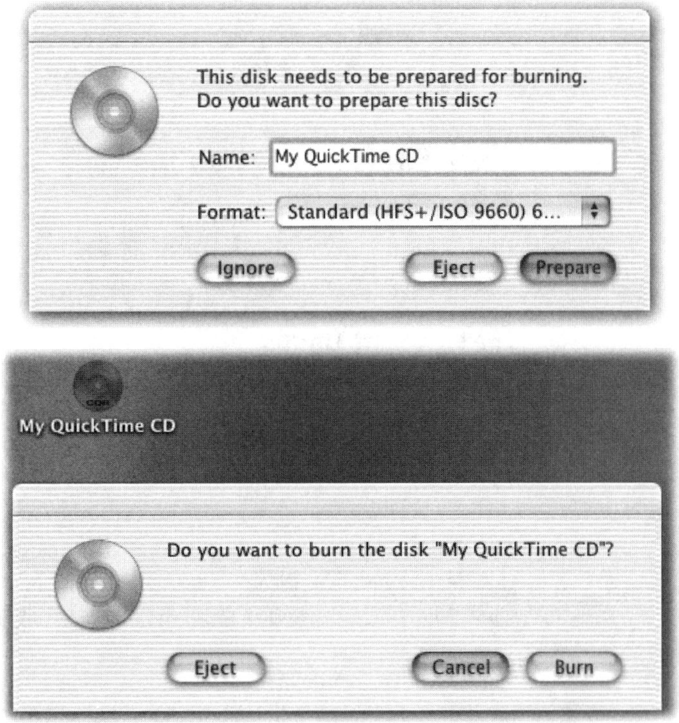

This disk needs to be prepared for burning.
Do you want to prepare this disc?

Name: My QuickTime CD

Format: Standard (HFS+/ISO 9660) 6...

Ignore   Eject   Prepare

My QuickTime CD

Do you want to burn the disk "My QuickTime CD"?

Eject   Cancel   Burn

3. **Click Prepare.**

   In a few seconds, the CD's icon appears on your desktop.

4. **Drag the QuickTime movie(s) onto the CD's icon.**

   These are, of course, the slide-show movies you've exported from iPhoto.

5. **Click once on the CD icon and then choose File→Burn Disc.**

   A confirmation dialog box appears (Figure 11-9, bottom). This is your last chance to bail out.

6. **Click Burn.**

   The Mac saves the movies onto the CD.

   When the process is complete, eject the disc. Then marvel that it will play equally well on Mac OS 9, Mac OS X, and Windows computers that have QuickTime Player installed.

Tip: If you have the software called Toast Titanium (*www.roxio.com),* an additional option awaits. You can open your exported iPhoto slide-show movie and then export it as a *VCD-compatible MPEG* file.

If you burn the MPEG movie file onto a CD, you'll have yourself what's known as a *Video CD.* It's something like a low-rent, low-quality DVD. It will play on most modern DVD players, thus offering you a handy way for computer-less people to watch your slide show on TV.

Slide-Show Movies on the Web

Chapter 9 offers complete details for posting your photos on the Web. But with just a few adjustments in the instructions, you can just as easily post your slide-show movies on the Web, too.

The Fast Start Option

Under ordinary circumstances, posting a movie involves quite a wait for your Web visitors. They click the movie's icon in hopes of viewing it—and have to wait while the entire 3-megabyte movie downloads to their computers. Only then can they begin watching it.

Tip: When you export your Web-bound movie from iPhoto, make the "movie screen" no larger than 320 pixels wide by 240 pixels tall. If you make your movie any bigger, Apple's HomePage service will just squish it down to 320 x 240 anyway, possibly resulting in distortion.

But if you have QuickTime Player Pro, you can create movies that start playing almost immediately when Web visitors click them.

To endow your movie with this power, open it in QuickTime Player Pro, and then follow these steps:

---

1. **Choose File→Export.**

   The "Save exported file as" dialog box appears. Make sure that the Export pop-up menu says "Movie to QuickTime Movie," and the Use pop-up menu says Most Recent Settings.

2. **Click Options.**

   The Movie Settings dialog box appears (Figure 11-9, bottom). Your job here is to format the Web movie so that it will look good without taking a long time to arrive in your visitors' Web browsers.

Figure 11-9:
Bottom left: These settings will help you prepare your movie for Web serving. After you've tried an export or two, you can play with the adjustments to customize your slide show even further.

Top right: These are good video settings for an exported slide-show Web movie.

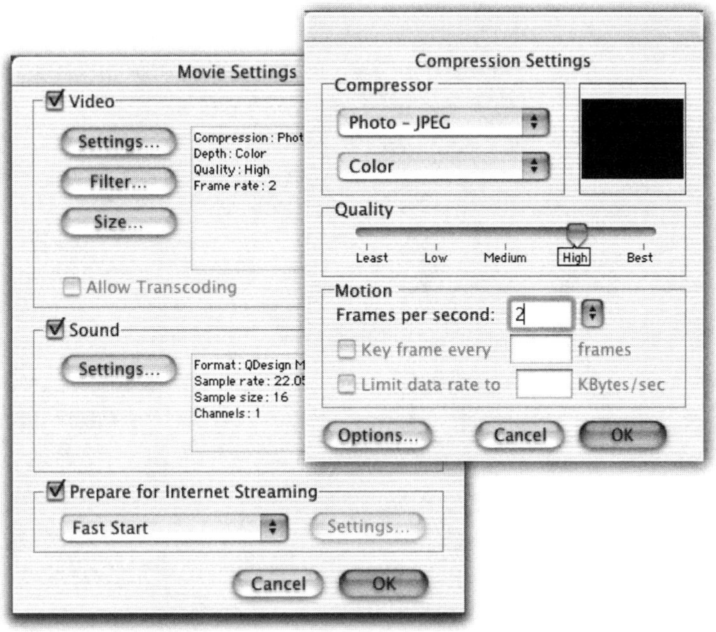

3. **Under Video, click Settings. In the Compression Settings dialog box (Figure 11-9, top), choose "Photo – JPEG" from the first pop-up menu.**

   This format is compact and high quality, making it a good choice for slide shows.

4. **In the "Frames per second" box, type whatever frame rate you used when you originally exported your movie from iPhoto.**

   For example *1* equals one frame (photograph) per second, *.5* flashes two frames per second, and so on.

5. **Drag the Quality slider to High or Best, and then click OK.**

   You return to the Movie Settings dialog box.

6. **Under Sound, click Settings. In the Sound Settings dialog box, choose QDesign Music from the Compressor pop-up menu, and then click OK.**

The QDesign Music format produces high-quality music at very small file sizes, which is just what you'd hope for in Web-played movies. (If your movie, by chance, has a spoken dialog track rather than music, use the Qualcomm PureVoice codec instead.)

You return once again to the Movie Settings box. Here, you should confirm that the "Prepare for Internet Streaming" checkbox is turned on, and that Fast Start is selected in its pop-up menu. These settings are responsible for the fast-playback feature described above, in which your viewers don't have to wait for the *entire* movie to download before playback starts. Instead, they'll only have to wait for a quarter or half of it, or whatever portion is necessary to play the entire movie uninterrupted while the latter part is still being downloaded.

7. **Click OK, then Save.**

Your slide show takes a few minutes to export. But once the process is complete, you're ready to upload the file to your Web site.

Note: Once you've optimized and exported your slide show in QuickTime Pro, don't use the File→Save or File→Save As command after making changes to the movie. If you do, you'll automatically turn *off* the Fast Start option you built in when you exported the movie.

It's OK to make further changes. But when you're finished, use the File→Export command again, repeating the previous steps, to preserve the movie's Web-optimized condition.

Uploading to the Web

When your movie file is ready, bring your iDisk onto the screen as described on page 177. Drag your movie file into the Movies folder, as shown in Figure 11-10.

Now open your Web browser. Go to *www.apple.com*, click the iTools tab, sign in if necessary, and then click the HomePage tab.

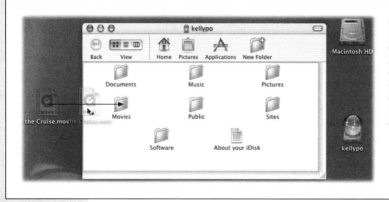

Figure 11-10:
Once you've brought your iDisk icon to the screen, drag your slide-show movie into its Movie folder. Be prepared to wait a very long time for both steps; the iDisk is not what you'd call a speedy mechanism.

Then create a movie-playing page like this:

1. **Click the + button underneath the list of existing Web pages you've made (Figure 11-11, lower right).**

   A list of canned design themes appears.

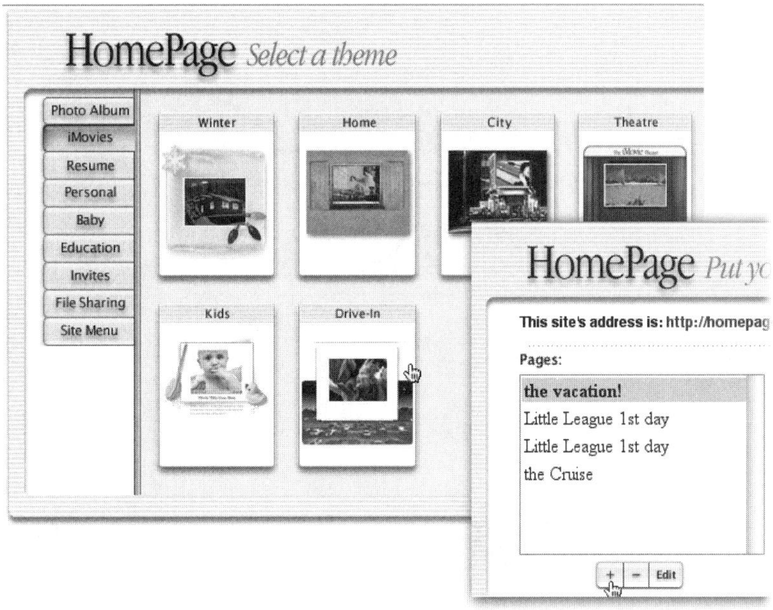

Figure 11-11:
Lower right: Creating a new Web page begins with a simple click on the + button.

Upper left: On the next screen, choose a design template from among the iMovie ones. This is idiot-proof Web design at its finest.

2. **Click the iMovies tab, and then click one of the movie templates (Figure 11-12, left).**

   Now a "big-screen" version of that template thumbnail appears.

3. **At the top of the page, click the Edit icon.**

   You can see this button in Figure 11-12. A "Choose a file" Web page appears, featuring a tiny list of movies you've dragged into your iDisk's Movies folder. Whichever one is first in the list begins to play immediately, just to remind you of what it is.

4. **Click the name of the movie you want, and then click Choose (Figure 11-12, inset).**

   You return to the Edit page. Ignore the fact that your actual movie doesn't yet appear in the placeholder frame.

5. **In the text boxes at the bottom of the dialog box, type a title and caption for your movie, if you like.**

   If you'd like a self-updating counter that shows how many people have viewed your movie, turn on the Show checkbox at the very bottom of the window.

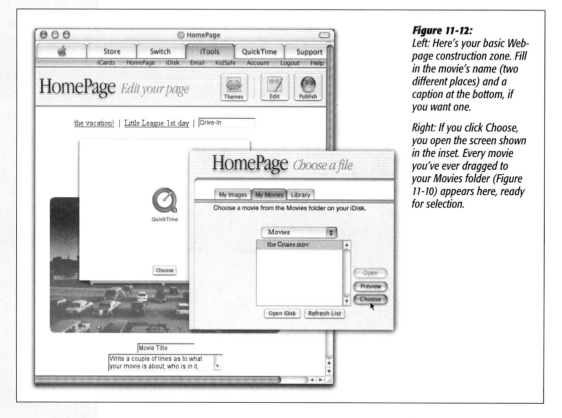

Figure 11-12:
Left: Here's your basic Web-page construction zone. Fill in the movie's name (two different places) and a caption at the bottom, if you want one.

Right: If you click Choose, you open the screen shown in the inset. Every movie you've ever dragged to your Movies folder (Figure 11-10) appears here, ready for selection.

6. **Name the movie page by typing a title into the text box just above the movie, and then click Publish.**

   Finally, a Congratulations page appears, letting you know the Web address of the finished movie page. Note the little button that offers to email this address to your friends, family, and agent, too—a handy feature, considering that this case-sensitive address is none too easy to remember *(http://homepage.mac.com/ yourname/iMovieTheater1.html).*

   You can also click the blue lettering of the address to view the movie yourself, right then and there—an almost irresistible offer. (For an example of a movie-on-the-Web made just this way, visit *http://homepage.mac.com/dstory* and click the "Haight St. Movie" link.)

Part Four:
iPhoto Stunts

4

Screen Savers, Desktop Pictures, and Plug-Ins

Y ou've assembled libraries of digital images, emailed heart-touching moments
to friends and family, published your recent vacation pictures on the Web,
authored a QuickTime movie or two, and even boosted the stock price of
Canon and Epson single-handedly through your consumption of inkjet printer cartridges. What more could there be?

Plenty. This chapter covers iPhoto's final repertoire of photo stunts, like turning
your photos into one of the best screen savers that's ever floated across a computer
display, plastering one particularly delicious shot across your desktop, and even exporting your shots to a Palm organizer. (Be honest: haven't you always wanted to do
that?)

Building a Custom Screen Saver

Mac OS X's screen saver feature is sensational. It's so good, it's been the deciding
factor responsible for pushing more than one Mac fan over the edge into making
the upgrade to Mac OS X. When this screen saver kicks in (after several minutes of
inactivity on your part), your Mac's screen becomes a personal movie theater. The
effect is something like a slide show, except that the pictures don't simply appear
one after another and sit there on the screen. Instead, they're much more animated.
They slide gently across the screen, zooming in or zooming out, smoothly dissolv-
ing from one to the next.

Mac OS X comes equipped with a few photo collections that look great with this
treatment: forests, space shots, and so on. But let the rabble use those canned screen
savers. You, a digital master, can substitute your *own* photos for screen-saver fodder.

Meet the Screen Saver

To get a feeling for Mac OS X's screen saver, choose →System Preferences (or click the System Preferences icon on the Dock) and click the Screen Saver icon. Click one of the prefab screen savers—Beach, Cosmos, Forest—and then click Test to try it out on your own screen. (Click the mouse to stop the show.)

Then, when you're ready to turn one of your own photo collections into a screen saver, duck into iPhoto and drag the pictures into an album of their own, if they're not already in one (Chapter 5).

Tip: Horizontal shots will fill your monitor better than vertical ones—the verticals will have fat black bars on either side to fill the empty space.

If you have an oddball camera (one whose photos have a 3:2 width-to-height ratio instead of 4:3) or an oddball screen (like the extra-wide PowerBook G4 screen), there's one more step. You might want to crop the photos (or copies of them) accordingly to maximize their impact.

Click the Share mode button, and then click the Screen Saver icon on the bottom panel. The dialog box shown in Figure 12-1 appears.

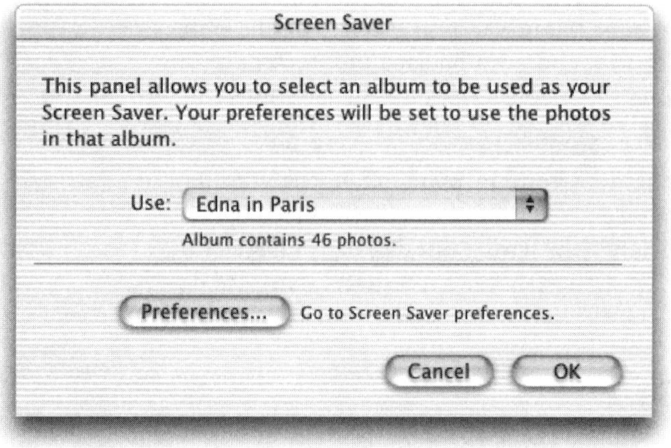

Figure 12-1:
After you hit the Screen Saver button, you're presented with this dialog box, in which you can choose an album for use with your Mac's screen saver. Click the Preferences button to open the corresponding panel of System Preferences, where you can specify when the screen saver should kick in.

Use the pop-up menu to choose the name of the album that contains the photos you want to grace your screen while you're away from the Mac. Click OK.

Ready to view the splendor of your very own homemade screen saver? If you have the patience of a Zen master, you can now sit there, motionless, staring at your Mac for the next half an hour or so—or as long as it takes for Mac OS X to conclude that you're no longer working and finally begin displaying your images on the screen.

If, however, you feel that life is too short as it is, open System Preferences. Click the Slide Show icon, and then click the Test button. See the box on the facing page for details on setting up and triggering the screen saver function.

Tip: Your screen saver slide shows will look best if your pictures are at least the same resolution as your Mac's monitor. (If your digital camera has a resolution of 1.3 megapixels or better, you're all set.)

If you're not sure what your screen resolution is, go to System Preferences and click the Displays icon (or just consult the Displays mini menu next to your menu-bar clock, if it appears there).

One-Click Desktop Backdrop

iPhoto's desktop-image feature is the best way to drive home the point that photos of your children (or dog, or mother, or self) are the most beautiful in the world. You pick one spectacular shot to replace the standard Mac OS X swirling-blue desktop pattern. It's like refrigerator art on steroids (Figure 12-2).

Creating wallpaper in iPhoto is so easy that you could change the picture every day—and you may well want to. Simply highlight a thumbnail, click the Share button, and click the Desktop button on the bottom panel.

UP TO SPEED

Screen Saver Basics

You don't technically *need* a screen saver to protect your monitor from burn-in. Today's energy-efficient monitors wouldn't burn an image into the screen unless you left them on continuously for two years, according to the people who actually design and build them.

No, screen savers are mostly about entertainment, pure and simple—and Mac OS X's built-in screen saver, the first in Mac history, is the most entertaining around.

When you click a module's name in the Screen Savers list, you see a mini version of it playing back in the Preview screen. Click Test to give the module a dry run on your full screen. (Moving the mouse or pressing any key kicks you out of test mode.)

You can control when your screen saver takes over your monitor in any of several ways. For example, in the **Acti-**vation pane, you can set the amount of time that has to pass without keyboard or mouse activity before the screen saver starts. The duration can be as short as five minutes or as long as an hour; or you can drag the slider to Never to turn the screen saver off completely.

On the **Hot Corners** pane, you can turn each corner of your monitor into a *hot spot*. Whenever you roll your cursor into that corner, the screen saver either turns on instantly (great for those times when you happen to be shopping on eBay at the moment your boss walks by) or stays off permanently (for times when you're reading onscreen or watching a movie).

In any case, pressing any key or clicking the mouse always removes the screen saver from your screen and takes you back to whatever you were doing.

Just three words of advice. First, choose a picture that's at least as big as your screen (1024 x 768 pixels, for example). Otherwise, Mac OS X will stretch it to fit, distorting the photo in the process. Second, horizontal shots work much better than vertical ones; iPhoto blows up vertical ones to fit the width of the screen, chopping off the heads and feet of your loved ones.

Finally, note that the second command in the Constrain pop-up menu (page 125) shows the exact dimensions of your screen, so that you can crop the designated photo (or a copy of it) to fit whatever oddball dimensions your monitor has.

And by the way: If public outcry demands that you return your desktop to one of the standard system backdrops, open System Preferences, click the Desktop icon, and choose from the Collections pop-up menu to restore one of the standard backgrounds.

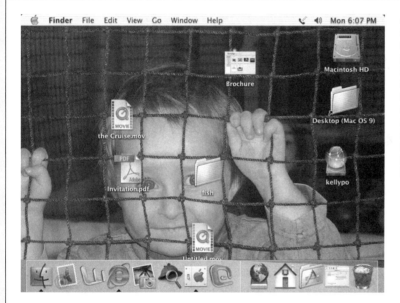

Figure 12-2:
Folders and icons may occasionally mar a desktop photo's full-screen magnificence, but look at the bright side: The fact that you're getting documents in your children's eyes will be all the more incentive for you to file them away in a folder, becoming a better housekeeper in the process.

Exporting Pictures

The whole point of iPhoto is to provide a centralized location for every photo in your world. That doesn't mean that they're locked there, however; it's as easy to take pictures out of iPhoto as it is to put them in. Spinning out a photo from iPhoto can be useful in situations like these:

• You're creating a Web page outside of iPhoto, and you need a photo in a certain size and format.

• Somebody else on your network loves one of your pictures and would like to use it as a desktop background on *that* machine.

- You want to set free a few of the photos so that you can copy them *back* onto the camera's memory card. (Some people use their digicams as much for *showing* pictures to their friends as for *taking* them.)

- You want to send a batch of pictures on a CD to someone.

Exporting by Dragging

It's amazingly easy to export photos from iPhoto: Just drag their thumbnails out of the photo viewing area and onto the desktop (or onto a folder, or into a Finder window), as shown in Figure 12-3. After a moment, you'll see their icons appear.

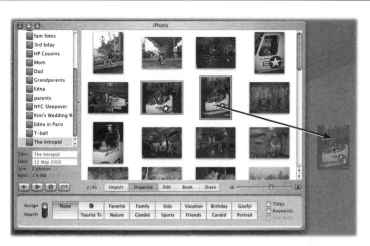

Figure 12-3:
This technique produces full-size JPEG graphics, exactly as they appear in iPhoto. Their names, however, are not particularly user-friendly: instead of "Timmy's First Solo Flight," as you named it in iPhoto, a picture might wind up on the desktop named 200205040035140.JPG or IMG_0241.JPG.

Exporting by Dialog Box

The drag-and-drop method has enormous virtue in its simplicity and speed. It does not, however, grant you much flexibility. It produces JPEG files only, at the original camera resolution, with iPhoto's own cryptic naming scheme.

To gain control over the dimensions, names, and file formats of the exported graphics, use the Export command instead. After selecting one picture, a group of pictures, or an album, you can invoke this command in either of these two ways:

- Choose File→Export (⌘-E).

- Click Share, and then click the Export icon in the lower-right corner of the window.

Either way, the Export Images dialog box appears, as shown in Figure 12-4. Click the File Export tab, if necessary, and then make the following decisions:

File format

You can use the Format pop-up menu to specify the file format of the graphics that you're about to export. Here are your options:

- **Original.** iPhoto exports the image in whatever format they were in when you imported them. If the picture came from a digital camera, for example, then this format will most likely be JPG.

- **JPG.** This abbreviation is shorthand for JPEG, which stands for Joint Photographic Experts Group (that's the group of geeks who came up with this format). The JPEG format is, of course, the most popular format for photos on the Internet (and in iPhoto), thanks to its high image quality and small file size.

- **TIFF.** These files (whose abbreviation is short for Tagged Image File Format) are something like JPEG without the compression. That is, they maintain every bit of quality available in the original photograph, but usually take up an enormous amount of disk space (or memory-card space) as a result. TIFF is a good choice if quality is more important than portability.

- **PNG.** This relatively new format (Portable Network Graphics) was designed to replace the GIF format on the Web. (The company that came up with the algorithms behind the GIF format threatened to exercise its legal muscle…long story.)

Whereas GIF graphics generally don't make good photos because they're limited to 256 colors, PNG is a good choice for photos (except the variation called *PNG-8*, which are just as limited as GIFs). The resulting files are smaller than TIFF images, yet exhibit even less compression-related quality loss than JPEGs. Not all graphics programs and Web browsers recognize this relatively new format, but the big ones—including iPhoto, GraphicConverter, Photoshop, and recent browser versions—all do.

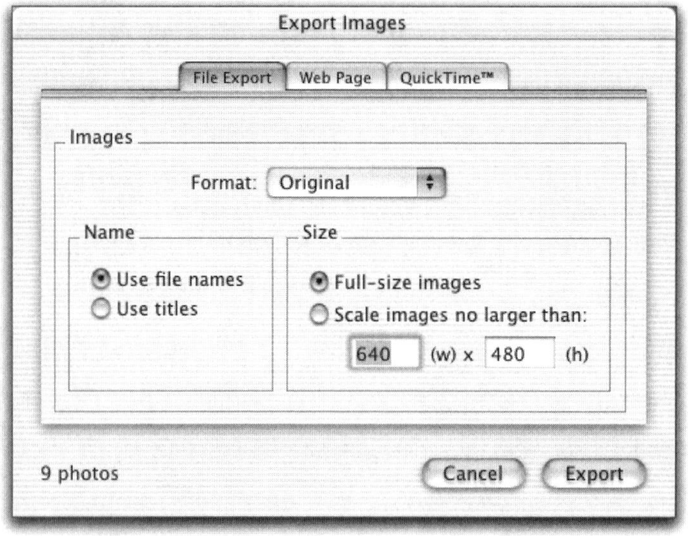

Figure 12-4:
The Export dialog box is where you control the file format, names, and dimensions of the pictures you're about send off from iPhoto. The number of photos you're about to export appears in the lower-left corner of the box.

Named option

As noted on page 103, iPhoto maintains two names for each photo: its *original file name*, as it appears in the Finder, and its *iPhoto title*, the one you may have typed in while working in the program. Click either "Use filenames" or "Use titles" to specify what names iPhoto gives the icons of the graphics you're about to export. (When you export just *one* photo, you're offered the chance to name it whatever you like.)

Size options

Remember that although digital camera graphics files have enough resolution for prints, they generally have far *too much* resolution for displaying on the screen.

As Chapter 9 makes clear, iPhoto offers to scale them down automatically whenever you email them or transfer them to the Web. If you turn on "Scale images no larger than," and then fill in some pixel dimensions in the boxes, you can oversee the same kind of shrinkage for your exported graphics. Points of reference: 1024 x 768 is exactly the right size to completely fill a standard 15-inch monitor, and 640 x 480 is a good size for emailing (it fills up about a quarter of the screen).

Plug-Ins, Add-Ons, and Beef-Ups

On one thing, friends and foes of Apple can all agree: iPhoto is no Photoshop. The program was deliberately designed to be simple and streamlined. This philosophy, incidentally, is what made smash hits out of iMovie (for editing video) and iTunes (for managing music files).

Yet Apple thoughtfully left the back door open. Other programmers are free to write add-ons and plug-ins: software modules that contribute additional features, lend new flexibility, and goose up the power of iPhoto.

And yet, with power comes complexity—in this case, power and complexity that Apple chose to omit. But at least this plug-in arrangement means that nobody can blame *Apple* for junking up iPhoto with extra features. After all, *you're* the one who installed them.

Some of the most important plug-ins and accessory programs are described in the relevant chapters of this book:

- **BetterHTMLExport** is designed to lend flexibility to the Web pages that iPhoto generates. (See page 185.)

- **Portraits & Prints** vastly expands iPhoto's printing features. It lets you create a multiple-photo layout on a single sheet of paper for printing. (See page 161.)

As the popularity of iPhoto grows, new add-ons and plug-ins will surely sprout up like roses in your macro lens (see page 262 for technical details). It's worthwhile to visit the Version Tracker Web site from time to time (*www.versiontracker.com/macosx*). When you do, type *iPhoto* into the search box and press Enter; you'll be surprised at the number of goodies just waiting for you to try. In the meantime, here's a sampling of the most interesting offerings.

Pictures to Your Palm Organizer

You can't always carry around your Mac to show off the brilliance of your iPhoto collection. But if you have a Palm organizer—and among the digerati, who doesn't?—you can carry around your photos on an electronic gizmo in your pocket. While ordinary citizens fumble with ratty, dog-eared photos in their wallets, you can smile patronizingly and whip out a tiny, shiny Palm that displays one perfect, bright colored photo after another.

The brains behind this operation is a little program called SplashData, which you can download either from *www.missingmanuals.com* or from its own home page (*www.splashdata.com/splashphoto/index.htm*). For $10, you get a little converter that lets you drag images directly out of iPhoto, ready to copy onto your Palm (or Handspring, or Sony) the next time you HotSync.

Using SplashPhoto

Start by opening both iPhoto and SplashPhoto. Position the windows so you can see both simultaneously, as shown in Figure 12-5.

Now just drag pictures from iPhoto into the SplashPhoto window, where you can then crop the pictures or adjust their brightness.

Finally, click Install. SplashPhoto obediently processes the pictures and prepares them for HotSyncing. The next time you connect your Palm device to your Mac and press the HotSync button, the photos are transferred automatically.

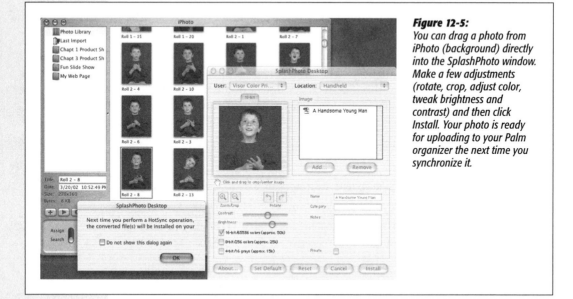

Figure 12-5:
You can drag a photo from iPhoto (background) directly into the SplashPhoto window. Make a few adjustments (rotate, crop, adjust color, tweak brightness and contrast) and then click Install. Your photo is ready for uploading to your Palm organizer the next time you synchronize it.

After the HotSync

Following your first HotSync, you'll discover the SplashPhoto viewer program installed on your Palm. Visit your Application screen and tap its icon to begin looking at your pictures.

You can view the pictures either individually or as part of a palmtop slide show, complete with transitions. The quality is amazing (see Figure 12-6). And once your colleagues and associates have picked their jaws up from off the floor, mention to them that you can beam both the SplashPhoto viewer and your pictures to them using the Palm's infrared transceiver. (This may be the only time complete strangers will ever ask for copies of your "wallet" photos.)

Figure 12-6:
You can display as many photos on your Palm organizer as you have memory to store them. (Each photo consumes about 28 K, and the SplashPhoto viewer program itself takes up about 100 K.) You can even run slide shows and beam the pictures to other Palm devices.

AppleScript Help: Where's That File?

AppleScript, of course, is the famous Macintosh *scripting language*—a software robot that you can program to perform certain repetitive or tedious tasks for you.

iPhoto itself isn't *scriptable*—that is, AppleScript gurus can't manipulate it by remote control with AppleScripts. Nevertheless, AppleScript can still play nice with it. When Apple first released iPhoto, for example, the company filled in some of the holes in the 1.0 version with a series of AppleScript programs. (For example, iPhoto 1.0 couldn't email photos at a scaled-down size, so Apple created an AppleScript script called Mail iPhoto Images.)

Thanks to the improvements in subsequent versions of iPhoto, you don't need most of these AppleScripts anymore. But one little program from this collection is still very handy and worth the download: Show Image File. It's for whenever you're looking at a photo in iPhoto and wish you could leap instantly to the Finder icon that represents it, so you can copy it to a disk, send it across a network, or whatever. (You might find Show Image File especially handy for finding the original source file for a picture that was part of an iPhoto 1.0 library, in which the picture files have unrecognizable file names.)

You can download this little script from *www.missingmanuals.com* or from *www.apple.com/applescript/iphoto*.

To use the Show Image File script, see Figure 12-7.

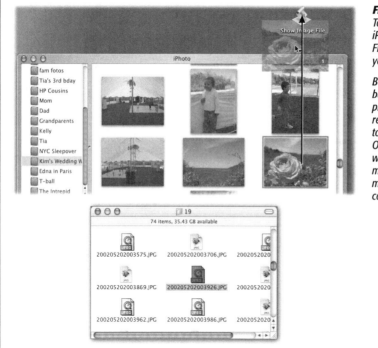

Figure 12-7:
Top: Drag a photo right out of iPhoto and onto the Show Image File icon, wherever it may be on your Mac.

Bottom: In a flash, you switch back to the desktop, where the photo's icon is highlighted and ready for action. (The best way to use the picture from here is to Option-drag a copy out of this window: renaming, deleting, or moving it behind iPhoto's back may cause the program complete confusion.)

CHAPTER 13

iPhoto File Management

W hen you don't have to buy film or pay for processing, photos have a way of piling up very quickly. Apple says iPhoto can hold an unlimited number of photos and, technically, that's true (as long as you have enough memory and hard drive space). But in reality, a gargantuan Photo Library winds up gasping for RAM and can make iPhoto behave as if you've slathered it with a thick coat of molasses.

As noted earlier in this book, about 2,000 photos is enough to slow down mere mortal 128-megabyte G3 Macs, and even a tricked-out, souped-up G4 RAM monster exhibits signs of strain as it approaches 10,000 photos.

For some photo fans, this comes as a distressing bit of news. You downloaded the software, entrusted your best work to it, even bought a book about it—and now you learn it's going to cop out on you in another six months.

Fortunately, a little knowledge can keep you happily in iPhoto at reasonable speeds. The trick is learning how to manage iPhoto's library files—wisdom that will also serve you when it comes time to *back up* your photo collection.

This chapter covers all of it: both iPhoto's behind-the-scenes filing system and what's involved in backing it up—namely, swapping photo libraries, transferring them to other machines, and merging them.

iPhoto Backups

Bad things can happen to digital photos. They can be accidentally deleted with a slip of your pinkie. They can become mysteriously corrupted and subsequently unopenable. They can get mangled by a crashed hard disk and be lost forever. Losing one-of-a-kind family photos can be pretty painful, so if you value your digital photos, you should back them up regularly.

Performing an iPhoto Backup

Fortunately, backing up even thousands of photos is a simple task for the iPhoto maven. After all, one of iPhoto's main jobs is to keep all your photos together in *one* place, one folder that's easy to copy to a backup disk, CD, or DVD.

That all-important folder is the *iPhoto Library* folder, which resides inside the Pictures folder of the Home folder that bears your name. If your user name (the short name you use to log into Mac OS X) is *corky*, the full path to your iPhoto Library folder from your main hard drive window drive is: Users→corky→Pictures→iPhoto Library.

As described in Chapter 4, the iPhoto Library contains not just your photos, but a huge assortment of additional files, including:

- All of the thumbnail images in the iPhoto window.

- The original, safety copies of photos you've edited in iPhoto.

- Various data files that keep track of keywords, comments, and any albums you've created within iPhoto.

To prepare for a disaster, you should back up *all* of these components.

To perform a complete backup, copy the entire iPhoto Library folder to another location. If you can copy it to a different disk, that's the best solution. (Copying it to another folder on the *same* disk means you'll lose both the original iPhoto Library folder and its backup if, say, your hard drive crashes or your computer is hit by an asteroid.)

One quick and convenient solution is simply to copy the iPhoto Library directly onto a blank CD—*if* your Mac has a CD burner and *if* your library folder is smaller than about 650 MB, which is the limit for a CD.

Tip: To find out the size of the iPhoto Library folder, highlight it and then choose File→Show Info (or press ⌘-I).

If the iPhoto Library folder is too big for a CD, you'll have to split it up. One way to do that is to whittle it down into separate iPhoto Library folders, as described in the next section.

Another way is to break up your Library folder onto different CDs by month or year. As shown in Figure 13-1, iPhoto keeps your photos organized in subfolders named after the day, month, and year the photos were created. You might decide to copy the 2001 folder onto one CD, the 2002 folder onto another, and so on.

Back up the iPhoto Library again every so often, or perhaps after each major batch of new photos joins your collection.

Note: Of course, you can also back up your photos by dragging their thumbnails out of the iPhoto window and into afolder or disk on the desktop, once you've tugged the iPhoto window to one side.

Unfortunately, this method doesn't preserve keywords, comments, album organization, or any other information you've created in iPhoto. If something bad happens to your iPhoto Library, you'll have to reimport the raw photos again and reorganize them from scratch.

Figure 13-1:
If your iPhoto Library folder is too big to fit on a single CD, you may have to back up the iPhoto Library in sections. The important thing is to copy all of the files and folders—even if they end up on separate disks—so you can reassemble the complete iPhoto Library if a disaster occurs.

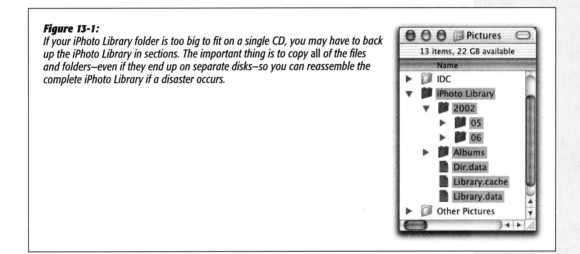

Multiple Photo Libraries

As you now know, iPhoto stores all your photos, thumbnails, and unedited originals in a single location: the iPhoto Library. (The same folder contains files called Library.cache, Dir.data, and Library.data—very important files that track your comments and keywords, album list, and master photo list, respectively. Don't touch any of these files!)

This arrangement works fine when your photo collection is small—maybe a few hundred files. But as your collection of digital photos grows into the thousands (and if you have a digital camera, this will happen *much* sooner than you think), the iPhoto Library files become dangerously bloated. iPhoto eventually starts slowing down as it sifts through more and more data to find and display your pictures. Before you know it, scrolling the photos in the main Photo Library "album" becomes an exercise in patience that would drive a Zen master crazy.

The answer, though not obvious, is simple: When one iPhoto Library becomes too large to manage comfortably, start a new one.

Splitting your photo collection into smaller libraries has a number of advantages.

- iPhoto is *much* faster, especially during scrolling, if the library contains a reasonable number of photos.

- You can keep different types of collections or projects separate. You might want to maintain a Home library for personal use, for example, and a Work library for images that pertain to your business.

- If you keep each library folder under 650 MB, you can neatly back each one up on a recordable CD. That's a much tidier system than the "back up by year" method described earlier.

Creating Additional Libraries

Unfortunately, iPhoto provides no built-in tools for retiring one Photo Library and starting a fresh one. You must fool it into creating a new one by using the following trick:

1. **Quit iPhoto.**

   Return to the Finder.

2. **Move the whole iPhoto Library folder out of the Pictures folder to a different location, or just give it a new name.**

   The idea is simply to *hide* this folder from iPhoto. You can drag it to a new folder on your hard drive, rename it something like Old iPhoto Library, or even stash it in a new folder called Old Libraries *inside* your Pictures folder.

   If you decide to move it, move the *whole* iPhoto Library folder. Messing around with the files and folders inside the iPhoto Library folder can cause problems.

3. **Open iPhoto again.**

   When iPhoto starts up, you'll find it completely empty. Because iPhoto can no longer find the folder it expects (iPhoto Library) in the place it expects to find it (your Home→Pictures folder), all remnants of your old Photo Library are gone. You're left with a blank window, ready to import fresh photos.

Note: Although starting a new library clears out your photos and albums, your existing keywords remain intact. That's because they're *not* stored in the iPhoto Library. Instead, the Mac stashes them in a separate preference file called *com.apple.iPhoto.plist*, which is in your Home→Library→Preferences folder.

What's happened is that iPhoto, unable to get its paws on an iPhoto Library folder, went ahead and created a brand new one. If you want proof, quit iPhoto, open your Home→Pictures folder, and take a look. What you'll see is a pristine iPhoto Library folder.

Using this technique, you can spawn as many new iPhoto Libraries as you need. You can archive the old libraries on CD, move them to another Mac, or just keep them somewhere on your hard drive so that you can swap any one of them back in whenever you need it.

As for *how* you swap them back in, well, you have three options: a hard way, an easier way, and a practically effortless way.

Swapping Libraries (Hard)

The photos and albums from your old Photo Library aren't really gone, of course. They're still stored safely in the *old* iPhoto Library. You can resurrect them at any time by following these two steps:

1. **Quit iPhoto. Take the new library folder out of the Home→Pictures folder.**

    Drag it into any other folder (or that Old Library folder, if you made one).

2. **Drag the original library folder back into the Home→Pictures folder, making sure you rename it *iPhoto Library*.**

When you open iPhoto again, you'll find the original photos back in place.

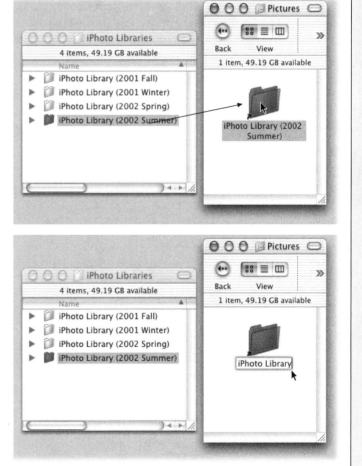

Figure 13-2:
Top: One way to manage your various photo libraries is to keep them in a separate folder, anywhere on your hard drive (left). When you want to swap one in—like the "iPhoto Library (2002 Summer)" folder here— put its alias into your Home→ Pictures folder. (The quickest way is to Option-⌘-drag it.)

Bottom: Rename the alias so that it says iPhoto Library. That's good enough for iPhoto, which will now display the photos in the "iPhoto Library (2002 Summer)" folder, wherever it happens to be.

Swapping Libraries (Easier)

You don't necessarily have to move the *actual* iPhoto Library back into your Home→Pictures folder. You can also make an *alias* of it.

In fact, you might want to set up the convenient arrangement shown in Figure 13-2. In this system, your actual iPhoto Library folders can reside anywhere on your hard drive, in any folder you like. They never have to leave that position, even when you want to install one as the current iPhoto Library folder.

Instead, all you have to do is put an *alias* of the iPhoto Library folder you want into the Home→Pictures folder. Then just make sure the alias is called *iPhoto Library*. Figure 13-2 illustrates this effect in greater detail.

Swapping Libraries (Practically Effortless)

If all this renaming, moving, and swapping of iPhoto Library folders strikes you as a little tiresome, confusing, and even risky, you're not alone. Brian Webster, a Mac software developer and self-proclaimed computer nerd, thought the same thing—but *he* decided to do something about it. He wrote iPhoto Library Manager, a free program that performs all this swapping and moving for you. You should waste no time downloading it from either *www.missingmanuals.com* or Brian's own site, whose address is *http://homepage.mac.com/bwebster*.

Once you've forced iPhoto to generate multiple iPhoto Library folders (as described earlier), you can use Webster's program to turn any one of them on or off with just a few clicks, as shown in Figure 13-3. You don't have to move your various library folders around—they can be anywhere on your hard drive—and there's no need to name them anything special.

Here are a few pointers for using iPhoto Library Manager:

- iPhoto Library Manager may have a New Library button (see Figure 13-3), but don't be fooled: It can't actually create new iPhoto Library folders. It's up to you to generate new iPhoto Library folders, as described in the previous pages.

  Then, once you've got yourself a duplicate iPhoto Library folder, hook it up to iPhoto Library Manager by clicking the New Library button in the lower-left corner of the window (see Figure 13-3) and then navigating to it.

- You still have to quit and relaunch iPhoto for a change in libraries to take effect. Conveniently, iPhoto Library Manager includes Quit iPhoto and Relaunch iPhoto buttons to make this easier.

- iPhoto Library Manager is fully AppleScriptable. If you're handy with writing AppleScript scripts, you can write one that swaps your various libraries automatically and instantaneously with a simple double-click.

- You still might want to investigate iPhoto Library Manager even if you have no intention of using multiple Library folders, thanks to another brilliant feature. iPhoto Library Manager lets several account holders on a single Mac share one iPhoto Library, as explained in the next section.

Tip: Sometimes library changes don't take effect when you quit and launch iPhoto from within iPhoto Library Manager. For more consistent results, manually quit iPhoto, use iPhoto Library Manager (which is a stand-alone application) to activate your desired library, and then launch iPhoto again.

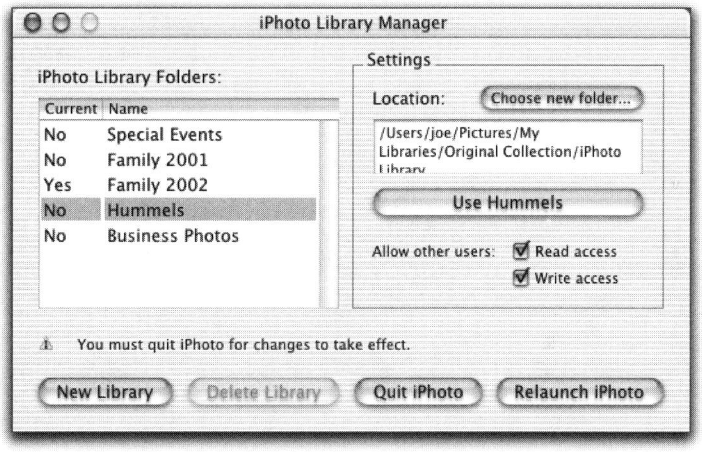

Figure 13-3:
Brian Webster's free iPhoto Library Manager is a must-have program that lets you switch between as many different iPhoto Library folders as you want. Just select a library folder from the list on the left, then click the Use [Folder Name] button. Double-click a library name in the list on the left to edit it. The names that you give your libraries within iPhoto Library Manager are independent of names of the corresponding library folders on disk.

Sharing Photo Libraries

Like the Unix under its skin, Mac OS X is designed from the ground up to be a *multiple-user* operating system. A Mac OS X machine can be set up with individual *user accounts* so that everyone must log in (that is, you have to click your name and type a password) when the computer turns on.

Upon doing so, you discover the Macintosh universe just as you left it, including *your* icons on the desktop, Dock configuration, desktop picture, screen saver, Web browser bookmarks, email account, fonts, startup programs, and so on. This *accounts* feature adds both convenience (people don't have to wade through other people's stuff) and security (people *can't* wade through other people's stuff). As you can imagine, this feature is a big deal in schools, businesses, and families.

This feature also affords each account holder a separate and individual iPhoto Library folder. (Remember, it lives inside your own Home folder.) The photos *you* import into iPhoto are accessible only to you, not to anyone else who might log in. If you and your spouse each log into Mac OS X with a different account, you each get your own Photo Library—and neither of you has access to the other's pictures in iPhoto.

But what if the two of you *want* to share the same library of photos? Ordinarily, you'd be stuck, because iPhoto can't make its library available to more than a single account holder.

There are two relatively easy solutions:

- **The geek's way:** Move the actual iPhoto Library folder into the Users→Shared folder on your hard drive. Then put one alias of that iPhoto Library folder into the Home→Pictures folder of each account holder. Now everybody can log in and work with the same iPhoto Library folder.

- **The simpler way:** Once again, use iPhoto Library Manager. This program makes it easy to share your Photo Library (or *libraries*, if you've created more than one) with anyone using your Mac (see Figure 13-4). Whole families or workgroups can view, edit, and update the same shared library of photos.

Figure 13-4:
To share your photo library with other user-account holders on your Mac, you simply have to turn on two checkboxes in iPhoto Library Manager, as shown here. First select the name of the library you want to share (left), and then turn on the "Read access" and "Write access" checkboxes.

THE OTHER WHITE MEAT

Another Free Librarian

iPhoto Library Manager isn't the only kid on the block. Another interesting (though much less sophisticated) library-swapping utility is iPhoto Librarian, a tiny AppleScript program by Scott Schroeder. Like iPhoto Library Manager, it's designed to let you point iPhoto to any number of different library folders, stored anywhere you like. (You can download it from *http://homepage.mac.com/scrufmeister*.)

iPhoto Librarian is a minimalist programming effort. When you launch it, you see a single dialog box with three buttons: Default, Choose, and Cancel. You click the Default button to open iPhoto using the standard iPhoto Library folder (the one in your Pictures folder), or Choose to point iPhoto to another photo library folder, which can be anywhere and named anything. Every time you want to switch libraries, you run iPhoto Librarian again to make the change.

As with iPhoto Library Manager, the iPhoto Librarian script doesn't create new libraries, it just points to other libraries that you've created using iPhoto. (If you point iPhoto Librarian to a plain folder of photos, as opposed to a true iPhoto library folder, iPhoto will open with no photos displayed at all.)

Merging Photo Libraries

You've just arrived home from your photo safari of deepest Kenya. You're jet-lagged and dusty, but your iBook is bursting at the seams with fresh photo meat. You just can't wait to transfer the new pictures into your main iPhoto Library—you know, the one on your Power Macintosh G4 with 1 gig of RAM and a 23-inch Cinema Display.

And then it hits you: How are you supposed to merge the libraries from two different Macs?

How Not to Do It

You certainly can combine the *photos* of two Macs' iPhoto libraries—just export them from one and then import them into the other. As a result, however, you lose all of the album organization, comments, and keywords you added.

Your next idea might be: "Hey, I know! I'll just drag the iPhoto Library folder from computer #1 into the iPhoto window of computer #2!"

Big mistake. You'll end up importing not only the photos, but also the tiny thumbnail versions of each photo (which are stored separately in the iPhoto Library folder) *and* the original versions of any photos that you've edited. You'll wind up with duplicates or triplicates of every photo in the viewing area, in one enormous, unmanageable, uncategorized, sloshing library.

The Best You Can Do

There is, however, a partial solution to the merging-libraries problem. It's not something you'll want to do every day—fortunately, you won't have to—but it's a good system of getting both the photos and their album structure from one photo library into another.

It has three potentially depressing drawbacks:

- This method doesn't preserve keywords or comments.

- This method is best for iPhoto libraries in which you *haven't* put photos into more than one album. You'll wind up with *real* duplicates of such photos, not just aliases (page 112). (Fortunately, many people don't make much use of that feature anyway, instead filing Enid's birthday pictures into only an Enid's Birthday album, Disney Trip pictures into only a Disney Trip album, and so on.)

- It takes a long time.

All right, you've been warned.

Now suppose you have two photo libraries that you want to combine. Maybe they're both on the same Mac, or maybe each is on a different Mac.

In any case, begin with the library, or the Mac, whose photos you want to *export* into the larger, combined one. If your intention is to merge the libraries of two different Macs, you should be working with the *outgoing* Mac, the machine whose photos will join up with a master library. (In the Kenya-safari example, you'd begin with the copy of iPhoto on the laptop.)

1. **Launch iPhoto.**

   Now you've got a good look at the album names in Library A.

2. **Create a new folder on the desktop. Give it the same name as the first album listed in the Photo Library.**

   If you don't have any albums yet, make just one folder on the desktop and name it whatever you want.

3. **Select the first photo album in the library, so that its thumbnails appear in the main iPhoto window. Choose Edit→Select All (⌘-A) to select all of the thumbnails. Using one thumbnail as a handle, drag them onto the correspondingly named folder on the desktop (Figure 13-5).**

   You've just exported all of the photos in the album into the desktop folder.

4. **Repeat steps 2 and 3 with each photo album.**

   In other words, keep going until all of the photos in the library have been copied to folders with matching names.

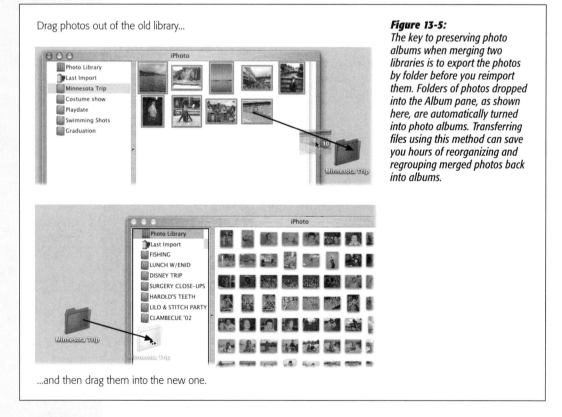

Drag photos out of the old library...

Figure 13-5:
The key to preserving photo albums when merging two libraries is to export the photos by folder before you reimport them. Folders of photos dropped into the Album pane, as shown here, are automatically turned into photo albums. Transferring files using this method can save you hours of reorganizing and regrouping merged photos back into albums.

...and then drag them into the new one.

5. **Quit iPhoto. Swap iPhoto Library folders.**

   If you're merging two libraries on the same Mac, swap the iPhoto Library folders either manually or using iPhoto Library Manager, as described earlier in this chapter. In any case, the master, soon-to-be-combined photo collection should now be before you in iPhoto.

   If you're trying to merge the libraries of two *different* Macs, skip this instruction. Instead, move to the second Mac at this point, the one that will serve as the final resting place for the photos you exported. Before proceeding, you'll have to connect the two Macs via a network, or find some other way to get your desktop photo folders onto the new Mac.

6. **One by one, drag the folders of photos from the desktop into the *Album pane* of the iPhoto window.**

   By dropping the folders into the Album pane (*not* the main photo viewing area), you not only import the photos, but also create a new album bearing the name of each folder.

Tip: Don't drag all of the folders in at once. To create separate albums from each folder of photos, you must add them one at a time.

---

7. **When you're done importing the photos, delete the folders on the desktop.**

   The folders were just temporary holding bins for the photos as you transferred them to the new library. Now that they've been imported into Library B, fresh copies of each photo have been stored in the iPhoto Library. You may as well delete the leftover duplicates on the desktop to save some disk space.

As noted earlier, this kind of surgery creates duplicate photos in your main Photo Library (the category at the top of the album list) if you used a photo in more than one album of the outgoing iPhoto collection. You might want to take a moment to weed them out at this point.

Splitting a Photo Library

You already know that among the advantages of having multiple iPhoto libraries, the idea of keeping your library under 650 MB for easy backup onto a recordable CD is an especially juicy one.

But what if you're reading this too late, and your iPhoto Library folder is already too big for a CD (Figure 13-6)?

Unfortunately, there's no tolerable way to spin out a subset of your pictures without losing their album structure, comments, keywords, and so on. You have no choice but to export them into a desktop folder (follow steps 2, 3, and 4 of the preceding instructions) and then delete them from your Photo Library.

That will certainly make your iPhoto Library folder smaller, which was the whole purpose of this exercise. Now, of course, you have to create a new library (page 246), move those exported pictures into it, and recategorize them in albums.

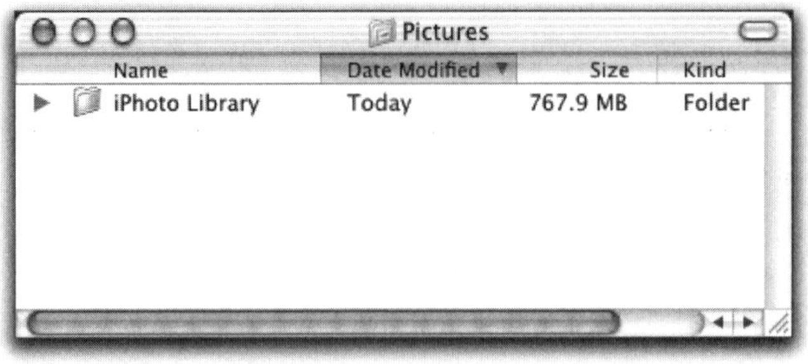

Figure 13-6:
Oh, bummer—the iPhoto Library is too big for a CD. This is the moment when you wish you could split the library, sending a chunk of it off into a separate library so that the first one could shrink to a reasonable size.

Beyond iPhoto

Depending on how massive your collection of digital photos grows and how you use it, you may find yourself wanting more file-management power than iPhoto can offer. Maybe you wish you could use more than fourteen keywords to categorize your files. Maybe you'd like to search for photos based on something other than just keywords and comments—perhaps by file type, creation date, or the camera model used to shoot them. Maybe you have a small network, and you'd like a system that lets a whole workgroup share a library of photos simultaneously.

To enjoy such features, you'll have to move beyond iPhoto into the world of *digital asset management*—and spend a little money. Programs like Extensis Portfolio ($650, *www.extensis.com*), Canto Cumulus ($100, *www.canto.com*), and iView MediaPro ($45, *www.iview-multimedia.com*) are terrific programs for someone who wants to take the next step up. (All three companies offer free trial versions on their Web sites.)

Here are a few of the stunts these more advanced programs can do that iPhoto 1.1.1 can't:

- Define an unlimited number of keywords.

- Create custom fields to store any other kind of information you want about your files—dates, prices, Web addresses, and so on.

- Track graphics files stored in any location on a network—not just in a specific folder.

- Catalog not just photos, but other file types, such as EPS files, QuarkXPress and InDesign documents, QuickTime movies, PowerPoint slides, and so on.

- Perform complex searches using multiple criteria, like "Find all JPEGs over 2 MB that contain the keyword 'yak' and have file names that start with the letter R."

- Share a catalog of images with dozens of other people simultaneously over a network.

- Rename an entire group of images en masse.

- Customize the fonts, colors, and borders of the thumbnail view.

- Create catalogs that can be read on both Mac and Windows. (iView MediaPro is Mac only, but Portfolio and Cumulus create cross-platform catalogs.)

- Display previews of "offline" photo files that aren't actually on the Mac at the moment (they're on CDs or DVDs on your shelf, for example).

- Handle tens of thousands of photos in a single catalog.

Some of the features in this list were obviously developed with professional users, like graphic designers and studio photographers, in mind. But this kind of program is worth considering if your photo collection—and your passion for digital photography—one day outgrows iPhoto.

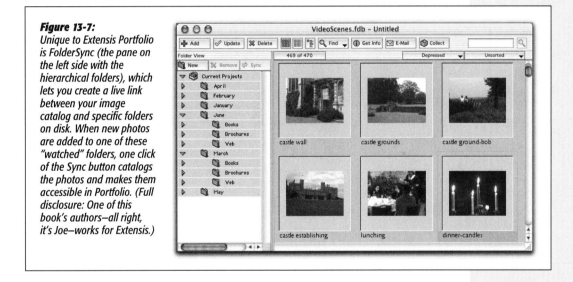

Figure 13-7:
Unique to Extensis Portfolio is FolderSync (the pane on the left side with the hierarchical folders), which lets you create a live link between your image catalog and specific folders on disk. When new photos are added to one of these "watched" folders, one click of the Sync button catalogs the photos and makes them accessible in Portfolio. (Full disclosure: One of this book's authors—all right, it's Joe—works for Extensis.)

Part Five: Appendixes

5

Troubleshooting

i Photo isn't just a Mac OS X program—it's a *Cocoa* Mac OS X program, meaning that it was written exclusively for Mac OS X. As a result, it should, in theory, be one of the most rock-solid programs under the sun.

Still, iPhoto does have its vulnerabilities. Many of these shortcomings stem from the fact that iPhoto works under the supervision of a lot of cooks, since it must interact with plug-ins, connect to printers, talk to Web servers, and cope with an array of file corruptions.

If trouble strikes, keep hands and feet inside the tram at all times—and consult the following collection of problems, solutions, questions, and answers.

Importing

Getting photos into iPhoto is supposed to be one of the most effortless parts of the process. Remember, Steve Jobs promised that iPhoto would forever banish the "chain of pain" that's part of digital photography. And yet…

iPhoto doesn't recognize my camera.

iPhoto generally "sees" any recent camera model, even if it's not listed on Apple's Device Compatibility page (*www.apple.com/iphoto/compatibility*). If you click the Import mode button and you see "No camera is connected" in the lower-left corner of the screen, even though the camera most assuredly *is* connected, try these steps, in order:

- Make sure you're turning on the camera only *after* connecting its USB cable to the Mac.

- Try turning the camera off, then on again, while it's already plugged in.

- If iPhoto absolutely won't notice its digital companion, use a memory-card reader as described in Chapter 4.

iPhoto crashes when trying to import.

This problem is most likely to crop up when you're bringing pictures in from your hard drive or another disk. Here are the possibilities:

- The culprit is usually a corrupted file. Try a test: Import only half the photos in the batch. If nothing bad happens, split the remaining photos in half again and import *them*. Keep going until you've isolated the offending file.

- Consider the graphics program you're using to save the files; it's conceivable that its version of JPEG or TIFF doesn't jibe perfectly with iPhoto's. (This scenario is most likely to occur right after you've upgraded either your graphics program or iPhoto itself.)

  To test this possibility, open a handful of images in another editing program, save them, and then try the import again. If they work, then you might have a temporary compatibility problem. Check the editing program's Web site for update and troubleshooting information.

- Some Photoshop users prepare images for the Web using a format called *progressive scan JPEGs* (an option in Photoshop's Save dialog box for JPEG files). iPhoto won't import these images. They must be resaved as Standard or Optimized JPEGs.

- If you're attempting to import hundreds of photos at once, break the import into batches. You'll have fewer problems with a couple of medium-sized imports instead of one big one.

- Some JPEGs that were originally saved in Mac OS 9 won't import into iPhoto. Try opening and resaving these images in a native Mac OS X editor such as Photoshop. Speaking of Photoshop, it has an excellent batching tool that you can use to automatically process mountains of images while you go grab some lunch.

iPhoto won't import images from my video camera.

Most modern digital camcorders can store your still images on a memory card instead of DV tape. If you're having a hard time importing these stills into iPhoto with a direct camera connection, try these tips:

- Take out the tape cassette before connecting the camcorder to your Mac.

- Try copying the files directly from the memory card to your hard drive with a memory-card reader or a PC Card adapter. Once the images are on your hard drive, you should be able to import them into iPhoto.

When I import from a Kodak Picture CD, I get a bunch of junk I don't want.

Kodak Picture discs include various support files that aren't actually graphics and shouldn't be imported into iPhoto. All you really want, of course, is the pictures.

To get them, put your Kodak disc in the CD drive, open iPhoto, and then choose File→Import. Navigate to and choose the PICTURES folder on the CD. iPhoto will now import the pictures and leave everything else behind.

Figure A-1:
Top: The first thing you have to do is make sure that Image Capture, not iPhoto, intercepts and downloads the photos when your digital camera is connected. Choose Image Capture's name from the Hot Plug Action pop-up menu. At this point, one click (on Download All) transfers the camera's pictures to your hard drive.

Bottom: If you click Download Some, you get this "slide-sorter" window, where you can choose the individual pictures you want to download, or use the buttons at the top to rotate or delete (from the camera) selected shots. In slide-sorter view, Shift-click or ⌘-click the thumbnails of the pictures you want. In list view, Shift-click or ⌘-click as though they're Finder list-view files.

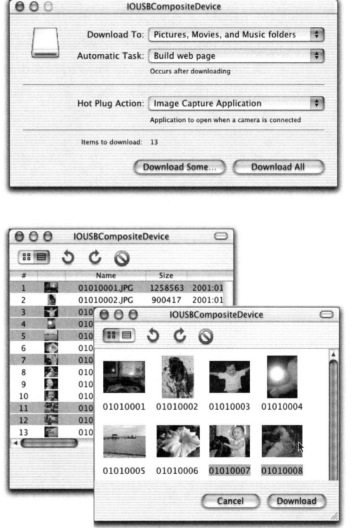

What if I don't want iPhoto to import all the pictures from my camera?

You can't tell iPhoto not to import them all—but you can use Image Capture, iPhoto's grandfather. It's a Mac OS X program that comes on every Mac. Although it doesn't perform even a hundredth of the feats that iPhoto can, it does offer one feature iPhoto lacks: *selective* importing.

First, however, you must tell iPhoto not to open automatically when you plug in your camera. You want Image Capture to do your importing, instead.

Change the preferences setting like this:

1. **Open Image Capture.**

   It's in your Applications folder.

2. **From the Hot Plug Action pop-up menu, choose Image Capture Application.**

   You could even choose another program to intervene when your camera is plugged in (by choosing Other).

3. **Quit Image Capture.**

From now on, Image Capture, not iPhoto, will open whenever you plug in your camera. As shown in Figure A-1, it offers just the feature you want: selective photo downloading to your hard drive.

Once the pictures are on your hard drive, copy them into iPhoto simply by dragging them (or the folder they're in) into the photo-viewing area.

Exporting

Clearly, "Easy come, easy go" doesn't always apply to photos.

After I upgraded iPhoto to the latest version, my Export button became disabled.

This problem is usually caused by outdated *plug-ins*. If you have any older plug-ins, such as an outdated version of the Toast Titanium export plug-in, disable it and then relaunch iPhoto to see whether that solves the problem.

Here's how to turn your plug-ins on or off:

1. **Quit iPhoto.**

   Return to the Finder.

2. **Highlight the iPhoto application icon. Choose File→Show Info.**

   You may have seen the Show Info box for other files in your day, but you probably haven't seen a *Plugins* command in the pop-up menu at the top (Figure A-2).

3. **Choose Plugins.**

   A complete list of the plug-ins you currently have loaded appears with a checkbox next to each item.

You may be surprised to discover that a number of iPhoto's "built-in" features are actually plug-ins written by Apple's programmers. Most of them are responsible for familiar printing and exporting options.

4. **Turn off the third-party plug-ins that you suspect might be causing the problem.**

   Figure A-2 should help you distinguish the legitimate Apple plug-ins from the unauthorized, non-Apple ones.

Figure A-2:
The plug-ins circled here are Apple's plug-ins, and are therefore OK. Any others should be turned off in times of troubleshooting.

Now open iPhoto and test the export function. If the technology gods are smiling, the function should work now. All that's left is to figure out which *one* of the plug-ins was causing your headaches.

To find out, quit iPhoto. Open its Show Info window again. Reinstate your plug-ins one by one, using the on/off switches depicted in Figure A-2, until you find the offending software.

Once you locate the culprit, highlight its name and then click the Remove button. (You may also want to check the Web site of the offending plug-in for an updated version.)

Tip: Here's another, somewhat more interesting way to remove a plug-in. Control-click the iPhoto icon; from the contextual menu, choose Show Package Contents; in the resulting window, open the Contents→PlugIns folder, where each plug-in is represented by its own, easily removable icon.

I get the message, "An unexpected error has occurred" when I try to export a HomePage photo album.

You've probably named one of your photos with an Option-key character (™, ®, ©, é, ç, ñ, è, ü, î, or whatever) or a *double-byte* character (Japanese or Chinese characters, for example). These are no-nos on the Internet, so iPhoto won't let you export them.

There's no solution except to rename the offending photos.

But you're not out of the woods yet. If you change the title of a photo *in iPhoto,* remember that you haven't changed the original file name of the JPEG file buried deep within your Library folder.

After you've changed your picture titles, therefore, you should export them to a folder on your desktop, delete the originals from iPhoto, and then reimport the set you exported. Doing so makes sure that iPhoto adopts their new, authorized names, both internally and externally. They should give you no further trouble.

My Sharing-mode panel doesn't even have buttons for Order Prints, Order Book, and HomePage!

Some of iPhoto's files are missing, or their Unix attributes have gotten hosed. Reinstall iPhoto.

Printing

How many things can go wrong when you print? Let us count the ways.

How can I tell if my printer is compatible with iPhoto?

There's no such thing, really, as an *iPhoto*-compatible printer. There is, however, such a thing as a *Mac OS X*–compatible printer, and that's what you care about. There's a list at this Web page: *www.apple.com/macosx/whatyoucando/applications /printcenter.html.*

If your printer is on that list, it should work in iPhoto too.

I can't print more than one photo per page. It seems like a waste to use a whole sheet of paper for one 4 x 6 print.

Check the following:

- Have you, in fact, selected more than one photo to print?

- Choose File→Page Setup. Make sure the paper size is US Letter (or whatever paper you've loaded). Click OK.

- Choose File→Print. Choose Standard Prints from the Style pop-up menu, click the print size you want (4 x 6 or 5 x 7)—and then, above all, turn off the box labeled "One photo per page." You'll now see both of your selected images side by side in the preview pane. They're ready to print.

I have an HP PhotoSmart printer, but I can't print from the 4 x 6 snapshot tray in iPhoto.

First verify that you have Mac OS X 10.1.5 and iPhoto 1.1.1 (or later versions). Also check for new printer drivers on Apple's Mac OS X downloads page: *www.apple.com /downloads/macosx/drivers.*

Then, in iPhoto, choose File→Page Setup. From the "Format for" pop-up menu, choose your HP printer's name. From the Paper Size pop-up menu, choose "4x6 Photo." Click OK.

Finally, choose File→Print. When the Print dialog box appears, choose Full Page from the Style pop-up menu. (Logic might suggest that you should choose Standard Prints instead of Full Page, but that won't work.)

Editing

There's not much that can go wrong here, but when it does, it *really* goes wrong.

iPhoto crashes when I double-click a thumbnail to edit it.

You probably changed a photo file's name in the Finder—in the iPhoto Library folder, behind the program's back. iPhoto hates this! Only grief can follow.

Sometimes, too, picture files become corrupted; that'll also make iPhoto crash when you try to edit them. Use the script described on page 240 to locate the scrambled file in the Finder. Open the file in another graphics program, use the File→Save As command to replace the corrupted one, and then try again in iPhoto.

iPhoto won't let me use an external graphics program when I double-click on a thumbnail.

Choose File→Preferences. Make sure that the Other button is selected and that a graphics program's name appears next to it. (If not, click Other, then Set, and choose the program you want to use.)

Also make sure that your external editing program still *exists.* You might have upgraded to a newer version of that program, one whose file name is slightly different from the version you originally specified in iPhoto.

My picture doesn't fit right on 4 x 6, 5 x 7, or 8 x 10 inch paper.

As described on page 125, most digital cameras produce photos in a 4:3 width-to-height ratio. Unfortunately, those dimensions don't fit squarely into any of the standard print sizes.

The solution: Crop them first, using the appropriate print size in the Constrain pop-up menu (see page 125).

I've really messed up a photo while editing it, and now it's ruined.

Highlight the file's thumbnail and then choose File→Revert to Original. iPhoto restores your photo to its original state, drawing on a backup it has secretly kept stashed away for your own good.

General Questions

Finally, here's a handful of general—although perfectly terrifying—troubles.

iPhoto's wigging out.

If the program "unexpectedly quits," well, that's life; it happens. This is Mac OS X, though, so you can generally open the program right back up again and pick up where you left off.

If the flakiness is becoming really severe, try logging out (choose →Log Out) and logging back in again.

Man, this program's slow!

Installing more memory is by far the best solution to this problem. iPhoto loves RAM like Madonna loves attention.

Keeping your Photo Library a reasonable size (page 245) and collapsing film rolls (page 95) are more immediate (and less expensive) fixes.

I opened iPhoto and my pictures are no longer there!

You must have moved, renamed, or deleted the all-important iPhoto Library folder (It's in your Home→Pictures folder.)

If you can't immediately find it (so that you can reinstate its name and folder location), look in your Trash.

If you still can't find it, use your Sherlock program to search for *thumbs.* If you're lucky, you'll turn up dozens of them—which means that the iPhoto Library folder is, in fact, somewhere on your Mac. Click one of the Thumbs folders to determine the location of the iPhoto Library folder, as shown in Figure A-3. At this point, you should be able to figure out how to rename the folder (to "iPhoto Library") and move it back to where it once belonged (your Home→Pictures folder).

I can't change an album's name.

Double-click its name, and then type in the new label.

I exported some stills from iPhoto, and iMovie won't import them!

The answer involves a good bit of thrashing through high-tech underbrush, but the solution is fairly satisfying.

Every operating system needs a mechanism to associate documents with the applications that created them. When you double-click a Microsoft Word document icon, for example, you want Microsoft Word to launch and open the document.

Mac OS 9 relies on invisible, four-letter *creator codes* and *type codes.*

The creator code of a Macintosh document identifies the program that will open it: MSWD for Microsoft Word, FMP3 for FileMaker Pro, and so on. The creator code tells the Mac which program to open when you double-click a particular document.

The *type code,* on the other hand, specifies the document's file format. Photoshop, for example, can create graphics in any of dozens of different formats: GIF, JPEG, TIFF, and so on. If you inspect your Photoshop documents, you'll discover that they all share the same *creator* code, but have a wide variety of *type* codes.

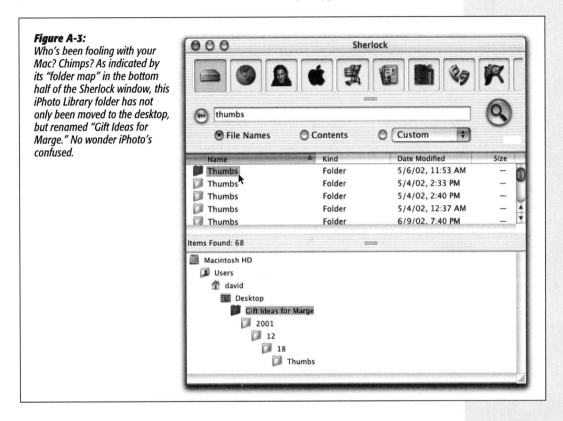

Figure A-3:
Who's been fooling with your Mac? Chimps? As indicated by its "folder map" in the bottom half of the Sherlock window, this iPhoto Library folder has not only been moved to the desktop, but renamed "Gift Ideas for Marge." No wonder iPhoto's confused.

In Mac OS X, however, plenty of documents don't have type and creator codes. Documents created by *Cocoa* programs generally don't, in fact—and iPhoto is a Cocoa program. (A Cocoa application is a program that was written for, and runs only on, Mac OS X.) That's because Mac OS X is based on the Unix operating system. In Unix, what determines which programs opens when you double-click a document is its *file name extension,* just as in Windows—a suffix following a period in the file's name, as in *Letter to Mom.doc.*

The bottom line is that Mac OS X offers *two different* mechanisms that associate documents with the programs that created them. The old type/creator codes are at work, especially in "Carbonized" versions of older programs; and where they're absent, the file name suffixes kick in.

So that's the problem: iMovie, having been written during the pre–Mac OS X era, expects its imported graphics to have the invisible type code *JPEG* when it imports still images—but JPEG files exported from iPhoto may not have them. (Some do, some don't, depending on where they came from before being imported into iPhoto.) iMovie has no idea what those pictures are supposed to be—never mind that their names end with *.jpg*—and chooses to ignore them.

The only solution is to add type codes manually, using a program like Type And Creator Changer. (It's a $5 shareware program available from *www.missingmanuals .com,* among other places.) As shown in Figure A-4, this program lets you assign a "type" to your code-less files.

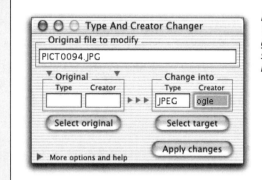

Figure A-4:
The Type And Creator Changer program reveals that this graphic did not have any type or creator codes at all (left side). Change the Type code to JPEG; the creator code doesn't really matter, for iMovie's purposes.

iPhoto, Menu by Menu

You could use iPhoto for years without pulling down a single menu—and most people probably will. But unless you explore its menu commands, you're likely to miss some of the options and controls that make it a surprisingly powerful little photo manager.

Here's a menu-by-menu look at iPhoto's commands.

iPhoto Menu

This first menu, Mac OS X's Application menu, takes on the name of whatever program happens to be running in the foreground. In iPhoto's case, that would be iPhoto.

About iPhoto

This command opens the "About" box containing the requisite Apple copyright, trademark, and version information. In iPhoto's About box, you'll also find some fascinating details about the recordings of the two J. S. Bach tunes—*Minuet in G* and *Jesu, Joy of Man's Desiring*—that are included as sample soundtracks for use with iPhoto's Slide Show feature. (Here, at last, you can learn that you've been listening to the guitar playing of Leo Kottke and Harvey Reid.)

There's really only one useful reason to open the About iPhoto window: It's the easiest way to find out exactly which version of iPhoto you have.

Preferences

Opens the Preferences window (Figure B-1), where you can twiddle with the following ten options:

- Add a drop shadow or thin frame to your thumbnails in the photo viewing area.

- Change the background of the photo viewing area from white to black—or any shade of gray.

- Align thumbnails to a grid in the iPhoto window (page 119).

- Put the most recently imported photos at the top of the iPhoto window instead of the bottom, when sorted by date (or the most recent film rolls at the top when sorted by film roll).

- Change the setting of iPhoto's Rotate button so that it spins selected photos counter-clockwise instead of clockwise.

- Choose how you want iPhoto to open photos when you double-click them. You have three choices: Open the photo for editing in the main iPhoto window, open the photo in a *separate* window, or open it using another program (which you choose by clicking the Set button).

- Tell iPhoto whether to search for photos using keywords or comments.

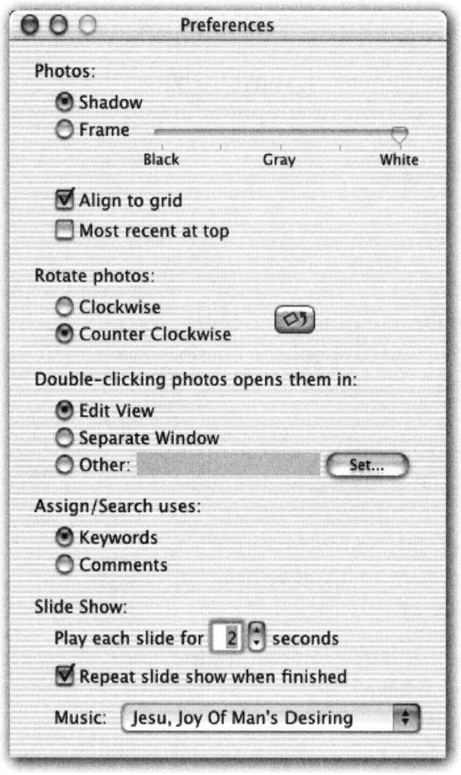

Figure B-1:
You'll probably be visiting iPhoto's Preferences window regularly, so remember the keyboard shortcut that takes you here: ⌘-Y. You need to open Preferences every time you want to change the factory-setting music track for a slide show or change your search criteria from comments to keywords (Chapter 5).

- Specify the timing of each slide in a slide show.

- Indicate whether or not you want slide shows to repeat.

- Choose the soundtrack for the standard slide show by selecting any MP3, AIFF, or WAV sound file.

Shop for iPhoto Products

This isn't so much a command as it is a shameless marketing ploy. It opens your Web browser and opens a page on Apple's Web site that offers to sell you digital cameras, tripods, printers, and other accessories.

Hide iPhoto, Hide Others, Show All

These aren't iPhoto's commands—they're Mac OS X's.

In any case, they determine which of the various programs running on your Mac are *visible* onscreen at any given moment.

The Hide Others command is probably the most popular of these three. It zaps away the windows of all other programs—including the Finder—so that the iPhoto window is the only one you see.

Tip: If you know this golden Mac OS X trick, you may never need to use the Hide Others command: To switch into iPhoto from another program, hold down the Option and ⌘ keys when clicking the iPhoto icon in the Dock. Doing so simultaneously brings iPhoto to the front *and* hides all other programs you have running, producing an uncluttered, distraction-free view of iPhoto.

Quit iPhoto

This command closes iPhoto, no questions asked. You're not even asked to save changes, because as you've probably noticed, iPhoto doesn't even *have* a Save command. Like Filemaker Pro, 4D, and other database programs, iPhoto—itself a glorified database—continually saves changes as you add, delete, or edit photos.

File Menu

Most of the commands in the File menu involve moving photo files into or out of iPhoto. This is also where you go to get information about specific photos and do all your printing.

New Album

Creates a new photo album in the Albums pane, and prompts you to name it. Shortcuts: pressing ⌘-N or clicking the + button in the main iPhoto window.

Import...

Lets you select files or folders of photos to add to your iPhoto Library. Use this command to take photos from your hard disk, a CD, or some other disk. Choose

Import, select the file or folder you want to add, then click the Import button in the Import Photos dialog box.

You *don't* use this command when you're bringing in photos from a camera, card reader, or Kodak PhotoCD. In that case, put iPhoto in Import mode, connect your camera or insert the memory card, and then click the Import *button* on the bottom pane of the iPhoto window.

Export

Opens the Export Images window. Its three tabs offer the following three different ways of copying photos out of iPhoto:

• **File Export.** Makes fresh copies of your photos in the file format and size you specify. You can export photos in their existing file format or convert them to JPEG, TIFF, or PNG format. You also can set a maximum size for the photos, so that iPhoto scales down larger photos on the fly as they're exported.

• **Web Page.** Publishes selected photos as a series of HTML pages that you can post on a Web site, featuring an index page with clickable thumbnails that open individual pages containing each photo. (See Chapter 9 for step-by-step instructions on using this pane to format the HTML pages and set image sizes.)

• **QuickTime.** Turns a series of photos into a self-running slide show, saved as a QuickTime movie that you can post on the Internet, send to friends, or burn to a CD. You can set the size of the movie, pick a background color, and add music (the sound file currently selected in Music section of iPhoto→Preferences) before exporting. You'll find more about going from iPhoto to QuickTime in Chapter 11.

Show Info

This command (or ⌘-I) opens the Photo Info window. Click the Photo tab in the Photo Info window to see information about a selected photo, such as its creation date and the camera model used to create it. Switch to the Exposure panel for details about the specific camera settings that were used to take the picture. (iPhoto gathers all this information by reading *EXIF* tags—snippets of data invisibly embedded in the photo files created by most of today's digital cameras.)

You can open the Photo Info window even when no photos are selected, but it won't have any info filled in. The data pops into the window as soon as you select a photo.

Tip: Once the Show Info window is open, you can leave it open. As you click different photos, the information in the window changes instantly to reflect your selection.

Duplicate

Just as in the Finder, this command creates a duplicate of whichever photo is selected and adds it to the iPhoto Library. If you select multiple photos, they'll all be duplicated.

If an album is selected (and no photos are), this command duplicates the album itself. The copy appears at the bottom of the album list, named Album-1 (or whatever number it's up to).

Revert to Original

The Revert to Original command restores edited photos to the condition they were in when you first imported them into iPhoto, reversing all the cropping, rotating, brightening, or anything else you've done. This command is active only if you've edited the selected photo at least once.

If the Revert to Original command is dimmed out, one of these conditions is probably true:

- You don't have a photo selected.

- The photo you've selected hasn't been edited, so there's nothing to revert to.

- You edited the photo outside of iPhoto in an unauthorized way (by dragging the thumbnail to the Photoshop icon in the Dock, for example). iPhoto never has the chance to make a backup of the original version, which it needs in order to revert the file.

   On the other hand, it's totally OK to edit photos outside of iPhoto—thereby activating the Revert to Original feature—if you do it by *double-clicking* the photo's thumbnail rather than dragging it. Page 135 has all the details.

Page Setup...

Opens the standard Page Setup dialog box for your printer, where you can select the paper size, orientation, and scaling of your print job.

Print...

Opens iPhoto's Print dialog box, where you can print contact sheets, greeting cards, full-page photos, or groups of photos in standard sizes like 4 x 6 or 5 x 7. See Chapter 8 for details.

Edit Menu

As you would expect, the commands in the Edit menu let you edit various parts of your photo library, such as keywords, photo titles, and the sort order. The standard Cut, Copy, and Paste commands operate on selected text and photos as normal.

Undo

Where would this world be without Undo? In iPhoto, you even have a *multiple* Undo; using this command (and its keyboard equivalent, ⌘-Z), you can reverse your last series of actions in iPhoto, backing out of your bad decisions with no harm done. How nice to know that if you go too heavy on the contrast, delete an important photo, or crop your grandmother's earlobe, there's a quick and easy way out.

Note, however, that the Undo command tracks your changes in each window independently. For example, suppose you're in the main iPhoto window. You enter Edit mode, where you crop a photo and rotate it.

Now you double-click the photo so that it opens in its own window. Here, you fix some red-eye and adjust the contrast.

As long as you remain in the new window, you can undo the contrast and red-eye adjustments—but if you return to the main window, you'll find that the Undo command will take back only your *original* actions—the cropping and rotating.

So while iPhoto can handle multiple levels of undo, keep in mind that each window maintains its own private stash of Undo's.

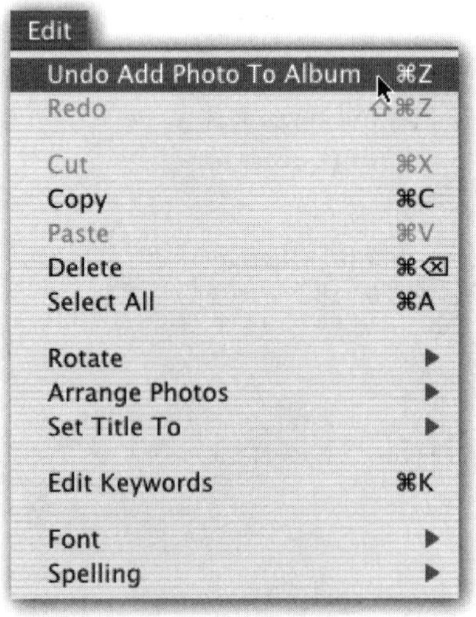

Edit	
Undo Add Photo To Album	⌘Z
Redo	⇧⌘Z
Cut	⌘X
Copy	⌘C
Paste	⌘V
Delete	⌘⌫
Select All	⌘A
Rotate	▶
Arrange Photos	▶
Set Title To	▶
Edit Keywords	⌘K
Font	▶
Spelling	▶

Figure B-2:
Just about any action you perform in iPhoto can be reversed with the Undo command. The menu command itself always spells out exactly what it's going to undo—Undo Add Photo to Album, Undo Cropping, and so on—so that you know which action you're backing out of. The one not-undoable action to keep in mind is deleting a photo from your Photo Library. Once you do that, your photo's gone.

Redo

Redo lets you undo what you just undid. In other words, it reapplies the action you just reversed using the Undo command.

Cut, Copy, Paste

These commands work exactly the way they do in your word processor when you're editing photo titles, comments, keywords, or any other text fields. In addition, they have a few special functions when they're used in certain parts of iPhoto.

- In a photo album (not the main Photo Library), you can select photos and use Cut to remove them from the album. (This doesn't delete them from the Photo Library, only from that particular photo album.) To move the photos to a different album, click the album's name, or click one of its photos, and choose Paste.

- You can assign photos from the main Photo Library to a specific album using the Copy and Paste commands. Select a file, choose Copy, click the destination photo album, and finally choose Paste.

- Cut, Copy, and Paste are all inactive when you're in Editing mode (Chapter 6).

Delete

When you're in an *album*, Delete behaves much like the Cut command: It removes selected photos from the album, but not your master library. (The difference: Delete doesn't put the photo on the invisible Macintosh Clipboard, ready for pasting elsewhere.)

When you're viewing the entire *Photo Library*, however, the Delete command does just what its name implies: It deletes the photo itself, permanently expunging it from the iPhoto Folder. iPhoto always warns you before deleting files, because there's no Undo.

Select All

This command behaves in three different ways, depending on when you use it in iPhoto.

- It selects all thumbnails visible in the viewing area—either those in the selected album or the whole Photo Library.

- In Edit mode, with a photo opened in the main iPhoto window, the Select All command extends the cropping rectangle to the very edges of the photo.

- When you're editing photo titles, comments, keywords, or any other text fields, the Select All command selects all of the text in the field you're editing.

Rotate

You can use the two Rotate commands in the submenu—Counter Clockwise or Clockwise—to rotate selected photos in 90-degree increments, switching them from landscape to portrait orientation as needed.

The Rotate menu command is by far the *least* convenient way to rotate your photos, however. Here are some alternatives:

- Click the Rotate button in the main iPhoto window, just under the Info pane.

- Option-click the Rotate button to reverse the direction of the rotation. (You specify the "main" rotation direction by choosing iPhoto→Preferences.)

- Press ⌘-R to rotate selected photos counter-clockwise, or Shift-⌘-R to rotate them clockwise.

Arrange Photos

Determines how iPhoto sorts the photos in the viewing area. You have these three options:

- **By Film Roll.** Sorts the photos chronologically, according to when each batch was first imported into iPhoto.

- **By Date.** Arranges the photos chronologically, based on the creation dates of each file.

- **Manually.** Lets you drag your photos into any order you like. (It's dimmed out unless you're in an album. In the main Photo Library, you must use one of the first two options.)

Set Title To

When iPhoto imports photos, it names each photo according to its original file name (in the Finder or in the camera). The Set Title To command lets you apply new titles to a whole batch of photos at once, according to one of these four titling schemes:

- **Empty** removes existing titles, leaving the title field blank for each photo.

- **Roll Info** fills in the title field with the name of the film roll which the photo was a part of.

- **File name** is the default setting; iPhoto simply copies the photo's original file name into the new title field.

- **Date/Time** titles each photo with its creation date and/or time. When you choose this option, a dialog box opens so you can choose a format for the date and time information (long format, short format, 24-hour clock, or whatever).

Edit Keywords

Lets you edit the keywords that appear in the lower pane in Organize mode. After you choose the command (or press ⌘-K), you can double-click a keyword to edit or replace it.

When you're finished editing, press ⌘-K again to leave editing mode, click the Done button in the Keywords "table," or choose the strangely worded Edit→Done Editing Keywords command.

Fonts

Opens the standard Mac OS X Font Panel, which is of little use except when using iPhoto's book-designing feature (Chapter 10). You can't change the font used to display titles, comments, or keywords.

If you *are* formatting a Photo Book, choose Edit→Fonts→Show Fonts (or press ⌘-T) to open the panel and make your selections. (Note the limitations described on page 204, however.)

Spelling

Use the Spelling commands to check for misspelled words within iPhoto. It's primarily useful when you're typing in the captions and photo names for Photo Books that you plan to order, as described in Chapter 10. Even then, you may find its use a bit cumbersome (page 205).

Window Menu

The Window menu is filled with all the standard Mac OS X window-manipulating commands.

Close Window

Closes the frontmost window *if* it happens to be a photo that you've opened into its own window for editing. (Neither Close Window nor ⌘-W closes the main iPhoto window; only clicking the red Close button does that, and it quits the program to boot.)

Zoom Window

Zooms any iPhoto window to fill your entire screen (although it's nice enough to avoid covering up your Dock). Choosing this command is the same as clicking the green Zoom button in the upper-left corner of any iPhoto window.

If you choose the Zoom Window command (or click the Zoom button) again, the window shrinks back to its original proportions.

Minimize Window

Collapses the frontmost iPhoto window into the Dock, in standard Mac OS X fashion. It's just as though you pressed ⌘-M or clicked the yellow Minimize button in the upper-left corner of any window.

Show/Hide Toolbar

This command is active only when you've opened a photo into its own window. Choose Show Toolbar to display the iPhoto editing tools across the top of the window and Hide Toolbar to get rid of them. (Clicking the small white glob of toothpaste gel in the upper-right corner of the window does the same thing.)

Customize Toolbar

Produces a customization panel that drops down from the toolbar, loaded with 20 different icons that you can drag to the toolbar to tailor it to your editing needs (page 132). After you've added and removed the icons you want, click the Done button to roll the customization panel back up into the toolbar. See Chapter 6 for much more about using and customizing the editing toolbar.

Bring All to Front

Every now and then, the windows of two different Mac OS X programs get shuffled together, so that one iPhoto window is sandwiched between, say, two Internet Explorer windows. This command brings all your iPhoto windows to the front so they're not being blocked by any other program's windows. (Clicking iPhoto's icon on the Dock does the same thing.)

Help Menu

In iPhoto, the Help menu has a single entry—iPhoto Help. Choosing it (or pressing ⌘-?) opens Apple's Help Viewer program.

Not surprisingly, the assistance available through iPhoto Help is pretty limited. The articles are extremely brief and the explanations tend to skim the surface, and many help screens are stored on Apple's Web site, meaning that you need an Internet connection to see them. But at least you've got a searchable reference at your disposal if you forget how to do something (or lose this book).

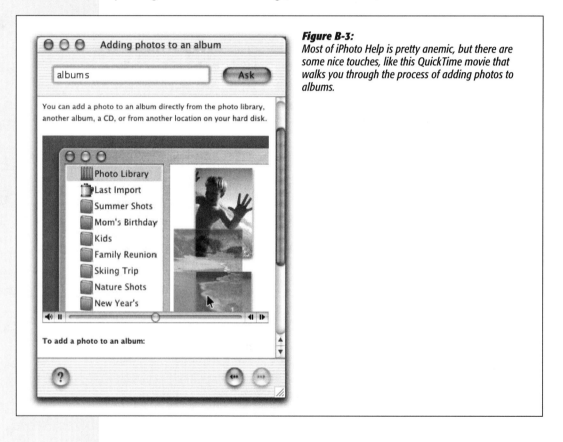

Figure B-3:
Most of iPhoto Help is pretty anemic, but there are some nice touches, like this QuickTime movie that walks you through the process of adding photos to albums.

Where to Go From Here

Your Mac, your trusty digital camera, and this book are all you need to *begin* enjoying the art and science of modern photography. But as your skills increase and your interests broaden, you may want to explore new techniques, add equipment, and learn from people who've become just as obsessed as you. Here's a tasty menu of online resources to help you along the way.

iPhoto and the Web

- **Apple's iPhoto site** features the latest product information, QuickTime tutorials, FAQ (Frequently Asked Question) lists, and camera and printer compatibility charts. There's even a feedback form that goes directly to Apple. In fact, each piece of feedback is read personally by Steve Jobs. (Just a little joke there.) *www.apple.com/iphoto*

- **Apple's iPhoto support page** contains answers to the most common questions and links to discussion forums where other iPhoto users share knowledge and lend helping hands. *www.info.apple.com/usen/iPhoto*

- **VersionTracker** is a massive database that tracks, and provides links to, all of the latest software for Mac OS X, including the cool iPhoto add-ons described in this book. *www.versiontracker.com*

- **The Mac DevCenter** features the latest iPhoto techniques for power users and programmers. *www.macdevcenter.com/mac*

Digital Photo Equipment on the Web

- **Imaging-Resource** offers equipment reviews, price comparisons, and forums all dedicated to putting the right digital camera in your hands. *www.imaging-resource.com*

- **Digital Photography Review** is similar: It offers news, reviews, buying guides, photo galleries, and forums. It's a must-visit site for the digicam nut. *www.dpreview.com*

- **Digital Camera Resource** is just what it says: a comprehensive resource page comparing the latest in digital cameras. *www.dcresource.com*

- **Photo.net** offers industry news, galleries, shopping, travel, critique, and community sharing. *www.photo.net*

Show Your Pictures

- **Fotki.com** is a thriving online community of photo fans who share their work online. Chime in with your shots, or just check out what everyone else is shooting. *www.fotki.com*

Online Instruction

- **ShortCourses.com** offers short courses in digital photography techniques and how to use current equipment. *www.shortcourses.com*

Online Printing

- **Shutterfly** is an alternative to iPhoto's built-in photo-ordering system. It's Mac OS X–friendly and highly reviewed (at least by *Macworld*). *www.shutterfly.com*

- **PhotoAccess** is another Mac OS X–friendly photo printing site that's also received high marks for quality. *www.photoaccess.com*

Index

Colophon

This book was written in Microsoft Word X on various Macs around the country.

The screenshots were captured with Ambrosia Software's Snapz Pro X *(www. ambrosiasw.com)*. Adobe Photoshop 7 and Macromedia Freehand *(www.adobe.com)* were called in as required for touching them up.

The book was designed and laid out in Adobe PageMaker 6.5 on a PowerBook G4 and Power Mac G4. The fonts used include Formata (as the sans-serif family) and Minion (as the serif body face). To provide the and ⌘ symbols, a custom font was created using Macromedia Fontographer.

The book was generated as an Adobe Acrobat PDF file for proofreading and indexing, and finally transmitted to the printing plant in the form of PostScript files.

International Distributors

http://international.oreilly.com/distributors.html • international@oreilly.com

UK, EUROPE, MIDDLE EAST, AND AFRICA (EXCEPT FRANCE, GERMANY, AUSTRIA, SWITZERLAND, LUXEMBOURG, AND LIECHTENSTEIN)

INQUIRIES

O'Reilly UK Limited
4 Castle Street
Farnham
Surrey, GU9 7HS
United Kingdom
Telephone: 44-1252-711776
Fax: 44-1252-734211
Email: information@oreilly.co.uk

ORDERS

Wiley Distribution Services Ltd.
1 Oldlands Way
Bognor Regis
West Sussex PO22 9SA
United Kingdom
Telephone: 44-1243-843294
UK Freephone: 0800-243207
Fax: 44-1243-843302 (Europe/EU orders)
or 44-1243-843274 (Middle East/Africa)
Email: cs-books@wiley.co.uk

FRANCE

INQUIRIES & ORDERS

Éditions O'Reilly
18 rue Séguier
75006 Paris, France
Tel: 33-1-40-51-71-89
Fax: 33-1-40-51-72-26
Email: france@oreilly.fr

GERMANY, SWITZERLAND, AUSTRIA, LUXEMBOURG, AND LIECHTENSTEIN

INQUIRIES & ORDERS

O'Reilly Verlag
Balthasarstr. 81
D-50670 Köln, Germany
Telephone: 49-221-973160-91
Fax: 49-221-973160-8
Email: anfragen@oreilly.de (inquiries)
Email: order@oreilly.de (orders)

CANADA

(FRENCH LANGUAGE BOOKS)

Les Éditions Flammarion ltée
375, Avenue Laurier Ouest
Montréal, QC H2V 2K3 Canada
Tel: 1-514-277-8807
Fax: 1-514-278-2085
Email: info@flammarion.qc.ca

HONG KONG

City Discount Subscription Service, Ltd.
Unit A, 6th Floor, Yan's Tower
27 Wong Chuk Hang Road
Aberdeen, Hong Kong
Tel: 852-2580-3539
Fax: 852-2580-6463
Email: citydis@ppn.com.hk

KOREA

Hanbit Media, Inc.
Chungmu Bldg. 210
Yonnam-dong 568-33
Mapo-gu
Seoul, Korea
Tel: 822-325-0397
Fax: 822-325-9697
Email: hant93@chollian.dacom.co.kr

PHILIPPINES

Global Publishing
G/F Benavides Garden
1186 Benavides Street
Manila, Philippines
Tel: 632-254-8949/632-252-2582
Fax: 632-734-5060/632-252-2733
Email: globalp@pacific.net.ph

TAIWAN

O'Reilly Taiwan
1st Floor, No. 21, Lane 295
Section 1, Fu-Shing South Road
Taipei, 106 Taiwan
Tel: 886-2-27099669
Fax: 886-2-27038802
Email: mori@oreilly.com

INDIA

Shroff Publishers & Distributors PVT. LTD.
C-103, MIDC, TTC Pawane
Navi Mumbai 400 701
India
Tel: (91-22) 763 4290, 763 4293
Fax: (91-22) 768 3337
Email: spdorders@shroffpublishers.com

CHINA

O'Reilly Beijing
SIGMA Building, Suite B809
No. 49 Zhichun Road
Haidian District
Beijing, China PR 100080
Tel: 86-10-8809-7475
Fax: 86-10-8809-7463
Email: beijing@oreilly.com

JAPAN

O'Reilly Japan, Inc.
Yotsuya Y's Building
7 Banch 6, Honshio-cho
Shinjuku-ku
Tokyo 160-0003 Japan
Tel: 81-3-3356-5227
Fax: 81-3-3356-5261
Email: japan@oreilly.com

SINGAPORE, INDONESIA, MALAYSIA, AND THAILAND

TransQuest Publishers Pte Ltd
30 Old Toh Tuck Road #05-02
Sembawang Kimtrans Logistics Centre
Singapore 597654
Tel: 65-4623112
Fax: 65-4625761
Email: wendiw@transquest.com.sg

AUSTRALIA

Woodslane Pty., Ltd.
7/5 Vuko Place
Warriewood NSW 2102
Australia
Tel: 61-2-9970-5111
Fax: 61-2-9970-5002
Email: info@woodslane.com.au

NEW ZEALAND

Woodslane New Zealand, Ltd.
21 Cooks Street (P.O. Box 575)
Waganui, New Zealand
Tel: 64-6-347-6543
Fax: 64-6-345-4840
Email: info@woodslane.com.au

ARGENTINA

Distribuidora Cuspide
Suipacha 764
1008 Buenos Aires
Argentina
Phone: 54-11-4322-8868
Fax: 54-11-4322-3456
Email: libros@cuspide.com

ALL OTHER COUNTRIES

O'Reilly & Associates, Inc.
1005 Gravenstein Hwy North
Sebastopol, CA 95472 USA
Tel: 707-827-7000
Fax: 707-829-0104
Email: order@oreilly.com

O'REILLY®

TO ORDER: **800-998-9938** • **order@oreilly.com** • **www.oreilly.com**
ONLINE EDITIONS OF MOST O'REILLY TITLES ARE AVAILABLE BY SUBSCRIPTION AT **safari.oreilly.com**
ALSO AVAILABLE AT MOST RETAIL AND ONLINE BOOKSTORES

**Large Print Car
Cartland, Barbara, 1902-
The love pirate**

GAYLORD M

·K
Hall
&Cᵒ.

*Also by Barbara Cartland
in Large Print:*

Alone in Paris
Bewildered in Berlin
Beyond the Stars
The Chieftain Without a Heart
A Dream from the Night
The Eyes of Love
Forced to Marry
Hidden by Love
Hiding
The Incomparable
An Innocent in Russia
Look With the Heart
Love and War
Love in the Ruins
The Loveless Marriage
Lovers in Lisbon
Lucky Logan Finds Love

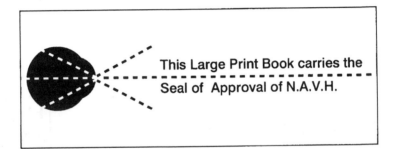

This Large Print Book carries the
Seal of Approval of N.A.V.H.